ED

WALKING *with* THE MUSES

WALKING *with* THE MUSES

a memoir

PAT CLEVELAND

with LORRAINE GLENNON

37INK

—

ATRIA

NEW YORK   LONDON   TORONTO   SYDNEY   NEW DELHI

ATRIA BOOKS   37INK

An Imprint of Simon & Schuster, Inc.
1230 Avenue of the Americas
New York, NY 10020

First 37 INK/Atria Books hardcover edition June 2016

37INK **/ ATRIA** BOOKS and colophons are trademarks of Simon & Schuster, Inc.

For information about special discounts for bulk purchases, please contact Simon & Schuster Special Sales at 1-866-506-1949 or business@simonandschuster.com.

The Simon & Schuster Speakers Bureau can bring authors to your live event. For more information, or to book an event, contact the Simon & Schuster Speakers Bureau at 1-866-248-3049 or visit our website at www.simonspeakers.com.

Interior design by Kyoko Watanabe

Manufactured in the United States of America

10 9 8 7 6 5 4 3 2 1

Library of Congress Cataloging-in-Publication Data

Names: Cleveland, Pat, author. | Glennon, Lorraine, author.
Title: Walking with the muses : a memoir / by Pat Cleveland (with Lorraine Glennon).
Description: New York : 37 INK, [2016] | Includes bibliographical references and index.
Identifiers: LCCN 2015041692 (print) | LCCN 2015044816 (ebook) | ISBN 9781501108228 (hardcover : alk. paper) | ISBN 9781501108235 (trade paper : alk. paper) | ISBN 9781501108242 (eBook)
Subjects: LCSH: Cleveland, Pat. | African American models--Biography. | African American women--Biography. | Fashion--United States. | Fashion designers--United States.
Classification: LCC HD8039.M772 U5365 2016 (print) | LCC HD8039.M772 (ebook) | DDC 746.9/2092--dc23
LC record available at http://lccn.loc.gov/2015041692

ISBN 978-1-5011-0822-8
ISBN 978-1-5011-0824-2 (ebook)

For my mother, Lady Bird the Artist, for the gift of life.
And for my husband, Paul van Ravenstein,
and our children, Noel and Anna.

When you wish upon a star, your dreams come true.

—Jiminy Cricket in Disney's *Pinocchio*
(Leigh Harline and Ned Washington)

prologue

DREAM LOVER

$\mathcal{B}$*orn* smack in the middle of the middle of the twentieth century (June 1950), I'm like millions of other baby boomers in that some of my most formative experiences have occurred inside a darkened movie theater. Like falling in love for the first time.

At some point around my sixth birthday, my mom began taking me to matinees at the RKO 86th Street Theatre, a slightly musty old movie palace roughly eleven blocks due south of our tenement apartment on the edge of Spanish Harlem. There, warm and toasty in winter and blessedly cool in New York's steamy summers, the two of us would sit, arms entwined, sharing popcorn and Raisinets, and stare transfixed at the big screen through hours of previews and double features (two movies for a buck—seventy-five cents for Mom and a quarter for my child's ticket).

Whatever new fare Hollywood served up, Mom and I would be there most Saturday afternoons to devour it.

For me, the only child of a single mother, male role models were in short supply, so my template for the ideal man was forged right there on that screen. Charlton Heston. Rock Hudson. Tony Curtis. And then one day a movie star came along who wiped all the others off the map: Warren Beatty. Mom and I went to see *Splendor in the Grass* the week it was released in October 1961. I didn't know it then, but our days of blissful moviegoing—just Mom and me, together in the dark—were nearing their end because she'd recently married a soldier from Georgia who would radically curtail her outings. I was eleven and Warren, who was making his screen debut in the male lead, was twenty-four. From the moment he appeared on-screen, as the rich Kansas high school football star Bud Stamper who's in love with the town's good girl, Deanie Loomis (played by an incandescent Natalie Wood), I was a goner. I couldn't have explained the effect he had on me—I was only eleven, after all, and until then I'd never experienced that thrill of pure longing for the opposite sex—but I knew instantly: *We were destined to be together*. Later that day, at home in my bedroom, I daydreamed freely. *Patricia Beatty. Mrs. Warren Beatty*. I tried out the name in my mouth a few times. I practiced writing it in my fanciest script. It was meant to be.

Imagine, then, the inner frenzy that descended when, fourteen years later, I spotted Warren in the flesh at the opening of an exhibition of photographs by Richard Avedon at a tony Fifty-Seventh Street gallery, an event attended by a who's who of prominent New Yorkers ranging from Andy Warhol to Norman Mailer. By then I had traveled all over the world as a model, met more boldface names than I could count (and bedded a few of them), and become friends with some of the most creative people of the time (including Warhol, who ended up being one of my wingmen that night). But when Warren Beatty walks in, even the most blasé girl in the world gets weak in the knees—not that I was that girl, anyway. I instantly reverted to the eleven-year-old from Spanish Harlem crushing on the movie star.

As it turned out, my feeble preadolescent fantasies never even came close to conjuring the awesomeness that was Warren. The actual man was so much more beautiful, more sensitive, more talented, more intelligent, more . . . well, *good in bed* than the dream lover who'd lived in my imagination. Our on-and-off affair, which lasted six years in all, was an unforgettable chapter in my life—a life that's been filled with despair and triumph, sickness and health, heartbreak and joy, lust and true love, and loads and loads of fun.

WALKING *with*
THE MUSES

chapter 1

EXILE ON MAIN STREET

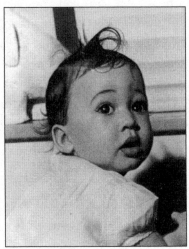

Me at nine months on a
good hair day, 1951.

$\mathcal{M}y$ mother drew pictures of me before I was born. The pregnancy was an accident, and as was her habit from the time she was a small child, Mom turned to art and her own imagination to escape an unpleasant reality: At twenty-three, she was about to become a single mother. (Her lover, Johnny Johnston, had gone back to his home country of Sweden after his visa expired, without even knowing I was about to show up on the planet.) Mom had just purchased a ticket to Paris on the *Queen Mary*. When she realized she was pregnant, she gave the ticket to her older sister, my glamorous Auntie Helen, a dancer who'd been living with Mom in an apartment on East 100th Street that functioned as a kind of nighttime salon for the African-American creative class in New York City.

As Auntie Helen danced her way across the Atlantic, my mom, alone

1

in her apartment, drew picture after picture of the baby whom, ready or not, she would soon welcome into her life. On June 23, 1950, she felt the first pangs of labor. She dressed up in her best high heels and a satin maternity dress she'd sewn for herself and walked halfway across the Queensboro Bridge to a little elevator that took her to Welfare Island (as Roosevelt Island was then called), a sliver of land that was home to the city's "charity hospital." The hospital complex had been designed by James Renwick, Jr., the architect of Saint Patrick's Cathedral, in a grand neo-Gothic style, but it had been allowed to fall into disrepair, and the surrounding buildings were abandoned and being used by the fire department as a practice location for firefighters to learn their trade. So my first glimpse of the world—into which, Mom always told me, I came barreling feetfirst—was this glorious ruin just outside the hospital's windows.

A week later, with me, Patricia Lee Ann Cleveland, in her arms, Mom put on those same high heels and took me home to the 100th Street apartment. The place was so old that one day, while I was asleep in my crib, the ceiling over my head started to crumble. Luckily, Mom whisked me away moments before the whole thing caved in. A few weeks later, a rat jumped into the crib to get milk from my bottle. Mom managed to kill the rat, but that was the last straw. She moved a few blocks south, to a high-rise on Lexington Avenue, on the edge of Spanish Harlem.

༝

I wasn't yet two when my father came back to America. He found out where my mom was living and paid us a visit. Mom dressed the two of us in our nicest outfits, and in walked a tall, handsome, long-limbed blond man carrying a can of Carnation evaporated milk (a request from my mother). He kissed my mom, looked at me, and sat down on the sofa. My mom placed me on his knee for the first and last time, saying, "This is your father." All I remember were his starched white collar, his deep blue satin tie, and his incredibly long legs, a physical characteristic he bequeathed to me. He handed me back to my mom and they chatted for a few minutes. Then he stood up and was gone forever.

Later, Mom told me he'd gotten married in Sweden soon after leaving New York, and that he'd come back only to tell her he had a son. From that day forward, my mom knew she was on her own when it came to raising me.

Mom continued the jobs she'd been doing—painting neckties that looked like regular ties from the front but inside featured naked women in the style of Vargas pinups; decorating store windows; and designing subway billboards—but her earning potential was limited by the racial discrimination of the era. She was forced to take drastic measures. When I turned two, my mother sent me to live with her brother, Randolph, out in western Michigan—in other words, in the middle of nowhere—in a little house he'd built by hand. My uncle, a World War II air force officer, and his wife, a stern former WAC (Women's Army Corps), had no children of their own yet, so they agreed to take me in until my mom saved up enough money to get on her feet. My uncle loved children; my aunt, less so. Nevertheless, these two provided me with my earliest experience of family life.

At first things were tolerable, but once my aunt and uncle had a baby boy of their own, my honeymoon (such as it was) was unequivocally over. On the coldest days of winter, my aunt would lock me out of the house and let me back in only when she heard my uncle's car pulling up the gravel-covered driveway. That crunching sound was my salvation. Once, Uncle Randolph came home early from hunting squirrel—my aunt made it into stew, which, not knowing any better, I thought was delicious—and found me shivering at the front door. He and my aunt had a big fight, and I heard her scream, "I didn't want her here! She's not your child, but you love her more than your own son!" My uncle never buckled, though. He was kindhearted and funny, constantly telling me jokes and calling me his little buddy. "We're going to be happy, okay?" he'd whisper in my ear. He always said we had a deal to be happy. And he hugged me—something my aunt never once did.

I turned three with no fanfare: no birthday party, cards, or presents. Of course, I was too young to know what I was missing. And in hindsight I realize that plenty of kids had less. Relatively speaking, I was one of the lucky ones. I did get presents the following Christmas, when a man from New York (who departed as quickly as he arrived) brought me two wrapped parcels: a tricycle and a miniature toy stove. I didn't understand what they meant or who had given them to me.

That summer Uncle Randolph took me with him to visit *his* uncle, my grandfather Albert's brother. My great-uncle Rep was a real American Indian, a Cherokee, who lived in the woods in a log cabin that looked lifted out of a cowboy movie. The only furnishings were a black potbellied stove, a wooden soapbox, a rocking chair, and a World War I army cot. Because Uncle Rep wore a bowler hat with an eagle feather sticking up at the back, I called him Eagle Feather. He smelled of tobacco that he smoked from a homemade corncob pipe, and he'd sit in the rocking chair and talk about President Roosevelt and tell hunting stories while pointing to the black bear and giant moose heads mounted on the walls and the uncannily lifelike stuffed squirrels, bats, and chipmunks scattered around the room. (I later found out that he was a professional taxidermist.)

I loved these outings; they were my only escape from endless drudgery. My auntie treated me like a servant, insisting that I make all the beds, complete with hospital corners. I tried my best with my tiny three-year-old hands, but she wanted perfection. As soon as a bed was made, she'd bounce a coin on the sheets to make sure they were sufficiently tight. If they weren't, she'd smack me across the hands and I'd have to make the bed again, by myself. She learned her bed-making technique in the Women's Army Corps and she wanted to make sure I got the lesson. I did; to this day, every bed I make has crisp hospital corners.

For dinner, she'd cook frozen peas. If I didn't eat them all, she'd smack me hard on the back of the head. If I cried, she'd stuff the peas in my mouth, saying, "You're nothing but trouble. I can't wait till your mother comes to take you back."

My mother? My pre-Michigan memories were murky. I thought *she* was my mother. So I'd sit there, confused, my mouth filled with peas, scared to death that if I didn't chew and swallow, she'd hit me again. Uncle Randolph had no idea that she was treating me this way, since he worked long hours at a Ford factory, building trucks on an assembly line.

Easter Sunday 1954 was a special day for us because my uncle was going to sing in the church chorus; I loved crooning along. I got up early, ate my fried sausages, and went to brush my teeth and comb my hair for church. As I climbed on the bathroom stool, I noticed myself in the mirror for what seemed like the first time. At three and a half, I found my reflection amusing and started making funny faces at myself. Then I saw a hairbrush and had a pretty good time running it through my hair until the brush got tangled up in my fluffy curls.

My aunt came in to see what was holding me up and immediately hit me across the back before grabbing a pair of nail scissors and lopping off all my curls. "It's because of you, missy, that I'm late for church," she said. "So there—you have no more hair to brush." She yanked me by the arm toward the door. I broke away, but she caught me, spanked me, and dressed me roughly, twisting my arms and neck, then dragged me down the hall to the living room. Sore and hurting, I started to sob. "Shut up, shut up!" she shrieked. "Who wants you?"

In the living room, my uncle was holding a big package. "Honestly, Randolph," my aunt said, "sometimes I think you care more about your sister's child than you do your own." Then she stormed out of the room.

"God's watching you," he called after her. "Do unto others . . ." Then he turned to me and said, "Don't worry about her, little buddy. We have to forgive her."

I hugged my uncle around the leg while he wiped my tears away with his handkerchief. He showed me the package—a big box wrapped in brown paper and tied with a string—and said, "This is for you." The box was almost as big as I was, and we opened it together.

As we tore off the outer wrapping, my pain disappeared. I saw something so beautiful it took my breath away: soft pink tissue paper. I thought that was the present until my uncle pulled out something from under the paper, and in that joyous moment, I swear, my lifelong love of fashion was born. He held up a pink ruffled dress, made of three layers of transparent organza, with tiny golden stars printed on the fabric. He dug deeper into the tissue paper and found a pair of black patent-leather Mary Janes, with tiny pearl buttons on the strap, and two small white gloves. Such pretty clothes! I started giggling with pure delight.

"This is all for you. It's from your mother."

Those words again: *your mother*. At that point, the concept of a mother was as unreal and magical to me as Santa Claus or the Good Witch. My uncle handed me the dress and said, "A little star dress for a little star, so you can shine bright." Then he hugged me and added, "You can wear this to Sunday school today."

My aunt threw a fit—we were already late, I was already dressed—

but my uncle won the day. "She should wear it," he said firmly. "It's Easter Sunday."

With a fed-up look, Auntie snatched the dress from my uncle. "Don't just stand there, Randolph," she said. "Get your son while I dress her again."

My old dress got stuck over my head as Auntie jerked on it to take it off. "Help!" I cried.

"*Quiet!*" Auntie hissed. "Your mother should be dressing you, not me. But no, she's in New York, doing whatever she wants, while I'm stuck with you. She should be sending money instead of fancy dresses."

One hot June day, I was taking a nap in the room where my little cousin and I slept in twin beds. The sounds of woodpeckers and insects and busy forest animals drifted into the room. Everything seemed to be buzzing. Most kids hate naptime, but I liked it because it was a chance to daydream and let my mind wander. I watched a fly dancing in circles around the ceiling, and I felt alive: For the first time I recognized that *this* was summer. It was like hearing music. I had just turned four.

Then the door of the room opened. I expected my aunt to be angry because I wasn't asleep, but she was ever so nice—not her usual self at all. "There's someone here to see you," she announced before leaving the room. In a moment, the door opened again and a very pretty lady entered. She was tall and slender, with bobbed hair. She wore large gold hoop earrings, an off-the-shoulder puffed-sleeve blouse, and a horsehair skirt with lots of petticoats underneath. Her tiny waist was cinched with a wide belt, and on her feet were high-heeled sandals. I'd never seen anyone dressed so stylishly. As she beamed me a smile and walked toward me, I noticed the poodle motif on her skirt.

"Doggie?" I said, pointing. Without saying a word, she held out her skirt and let me touch the felt poodles, with their red sequin eyes and little gold chains as collars. I was entranced by this angel who had come to visit me.

She sat with me, and I touched her. She didn't get angry, like my aunt would have. And then she hugged me, wrapping me in the scent of rose perfume. As we broke the embrace, she asked, "Do you know who I am?" I looked down shyly and shook my head. She held my little hands in her long, slender ones, and I noticed the charm bracelet she wore. I withdrew my hands from hers in order to play with the charms. And she let me. "I'm someone who loves you very much," she said. "And I want you to come live with me." I stared at her, the charm between my fingers forgotten. "Do you know I'm your mommy?"

And suddenly I did know. I knew from her hug. I knew because I had asked God for a beautiful mommy, and now here she was.

My mom stood up, and my aunt walked in. What a contrast! There was the nice, glamorous female on one side and the mean, plain one on the other. When I looked at the glamorous one, she stretched her arms out to me. I flew into them like a lost bird.

chapter 2

A ROSE IN SPANISH HARLEM

My mom, Lady Bird Cleveland, at
nineteen, in New York City, 1945.

My mother, Lady Bird Cleveland, was born on July 24, 1926, to
Nannie Edwards from North Carolina and Albert Cleveland from
Georgia. The family lived in Cornelia, Georgia, in a house that's still
standing today. Nannie, whom I know only through stories, was born in
1893, three years before *Plessy* vs. *Ferguson* made "separate but equal" the
law of the land; thirty years after the Emancipation Proclamation; and
274 years after the first Africans were brought to Jamestown, Virginia,
as de facto slaves (at that time, slavery as an institution didn't exist, so
technically, they were indentured servants). Nannie's parents were born
into slavery, and she didn't fare much better. Her family was separated,
as slave families often were, and she grew up with no relatives except her
sister, Leanna, who became a Sunday school teacher in St. Louis, where
she taught a local girl named Josephine Baker to sing and play the piano.

Leanna encouraged young Josephine to go into show business as a ticket out of town.

Meanwhile, Nannie (whose real name was Nancy, but everybody called her Nannie, because she took care of children from the time she was a child herself) made her way to North Carolina, where, by the grace of God, a black family took her in and made sure she got an education. In 1910, at seventeen, Nannie enrolled at Spelman College (then called the Spelman Seminary for Young Women) in Atlanta, a prestigious institution named after Laura Spelman, the abolitionist wife of John D. Rockefeller, which was (and still is) considered the African-American Ivy League.

Even with an education, a Negro had very few opportunities in that era, and there was virtually no career path for an educated Negro woman like Nannie. So in 1912, when she was twenty-one, Nannie took the conventional route and found a young man to marry: a soldier named Albert Cleveland. Because he had blond-red hair, light skin, and freckles (courtesy of his Irish-Scottish blood), Albert was considered a Caucasian, though he was a quarter Cherokee.

Lady Bird, Nannie and Albert's fifth child, was pushed off her mother's lap at the age of ten months to make room for the sixth, my aunt Frances. From there, things only got tougher for Mom. In the Deep South, in the foothills of the Blue Ridge Mountains, being black, or even Indian, meant your family could be run off their land at any time for pretty much any reason.

Everyone—from small children to old folks—was expected to fend for themselves. Nannie made shoes out of old tires, using the rubber as soles; you could almost call them an early version of today's fancy running shoes. But they wore out quickly, because running was one of the things you had to be good at if you were black and wanted to stay alive. Every so often, the Ku Klux Klan would show up at the Cleveland house, and Nannie would have to figure out how to get rid of them. The family was on guard at all times, and as a result of living like this day in and day out, little Lady Bird, my mother, developed plenty of grit.

As a way to earn extra money, Nannie created a kind of bed and board for black circus workers who had no place to stay when the circus came to town. She made corn liquor (a Prohibition specialty) and hired piano players from New Orleans to entertain in the evening. People came from far and wide to hear the music and to listen to Nannie, seated under a single lightbulb (the first in the black section of town) tell stories from the old days, including the one about the girl named Josephine Baker who ran away to Paris because Nannie's sister advised her to get the hell out of St. Louis. My mom slept on a nearby mattress made of straw and often fell asleep to the tunes coming out of the old roller piano and the same metal washboard on which she did the family's laundry.

Music and art were my mom's salvation. Nannie taught her how to draw the Indian head on a nickel, because an ad said, "If you can draw this, you can be an artist." From there, Mom started drawing everything she saw. When she got to her one-room schoolhouse, she'd draw in the middle of her lessons, and the teacher would catch her and rap her on the knuckles. Then she'd be sent outside to pick a hickory stick that the teacher would use to give her a whipping in front of the class. Mom kept on drawing, no matter how high the price. When the teacher stepped out of the room for lunch, Mom would draw a cartoon of her, and her classmates would all laugh. Then she'd have to suffer the old hickory stick again. Oh, the perils of being an artist!

Mom grew up fast. Between school, her work sweeping floors at a local beauty parlor, and all her chores at home, she picked up quite an array of skills. She could sew clothes and grow food; make music and draw; and wash clothes and clean house. And with the KKK around the corner and her own philandering father squandering his paycheck on the town whore, Mom had witnessed enough by the time she was ten to know the lowest depths of human behavior: manhandling of women, fighting over skin color, and gambling and drinking to the point where a grown man might just kill another one for a dollar.

All the Clevelands felt the strain, especially Nannie. One day while Mom was finishing her math homework, she looked up and saw her forty-six-year-old mother take her last breath. Nannie died just like that, probably from exhaustion and putting up with her two-timing husband.

Poor Mom, left motherless at age twelve with no one to guide her besides a not much older sister, Sally, who filled in as her mother, just as Mom did for their youngest sister, Frances. Many meals of salt-and-pepper sandwiches followed, until Sally decided my mom would be better off up north in New York with their much older sister, Kitty.

It was June 1940, just weeks before Mom's fourteenth birthday. In Europe, World War II was already raging. Mom went right to work taking care of Kitty's four children, since Kitty was pregnant with a fifth. Mom became the nanny and the maid, changing and washing diapers, then hanging them out to dry. That September, she began attending Wadleigh High School in Harlem, where she took all the usual subjects. The teachers soon noticed her aptitude for drawing and put her in a special class with other talented students. Some played piano, some wrote poetry, but Mom was the only painter—the school didn't even have an art teacher—so she got first dibs on any art supplies the school had. One particularly observant teacher, Mrs. Kuhn, entered Mom in a citywide art contest sponsored by Macy's department store. Mom's submission—*Tired Woman,* an oil painting of a bent-over laundress (which, like all Mom's fine art, sent a strong social message)—won first prize: a scholarship to Pratt Institute. But Mom was too young for college. She was also unprepared: She spoke ungrammatically, with a heavy Southern accent, so she'd been moved back two grades.

By the time she turned sixteen, Mom had been joined in New York by another older sister, Helen, who was running away from an early forced marriage. Helen squeezed into Kitty's overstuffed house and immediately got herself a job as a welder in a navy shipyard, which had plenty of openings because of the war. The first thing Auntie Helen bought with her paychecks was a red fox fur that she shared with Mom, who was becoming obsessed with fashion. Yearning for both freedom and sophistication, the sisters decided to move into their own apartment, on East 161st Street. It was barely larger than a kitchen table, but it sure beat living in the Bronx with five kids and a pee-soaked sofa for a bed. From their base, they explored the city, venturing out to the Savoy Ballroom and other pillars of Harlem nightlife. They danced and listened to the big bands with the African-American luminaries of the day—the boxers, musicians, and singers.

With a new apartment and a high school diploma, Mom was ready to take on the world with her art. Her work on store windows and billboards was beginning to get some recognition, and her income from painting the peekaboo neckties helped make ends meet. Meanwhile, Helen joined the dance troupe started by Katherine Dunham, the groundbreaking dancer and champion of African-American choreography. After a few years, Mom and Helen moved farther downtown to 100th Street, between Park and Madison. Every day Mom would sew a dress that she'd wear that night when she and Helen visited the jazz clubs all around the city. Because there weren't many clubs for blacks, the city also came to them: The sisters' living room became a kind of after-hours hangout where all the artists, musicians, and performers they knew would come to play. In many ways, these soirées were an urban version of the gatherings their mother, Nannie, used to host back in Georgia.

In the winter of 1947, my mom met my father, Johnny Johnston, at an uptown jazz club called Carl's Corner. Johnny, a saxophonist who revered Charlie Parker, had come to the United States from Sweden to nurture his love of American jazz. His English was shaky but adequate, and his and my mom's shared passion for music and art fueled their love affair.

And so it came to pass that my mother, a half-black, part-Cherokee, part-Irish fine artist, and my father, a Swedish descendant of Vikings, made beautiful music together. The two of them went to every club in Harlem and danced every night into the wee hours until, two years into their romance, my dad's time in America was up and he had to go back to Sweden. I was conceived that autumn, a few weeks before he left.

chapter 3

A LOVE SUPREME

A day at the zoo with
my mom, 1955.

Looking back, I see those early years in New York with my mom as a time of enchantment. As an artist, she had a way of creating a special world around her, and if having a young daughter cramped her style, I never knew it. My aunt Helen was still in Europe when I came back to the city from Michigan, so Mom was renting out her room to a shapely light-skinned young black woman called Miss Livingston. Auntie Helen had met her only briefly and was unaware that Miss Livingston was one of the best-known call girls in Harlem. When word got out that she was staying at our house (most likely she put out the word herself), the Harlem hotshots were at our door like a pack of wolves. Among them were the notorious gangster Bumpy Johnson and the boxer/actor Coley Wallace, who defeated future heavyweight champion Rocky Marciano in 1948 when they were both still amateurs. Later, in 1953, Wallace played Joe Louis in the biopic about the pioneering boxer.

On Saturday nights, Miss Livingston would invite these men—and all their friends, and even stray guys and their girlfriends whom she picked up at Red Randolph's bar on Seventh Avenue and 123rd Street—over to Mom's apartment. Come Sunday they'd still be there. The place constantly reeked of cigarettes and whiskey.

There was one very nice man who came to call on my mom, the actor and comedian Mantan Moreland, who played Charlie Chan's chauffeur in the movies. Mantan had nothing to do with Miss Livingston and was very nice to me, making me laugh with his funny faces and stories.

Then there were Timmie Rogers, the comedian and musician; James Edwards, another actor; and Noble Sissle, who wrote musical comedies and really liked my mom, but at sixty-five or thereabouts, he was too old for her. At the time, of course, I had no idea who these guys were, but all of them told me they were my uncle, so that was what I called them.

Since Mom needed the rent from Miss Livingston, she and I slept in the same room. It was wonderfully cozy, and I knew I had someone near who loved me and would never hit me. Mom sang to me, played the music from *Peter and the Wolf*, and read me children's stories like "The Three Little Pigs." That particular tale taught me some important life lessons: Don't let the wolf in the door, and build your house out of bricks, not straw.

One night a half-dressed, clearly drunken man staggered into our bedroom instead of Miss Livingston's. Mom had reached her limit. She felt it was no longer safe to have Miss Livingston around and asked her to leave. There went the rent money. But then, by some miracle, my aunt, who'd been working on the French Riviera as a seamstress and dancer, decided to come back to the United States.

I'll never forget her arrival. Mom and I went over to the boat docks on the Hudson River, on Manhattan's far west side. We looked down at the *Queen Mary* from the observation deck and saw this pretty lady standing on the top deck, waving up to us. When we met her at the gangplank, she was incredibly glamorous: curvaceous, wearing sunglasses, and dressed, she told us, in "a real Dior" suit. Mom and I weren't too shabby ourselves, even though Mom had sewn everything we were wearing. She was a designer at heart and would use any excuse to dress up, so while our clothes may have been homemade, to me they looked like couture—not that I had the foggiest idea what couture was. But I did know that the three of us together made an awfully pretty picture.

With Auntie Helen reinstalled in Mom's apartment, life became both calmer and more exciting than anything I'd ever known. The small-town code I'd gotten used to in Michigan—where not showing up for church on Sunday meant the townspeople would call you a sinner—was nowhere to be found. Though I said a prayer every night at bedtime, the three of us didn't go to church, because Mom said God lived in our hearts, not in a building. My first Easter in New York couldn't have been more different from the ones in Michigan: Mom sewed pastel dresses and cute little spring jackets for all three of us, and we wore them as we marched down Fifth Avenue with thousands of other stylish New Yorkers in the Easter parade. Mom and I celebrated Christmas by going to Macy's to meet Santa Claus.

It was a time of many firsts: my first visits to the Bronx Zoo, to the Metropolitan Museum of Art, to the beach. I was photographed for the first time by a professional and got my first ride on the carousel in Central Park. I'm not sure if New York was called the Big Apple back then, but that's exactly what it felt like to me: a shiny apple that I was taking a delicious bite of.

The biggest first of all was that I finally felt safe.

❦

Mom seemed her truest self when she was painting. I'd watch her every brushstroke until late in the evening, when I'd fall asleep in a big chair with a mental image of her in front of the easel and the smells of turpentine and linseed oil wafting through the air. (This environment was nothing if not stimulating to my senses.) My aunt had brought back Lanvin, an expensive French perfume, in lovely large bottles, and its fragrance mingled with the scent of my mom's art supplies to create an extremely specific aroma that for me was the very essence of home.

Though Mom was painting a lot and indulging her love of fashion (she constantly brought home dress patterns and fabrics she found on sale), money was always scarce. So to ensure a steady paycheck and to leave her days free to be with me, she took a night job as a nurse's aide. My aunt watched over me while Mom was at work.

That meant I spent many evenings with Aunt Helen at Katherine Dunham's School of Dance, located in a studio on West Forty-Third Street off Broadway. I was transfixed by Dunham, who was the first person I'd ever seen dressed "African-style," in a long skirt and a headdress. As the dancers warmed up before class, Dunham would invite me to join in, and I'd try my darnedest to keep up with all the students doing *grand pliés* and *battements frappés*. But I was so small that all I could muster was hanging off the practice barre. Dunham would laugh, and the dancers started calling me their little monkey.

When she was instructing, Dunham sat on a tall stool with the tips of her bare toes touching the floor as if *en pointe*. But when she was teaching, she'd get off the stool and demonstrate how something was done, dancing with grand movements, uttering not a word and stretching her limbs so far out that she looked twice her actual height. A drummer would accompany her on his African drums, and the other dancers—whether students or members of the troupe—would follow her movements exactly. There were several celebrities in the class, including Marlon Brando and Sidney Poitier, but what did I know? To me, they were just ordinary people, darting here and there around the studio.

Our living room had wall-to-wall mirrors on one side, and sometimes Auntie Helen would invite the dancers over to rehearse a number they were working on. My mother, who was not the natural performer that Auntie Helen was, played the conga drums. Rehearsals often turned into parties, with other drummers playing and bare-chested men dancing.

Late one summer night, when I couldn't sleep, I joined the party. At this point, I was so used to hearing the rhythm of the drums that all of the commotion was normal to me. The dancers were practicing the limbo for one of their shows, and when I walked into the room, I saw my auntie gyrating wildly under the limbo stick. (This was years before Chubby Checker made the limbo, a dance that originated in Trinidad, known to ordinary Americans.) She boogied over to me and said, "Now *you* dance." Well, I shook and shimmied just as my aunt told me to, and everybody clapped. Putting on my little show was so much fun that

I went back to bed happy, dreaming of when I could dance for them again. Mom had other plans. She decided it would be better for me to stay somewhere more wholesome on the weekends, away from all the adult shenanigans. So off we went to Connecticut to see my godmother, Henriette Metcalf, a wealthy widow who lived in a renovated barn in Newtown.

chapter 4

SOPHISTICATED LADY

Me at six, at the Connecticut home
of Henriette Metcalf, 1956.

Henriette Metcalf had been married to Willard Leroy Metcalf, an American painter known for his impressionist-style landscapes. When Willard died of a heart attack in 1925, he left Henriette most of his paintings and all of his money—thus enabling her affluent, gracious way of life in Connecticut. Getting to know her was one of those experiences that, though I wouldn't realize it until I was much older, affected me profoundly. Through her, I was exposed to a way of life I'd never encountered—one of easy affluence steeped in culture, good manners, and reverence for art above all else.

My mom was just fifteen when she met Henriette at the citywide reception where Mayor La Guardia presented Mom with the Pratt scholarship for her painting *Tired Woman*. Madame Metcalf (as she preferred to be called, since she'd lived in France for many years) was in the audience and, impressed with Mom's talent, invited her to come visit. Madame Metcalf became my mother's advocate, introducing Mom to the "right" people in the art world, many of whom asked Mom to paint their portraits. When I was born, Madame Metcalf became my godmother.

One summer weekend when I was five, Mom and I got dressed up and took the train to Connecticut. When the conductor called out, "Dan Berry," we got off. There to meet us was a tall man with an odd accent (Mom said it was Dutch), and as he drove us through the countryside, he told us he'd had to eat tulips when he was a teenager in Holland during the war, but now he planted them for beauty.

We finally arrived in Newtown. I looked out the window at a glistening new world: enormous country houses, acres of farmland, and flowers of every size and color, like the ones in storybooks. It was all I could do to keep my tongue from hanging out of my mouth in amazement.

Henriette Metcalf was standing at a white picket fence under a trellised archway covered with tiny white roses in front of a big white barn that had been converted into a house. I stared at this tall, slim woman with pale, almost pure-white skin and shiny light-blond hair. She was in her late sixties but seemed much younger, dressed in a wraparound denim skirt with large patch pockets, a simple lemon-colored sweater, and funny cork-bottomed sandals. She welcomed us with open arms, saying something in French. "*Bonjour, ma petite . . .*" As she bent down to hug me, I noticed her brooch—a big cluster of stones in a deep dark red, like the color of the wine my Aunt Helen drank. I didn't know a ruby from a shiny piece of red glass, of course, but somehow I intuited that her jewelry was rare and valuable, and it fascinated me.

Henriette took my hand in hers as she led us indoors and up the stairs toward the guest room. I looked down onto an enormous open space and saw a living room dotted with red velvet sofas and a very old-looking baby grand piano covered in a large Spanish shawl. There was art everywhere. Even the wood-paneled walls had been painted by Henriette's husband with family portraits and pictures of flowers and forests.

We went upstairs past the book-filled loft library, then a room that was empty except for a round table with a vase full of red roses, before arriving at our room, which was wallpapered in an intricate floral pattern and flooded with sunlight. It was so quiet that I could hear the bees buzzing softly just outside the window.

I climbed up on the big four-poster bed and immediately conked out. When I woke up, I went to look for my mom and found her in the room across the way, sitting at an easel touching up a portrait of a young man. I wanted to watch her, but she said I was distracting her and sent me away to play.

Wandering back down the staircase, I found my way into the garden. There, strung up between two birch trees surrounded by wildflowers, was a hammock. I climbed in, leaned back, and discovered something I'd spend the rest of my life searching for: *peace.* I lay there for hours, swinging gently and looking at the sky, daydreaming and inhaling the perfume of the natural world. Eventually, Madame Metcalf returned and introduced me to her three adorable gray poodles, who wriggled into the hammock with me, licking my face and making me laugh. Then Madame Metcalf led me to a tree house furnished with checked curtains and a child-size rocking chair. I gasped in pleasure. "You can play here," she said. "I had it built for my grandchildren, but they hardly ever come anymore."

As I played, I wondered why some children had all these fine playthings and I didn't. It was a troubling thought, and in retrospect, I see it as my first conscious perception of class, of the existence of haves and have-nots. At the time, though, I shrugged it off and simply enjoyed the luxuries at hand.

The next morning, as my mother painted, Madame Metcalf showed me her doves, twenty in all, which she kept in a walk-in birdhouse. I held several, stroked them, and learned how to coo exactly as they did. Next, she brought out a pony, which I rode around the yard. She showed me her garden and Mr. Metcalf's collection of bird eggs. She said the name of every bird, egg, and flower in both English and French and made me repeat the words after her.

It was a three-day weekend, and Madame Metcalf had charity events to attend (she was fond of any cause involving animals), so with Mom hard at work, I had the run of the place. Until Mom decided to do a painting of me. "I don't know why I'm painting everyone else's children," she said. "I want a portrait of you." She stretched a canvas, sat it against a chair, took out her paints, and asked me to sit in a puddle of light in the middle of the bed. She handed me a large storybook. "Here, Henriette wanted you to have this. It's called *Madeline,* and it's about a little girl who lives in Paris." She pointed to the cover. "See, there's the Eiffel Tower; it's a symbol of the city." Then she sat back down behind her canvas. "Now you can pose for me."

How do I do that? I thought, shifting and moving my body into all sorts of positions.

"Just sit without moving," she said in a soft voice. "You can do that." And I could. I could do anything she wanted me to, as long as we were together. So I sat there without moving, the book open on my lap, as if I were reading.

"That's good," Mom said. "Just read your book."

I kept my eyes glued to a page that showed the little red-haired girl with the big yellow hat staring at a tiger in a zoo. I wanted a hat like that. Without looking up, I could hear my mom's brushstrokes. I'd move just my eyes to look up through my eyelashes, and I'd catch her stealing a glance at me from behind the canvas. It was like a game of peekaboo. Every time our eyes met, she smiled, and I felt like the most important person in the world.

I asked, "Am I a good model, Mommy?" I was trying so hard not to fidget.

"You're a very good model."

I knew I *was* a good model, because my mom said so. She finished that portrait in one day, and the next morning she had to go back to work in the city. So there I was in that big barn house with Madame Metcalf, her menagerie, and the silence, broken only by the sound of the doves and the grandfather clock chiming out the hour.

Madame Metcalf encouraged me to go up to the library to select a few children's books. As I browsed the shelves, I noticed lots of old-timey photographs propped among the books. I was so deep in exploring them that I didn't hear Madame Metcalf come up behind me.

"They're lovely, aren't they?" She bent down to my height and put her arms around me. "I was young once, my dear, and living in Paris." That place again: *Paris.* She took a deep, sad breath. "That was when my husband was alive. He was an artist, like your mommy." She took a round-framed photo off the shelf and held it next to her heart. "We didn't have much money, but we had art and many friends. We knew the greatest artists, actors, and opera singers of the era. And ballet dancers, like the great Nijinsky." She pointed to a picture with handwriting on it. The man in it was dressed in tights and wearing lots of eye makeup; he looked like a forest fairy.

One by one, she showed me her friends in the old photos: Sarah Bernhardt, Henri Matisse, Pablo Picasso. She picked up a photo of a woman named Helen Keller who, according to Madame Metcalf, had picked blueberries with my mother before I was born. Then there was Isadora Duncan ("A dancer and an American like you," Madame Metcalf said, "who fled to Europe for artistic freedom") with her arms stretched up to the sky. I loved the way she looked: so free. I wanted to dance with her. Oh, let's face it: I wanted to *be* her.

I had fallen in love with the glamorous expat life of 1920s Paris that Madame Metcalf described—a life that, even at five, I yearned for so fiercely I could taste it. It would be another fifty years before I found out that Madame Metcalf's adventures in Paris had been a bit more complicated and a lot more scandalous than she'd let on. (I chalk up her less than total honesty to my being too young to understand.)

In actuality, the Metcalfs divorced in 1920, after nine years of marriage and two sons, and in 1921 Henriette, who worked as a translator and as an editor for French *Vogue,* embarked on a tortured sixteen-year love affair with Thelma Wood, an American sculptor who lived in Paris and was part of Gertrude Stein's inner circle. Thelma was the inspiration for the classic novel *Nightwood,* written by her former lover Djuna Barnes, who considered Thelma the love of her life. Barnes never quite got over the fact that Thelma left her for Henriette, who was the model for another character in *Nightwood.* Still, when Willard Metcalf died in 1925 (not long after the Corcoran Gallery in Washington, DC, mounted a huge retrospective of his work), he left all of his money and most of his extraordinary paintings to his ex-wife.

That first stay in Connecticut lasted for two weeks. Madame Metcalf explained that she wanted to instruct me in social correctness. She spoke in French and introduced me to egg cups and the soft-boiled *oeuf,* which I had to carefully break open with a little silver knife. I ate it with a silver teaspoon embossed with a coat of arms and a fleur-de-lis. "Etiquette, Patricia," she'd say, "it's all about etiquette."

Surrounded by both nature and culture, I experienced a tangle of strange new emotions: Being without my mom made me sad, but so did the thought of leaving this world and being back in our apartment in the hot, smelly city.

Fortunately, Mom and I visited Madame Metcalf almost every weekend that summer. Country life in Connecticut became a part of our routine, and it was heavenly. My mother was happy, too, because her social life was heading in the right direction. Madame Metcalf introduced her to Carl Van Vechten, the famous photographer and patron of the Harlem Renaissance; he loved my mother's art and photographed her many times. Once she took me with her to his studio, and he photographed the two of us together.

Mom met another new friend through Madame Metcalf—an opera singer who lived in a nearby Connecticut town. On our visit to the singer's house, Mom told me that I need to be extra well behaved, and that I should curtsy and say "pleased to meet you" when I was introduced. The house was on a little hill, and when we arrived at the door, we were greeted by a black woman dressed in a black uniform with a white apron and a little white hat. Mom whispered that she was the maid. I'd never seen a maid or a house as grand as this one. It had a marble foyer and a big chandelier and a tall staircase. The maid led us up the stairs to a pink room with pink shag wall-to-wall carpeting. The room was round— something else I'd never seen—and up on a round platform rested a round bed. The maid closed the door behind us, and as we stood there, a lovely brown lady walked in. She was dressed in a fancy pink dress and had shiny black hair and dark, intelligent eyes.

She bent down to me and said, "So you're the little girl Madame Metcalf told me about. I love your mother." She hugged Mom and asked, "How does my dress look?"

My mom noticed that the hem was slightly uneven and said, "I think you need to take it up a little on one side."

"Oh, goodness," the lady said, sighing. "I don't have time; I'll have to change."

My mom said, "I can hem it for you."

"You can do that?" the lady asked, astonished.

Of course she could. Mom was a master seamstress who spent hours every day dreaming up new clothes and creating them in our apartment. So she fixed the hem while the lady stood there. When Mom finished, the lady said, "I had this dress especially made for tonight's party. You saved me. Thank you."

"You're welcome, Mrs. Anderson," said Mom.

"You know you can call me Marian."

"Yes, yes, I forgot," Mom said, smiling sweetly.

"We've invited several producers tonight. I hope they all make it. There will be a few new singers." Marian turned to me and asked, "Do you sing?"

"Yes," I said, launching into "Twinkle, twinkle, little star . . ."

"That sounds good," she said.

"Can you sing, too?" I asked.

"Sometimes, but never at home."

I thought that was odd, because my mom and I were always singing at home. Then Marian took me by the hand, and the three of us went into the party. Somehow I ended up back in Marian's bedroom, on her bed. My eyes flickered open and shut, and I saw Marian and my mom watching over me. Then Marian sang softly in my ear. "Twinkle, twinkle, little star . . ." And I woke up.

That's all I can remember of my first visit with the great Marian Anderson. My mom and I returned to Mrs. Anderson's many times. She had no children of her own, and she asked to be my second godmother.

Both these godmothers, Henriette Metcalf and Marian Anderson, just wanted to help my mom, a gifted but struggling artist. For me, though, these women were revelatory: They showed me a different way of living and gave me something to aspire to. And they spent time with me, explaining everything from nature to manners, crocheting, and—the most essential lesson of all—how to be contented all by myself.

chapter 5

TEACH ME TONIGHT

My mom (*seated*) and Aunt Helen in our living room,
getting ready for one of their costume balls, 1958.

The following fall, just after I turned six, Madame Metcalf had the idea
to send me to school in Switzerland. She offered to pay for it, thinking
that it would not only give me a safe place where I could get a great
education, but also, most important, it would free up my mom to work
on her art.

Mom nixed Switzerland but agreed that a private school in the city
was a good idea. The next thing I knew, Mom and I were taking a bus
to Fifth Avenue and Seventy-Ninth Street. When I asked where we were
going, she said, "We're checking on a really good school for you." It was a
cold evening, so I was wearing a plaid wool skirt, itchy kneesocks, a new
pair of Mary Janes that felt heavy on my feet, and a navy blue reefer coat
with gold buttons and a velvet collar. I looked every inch the rich New
York City private school girl. In reality, of course, I was anything but.

We arrived at an ornate limestone building that seemed palatial. But then I caught a glimpse of my first nun: She was tall and dressed in black from head to toe, except for a white band around her forehead and neck. Though she smiled, something about her scared me. She tried to take my hand, but I pulled away. Then she directed her first words at me: "You are *not* well behaved." She showed us into an office where there was another, much meaner-looking woman dressed the same way. This nun said, "We should keep her here starting today."

When I heard that, I jumped up from my chair, howled, "Nooooo!" and flung myself at my mother and hugged her tightly around the hips. The first nun tried to pry me loose, but I howled some more. The scuffle escalated and Mom saw the terror in my eyes. That was when she looked the nun straight in the eye and said coldly, "Take your hands off of her." I knew that tone: Mom was furious. She put her arm around me, and as we headed for the door, the second nun said, "You will regret this decision. Once you leave, we will not take her back."

The fresh night air outside was such a relief. We walked east in the chill and caught the bus home. There was no more talk about private school, in Switzerland, New York, or anywhere else. A few weeks later, I enrolled at the regular public elementary school down the block from where we lived.

☙

As far as I'm concerned, my true education centered on the creative mess that existed in our living room. And what a glorious mess it was: There were sequins, strings of pearls, peacock feathers, large exotic fans, beads, and bent wire coat hangers loaded down with fabrics. The floor and sofas were covered with colored paper and tulle, as Mom and Auntie Helen went into a creative frenzy trying to make the deadline for various costume balls they hoped to attend. And I was in the middle of it all, absorbing everything, loving every minute.

I'll never forget a costume they made for New York City's Beaux Arts Ball in 1958, not long after the Soviets sent the first satellite, *Sputnik 1*, into outer space. *Sputnik 1* was followed a month later by *Sputnik 2*, which had a dog on board. In our living room, Mom and Auntie Helen were working on a four-foot-high replica of Planet Earth; the big round ball was covered in tulle, with green fabric representing the continents and hundreds of light blue sequins indicating bodies of water. As usual, I was prancing around the room, twirling ribbons and waving feathers. But I stopped midtwirl when my auntie lowered the globe over my mom. Her legs, covered in fishnet stockings sewn with hundreds of rhinestones, were the only part of her that showed. "Turn the light out, so we can see how it looks in the dark," Mom said. I ran and flicked the switch.

There she stood, my mom as Earth, lit up from within, legs glittering like the brightest constellation in the night sky. Attached to the globe by a wire was a little toy dog inside a transparent plastic ball, lit by a tiny bulb. As my mom the Earth stood still, the little ball started to orbit her.

"Can you see the *Sputnik* going?" her muffled voice asked. "Is it going?"

"Yes, yes! It's working!" Auntie Helen cried, jumping up and down and clapping.

It was magical. My mother could figure out how to make something look so real that I felt I was in outer space, gazing back at a wondrous world. That was *my* space travel—living within my mom's boundless imagination. I couldn't have asked for a better teacher.

The next day, the newspaper carried a photo of Mom in that costume. The caption read, "This year's winner of the Beaux Arts Ball, Lady Bird Cleveland." The prize was a trophy and some cash, which we always needed.

There were many competitions, many nights out, and many interested suitors coming to call on Mom and Helen, who were attractive young single women. Sometimes Mom would go out and Helen would stay with me, and sometimes it was the other way around. (They were both nurse's aides at Bellevue Hospital, but they worked different shifts.) I loved to watch them get ready. I'd sit at the kitchen table, and Mom or Helen would stand in front of the small mirror on top of the refrigerator, applying makeup. "Painting your face is a lot like painting a canvas," Mom would say. "You have to consider the image from every angle." Then she would highlight her eyes and add a little beauty dot just below her right eyebrow. "There, I'm finished," she'd say with satisfaction. "The beauty mark is like the period at the end of a sentence." Then she'd punctuate *that* statement by giving me a kiss on the cheek.

One night Mom took me to the Apollo Theater in Harlem to see a show called the Jewel Box Revue. A friend of hers, whose portrait she'd just painted, was performing in it. We sat in the first row, so close to the stage that I could see the dancers' hairy legs. I was totally confused. Suddenly, I realized the entire chorus of dancers was made up of men in dresses, moving and singing like women. Then a lady in a sparkly red gown came out to the middle of the stage and sang "Santa Baby."

Mom nudged me and whispered, "That's my friend." Just then, the lady spotted us and turned to sing in our direction. Looking directly at me, she purred the words "hurry down my chimney tonight."

The lady's name was Eartha Kitt, and she was just one of dozens of big-time musicians Mom hung out with. One night Mom came home fuming. "I will never go to her house again!" I heard her say to Helen. "I told her she was being nasty." Years later, my mom explained what had happened. The person she was mad at was Billie Holiday, who had pressured Mom to shoot heroin with her. When Mom refused, their friendship ended.

chapter 6

THE BIRTH OF THE BLUES

Me at nine on a day out with Mom,
who's learning to play golf with
Jackie Robinson, 1959.

It was December 1959, and Mom and I were hanging ornaments on our Christmas tree when a soldier walked into the living room. His uniform was a virtual rainbow of red, blue, and yellow stripes. His arms were loaded down with presents.

"Hey," Mom said jokingly, "who let you in?"

"When you leave the door open . . . ," he said, kissing her on the cheek. I should have been suspicious, but I was too distracted by the presents.

"This is Sonny," my mom said. "We grew up together in Georgia."

"These are for you," he said, handing me several brightly wrapped packages.

I was overjoyed, though it's obvious now that the presents were a bribe intended to secure my cooperation with what was about to transpire.

I tore into the first package. Inside was a bubblegum machine, the kind you stick a penny into to get the gum out. "Here," Sonny said, handing me a shiny new penny. "It won't work without this."

I took the coin and put it in the machine, and out popped my prize. Mission accomplished: He'd bought my compliance for the price of a sweet, colorful ball of gum. I was so busy with my little machine, digging out the penny so I could get another gumball, that I barely noticed they were kissing for real, on the lips. Nor did I notice that he'd slipped a diamond ring on my mom's finger. Then Sonny gave me another box, this one very small. I opened it and inside was a silver chain with a cross made of real diamonds. "I bought it in Korea," he said. "Look inside the center." He pointed to a tiny clear stone. "You'll see someone special."

I looked, and there was a miniature picture of Jesus as a shepherd. It was the most extraordinary thing I'd ever seen, and that cross instantly became my most prized possession. "I love it!" I said as Sonny fastened the chain around my neck.

Sonny was a sergeant in the US Army and had earned his stripes and badges from having seen action in Normandy and Germany at the tail end of World War II and in Korea. He had just come back from Vietnam, where the US military presence was starting to heat up, though it was not yet a full-blown war. Sonny was only in his early thirties, but to me, he was old and worldly.

That spring, Mom and I traveled via a special bus for servicemen's wives, children, and girlfriends to Fort Dix, New Jersey, to visit Sonny at his military base. I was the only child on board. It was nighttime when we drove through a big gate with barbed wire, then on to the barracks that served as the guesthouse.

The next day, as Mom and I walked to meet Sonny at the canteen for lunch, we saw soldiers marching in formation. A private escorted us to an old airplane hangar filled with soldiers sitting at long tables. Mom and I waited at the entrance as soldiers filed in. This must have been their free time, because they seemed lighthearted and happy, smiling and flirting with Mom on the way to their meal. With her bright red lipstick, flared skirt, and highest heels, she made quite a contrast to the soldiers in their drab uniforms. I thought she looked like a movie star.

Then Sonny arrived, and it was like we were with a VIP. One of the soldiers snapped to attention and saluted "Sergeant." Mom, Sonny, and I joined the line of soldiers to get what they called "slop." But we were in luck: It was steak day. Plates loaded, we sat at the long table and ate. I was the only child around, so the soldiers told me jokes, played games with me, and even bought me a Coca-Cola. It tasted like nectar. I had a fabulous time.

The following week, Mom told me that Sonny had gone back to Vietnam. We didn't see him for a long time, and life went on as usual. Mom and I went ice-skating in Central Park and then to the much fancier rink at Rockefeller Center. I even got my own ice skates, which we decorated with red-and-white pom-poms that we made. We also made doll clothes and doll furniture. We went out to eat Chinese food, and Mom taught me how to use chopsticks. For Saint Patrick's Day, she sewed me a majorette's outfit—boots, hat, and a green circle skirt with fringe—and we marched together in the parade, feeling very Irish. (We did have that teeny drop of Irish blood, after all.) At night, before she went to work, she and I would cuddle up on the sofa and watch old movies or Bugs Bunny cartoons on television, and I'd fall asleep. It was almost too good to last—and it didn't.

One day that spring, when I was across the hall playing with the neighbor kids, my mom called and asked me to come home. I walked in the door, and there they were, my mom and Sonny, being married by a preacher.

I was sent to sleep with Aunt Helen in her bedroom that night. After a month of this, Auntie moved to California, and Sonny took up permanent residence in our home. I was grief-stricken to lose my aunt, whom I loved dearly. But that sadness was nothing compared with the sorrow I felt over the loss of my one-on-one romance with my mother.

My stepfather wasted no time in taking over, and he ruled the roost with an iron hand: There was no more dressing up or going out. Our fun-filled bouts of creativity seemed to fade into a mundane routine of work, food, sleep. One night when Sonny was gone—he'd become a taxi driver and often drove in the evenings—Mom went to a party with some friends, and when she got home, Sonny started yelling at her and waving a gun around. He threatened to kill her if she ever went out without him again.

My only escape from the gloom was to dream my way out. I began cutting out pictures I loved from magazines and pinning them up on my bedroom wall as reminders of the big wide world outside those four walls. Because Mom worked at night, she'd often be asleep when I got home from school, while Sonny watched television in the next room. In this way, I learned to be a quiet person. At first this was so as not to disturb Sonny and his hair-trigger temper, but eventually, I realized that being quiet fostered my creativity. Amid the emotional tumult of that household, it gave me a chance to hear myself think. It's a technique I've used many times throughout my life.

On the rare occasions when Mom did have a spare moment, she taught me how to paint. We'd practice drawing eyes, because eyes, she said, were the most important feature on a person's face. So I spent a lot of time drawing, or reading, or studying. When Mom was asleep, I'd dance silently around the house from room to room, with songs from Broadway and movie musicals playing in my head. On weekends I'd go to the movies or walk in Central Park. These were activities I used to love doing with her. Now I did them alone.

Sometimes Helen would come back for a brief vacation when her love affairs went south. We'd pick up almost where we left off, with Helen and Mom back to doing and making all sorts of clever things. But my stepfather smothered fun like a blanket on a fire; all he cared about was watching war movies in the middle of the day and smoking big cigars. At night he'd have nightmares and wake up screaming. He slept with a pistol under his pillow and his shoes on. I asked him why he did that, and he said, "Never take your boots off." In a crazy way, it reminded me of Auntie Helen, who'd say, "Never take your eyelashes off." Sonny's fear was being shot dead; Auntie's was of being caught looking ugly.

I tried hard to make my mom happy, but sometimes it seemed there were no more smiles left to wring out of her. I ran errands and shopped for our groceries. On the weekends I'd do the laundry and ironing. Sonny barked orders at me like the drill sergeant he was, and if I didn't carry them out to his satisfaction, he'd threaten to beat me.

Once I walked in on a terrible fight between Sonny and my mom. I'd burst into the apartment crying, tears and blood running down my face, because a neighbor kid in another apartment in our building—a hateful bully—had hit me in the face with a brick. And there was Sonny, screaming at my mom and holding his gun to her head. I was terrified, but my adrenaline must have kicked in: Suddenly, I was lunging at him to keep him from shooting her. He was drunk and swatted me out of the way. Then he grabbed me, pulled off his belt, and repeatedly brought it down across my back—*hard*. The only consolation was that he got so busy hitting me that he forgot about hurting my mom.

I would have happily taken more beatings if that could have protected Mom from Sonny and his never-ending rage, which grew more extreme and violent with each passing year. Mom was too scared of him to fight back, and I was still too young to be the boss of my own life. I fantasized about the moment when I'd be old enough to say, *I'm leaving, and I'm taking Mom with me. You can go straight to hell.*

Such was my life from ages eleven to fifteen. Thankfully, I did have one friend I'd jump rope with. But even pursuing that friendship had its complications. She lived nearby, but to get to her apartment, I had to pass kids on the block who'd hiss at me and pick fights because I was funny-looking. I was too light to be black, too black to be white, and too skinny to be pretty. I worked out a system: I'd run up beside an adult who was walking in the same direction and stay at his or her side, out of sight, until I was safely at my friend's building. So much for being a carefree child.

chapter 7

ALL SHOOK UP

Me at fourteen, posing for
a modeling test shot in the
first dress I ever made.
Courtesy of Adelaide Passen.

$\mathcal{S}$*ometimes* I think Sonny's anger rubbed off on me, which often happens to kids raised in a violent home environment, as mine became. I no longer went cheerfully to school, as I'd done before Sonny entered our life. Now I seethed in fury at the bullies who made junior high a living hell for me.

One afternoon I was leaving school with my books strapped tightly in my book belt when I spotted the clique of mean girls who dominated my school's social scene. I ignored them, but the moment I walked out of the school doors, they followed me, as they'd been doing for several days.

"Hey you, Skinny!"

"Olive Oyl! Where's Popeye?"

"Toothpick!"

"Giraffe!"

Yes, I was tall. And maybe I did resemble a giraffe next to them. It was the truth of the jeers that made their sting especially harsh. By the time I was a block away from the school, the girls grew bolder. One by one, they came up behind me and pulled my long ponytail. They followed me all the way to the subway entrance. That's when I decided I'd had enough.

"You skinny! Bony! Stick!" they screamed. "Your mama's so skinny, she looks like jail bars."

I stood still without turning around, and all five of them huddled right behind me, pushing and shoving their weight into me. "Stop it!" I said. Nothing more.

Then one of them punched me in the side. That did it. I lifted my books and rammed the girl in the face. Another grabbed my hair, and I kneed her in the chest. Before I knew it, we were on the ground, scuffling on the rough pavement. The five of them jumped on top of me— each girl was about twice my weight—and I saw darkness and prayed for someone or something to help me.

But the kicking and screaming got rougher. I was fighting for my life. Finally, using all my strength, I clutched at the group leader's throat and didn't let go. She was gasping for breath, and the other girls jumped off of me to try to pry my hands off their friend's neck. I choked her harder, so hard that her face turned blue. I realized I had a death grip on her, and I actually felt my power surging. I hated her and she hated me and I was about to triumph by killing her.

The other girls were screaming "Get off!" but it was as if I'd gone deaf. I just kept squeezing her throat. Everything got quiet. The gang was eerily silent. In that hushed moment, I eased my grip on her as it dawned on me how close I was to choking someone to death. I got up off the girl and could feel my scraped, gravel-covered knees burning and bleeding. "Don't you ever touch me again," I said coldly, and turned on my heel.

I walked slowly into the subway station, onto the train platform. And then I saw the gang again. Before I knew what was happening, they'd surrounded me. They started shoving me as hard as they could, until I was at the very edge of the platform. They were trying to push me onto the tracks.

Thank God a man standing nearby saw all this, and he scared the girls off by waving his briefcase at them. The train came, and I got in and collapsed on a seat. I didn't stop shaking until I got to the door of our building.

High school didn't start off much better. My school was on the west side, off Eighty-Sixth Street, so instead of riding the subway, I took the crosstown bus through Central Park. My first semester was miserable. The other students harassed me on a daily basis about the way I looked and dressed. I tried to avoid trouble, but one afternoon I was hurrying across the schoolyard to meet my mom when three girls came up and threw a soda bottle at me. I was wearing my raccoon coat, which I'd bought for ten dollars in a secondhand store. I was so proud of that coat, the first fur I'd ever owned. I walked faster, but they were right behind me, running and hurling insults. Then I heard a deeper voice yelling in Spanish, and a beautiful boy with raven hair caught up with me. Believe it or not, he was wearing a raccoon coat, too. He took me by the arm and told me to keep walking.

His name was Juan Fernandez, and he was also new to the school. Unlike me, he seemed completely at ease with himself. "You're a star," he whispered in a magnificent Dominican accent. "We must forgive them—they're mere mortals." I knew instantly that I'd met a kindred spirit.

My other savior was the after-school drama club, which I joined because the principal said it was a way to get extra credit. I'd never been part of a group of young artists, and by the middle of the term, I understood that at long last I'd found my tribe. I made a few friends, including a girl named Frances and a cute, witty boy named Ray Robinson, Jr., whose father was the famous boxer Sugar Ray Robinson. I immediately developed a crush on him.

The big difference between these kids and me was that they were seniors and I was a fifteen-year-old freshman—a vast chasm when you're in high school. They also smoked cigarettes and drank alcohol. I did neither.

We began going out to a club on Fifty-Third and Broadway called the Cheetah, the first big disco in New York City, which held a teen night on weekends. We'd all pile into our friend's pizza van—it belonged to his dad—and go out dancing until three in the morning. I needed clothes to wear, so my mom taught me how to sew. These were precious times, sitting in the living room with my mom again, in a whirl of creativity and fabric, coming up with some pretty wild styles. Usually, Mom would suggest lowering the hem by five inches, and I'd suggest raising it by five inches, and then we'd compromise by raising it four. We mixed new looks with antique clothes from the twenties and thirties, and thus my style was born.

We'd even rip apart old clothes to repurpose the expensive fabrics into modern designs. And it was as if, with every stitch, my mom was threading her dreams of fashion and design into mine. The backlash from my classmates continued during the school day, but once the stars came out, I was on top of the world, heading to the club, joining in the line dances that were the latest craze. The girls would be on one line, standing opposite the boys on the other, everyone moving in sync to the R&B music, doing the Popeye, the Cleopatra, and a little bit of the twist. I wore anything and everything my mom and I dreamed up, and my wardrobe was starting to get noticed.

One night I went to the Cheetah with Frances, who was now my closest friend. All I wanted to do was dance with Ray, but he was quite the playboy and barely noticed me. I sort of slid off to the side, and as I stood there, looking longingly at him, I heard a male voice say, "You know that guy you're looking at?"

"Yeah," I said.

"He's a friend of mine." Then he said, "Wanna dance?"

The guy's voice was vaguely familiar and so smooth I almost swooned. *He could be a newscaster,* I thought. Then he said, "My name is Frankie Crocker, what's yours?"

Frankie Crocker? As in the number-one-disc-jockey-in-the-whole-region Frankie Crocker? No wonder his voice sounded familiar: I listened to his show every night. He was the original Soul Man, a pioneer in black-format radio who singlehandedly brought R&B to millions of teens. His program was the heartbeat of the city, especially for young black teenagers—*the* total black experience in sound. Before spinning a record, he would always tell little stories, complete with enigmatic, thought-provoking phrases like "Wherever you go, there you are," or "You don't have to be a pauper to be unhappy," which would match the theme of the song he was about to play. He'd always sign off with something inspiring, like "You can't run away from your destiny."

Clearly, he was *my* destiny that night. Frankie, who later became known for wearing silky open-necked shirts and lots of gold chains, was impeccably dressed in a three-piece suit. He took me by the hand, and we danced in line. Ray came over. "You're dancing with Frankie?" he said to me.

"Hey, I found her," Frankie said.

"Well, she's with us," Ray replied. *Suddenly, he's jealous? That's a positive development,* I thought.

We compromised and all danced together. Ray knew Frankie through his dad, because Frankie had interviewed Ray Sr. for his radio show. After we were good and tired from dancing, we all decided to go to the beach. Ray and I got into Frankie's fancy convertible, me in the front seat with Frankie and Ray in the backseat with the girl he was after. Off we went into the night, with loud Latin music playing. The other kids went ahead in the van.

We drove to Coney Island, way out in Brooklyn. We all sat under the boardwalk and looked out at the Atlantic Ocean, listening to the waves and feeling the midnight mist. But I was distracted: Ray was making out with that girl, and it upset me. Frankie saw the distraught look on my face and asked, "You want me to take you home?"

From that moment on, Frankie was my friend. He'd invite me over to his apartment, and we'd take his two huge Afghan dogs for a walk. Dressed in beige cashmere pants, a beige sweater, and a beige fur coat, Frankie was flamboyant. Because he was so tall and slim, the outfit made him look like one of his blond Afghans. He also liked expensive cars (one of many reasons his nickname was "Hollywood"), and he'd take me for drives in his champagne-colored Rolls-Royce and his small silver Porsche for two, where we'd listen to his taped show while we rode. And it was thrilling when he'd send me—*me!*—cryptic messages on-air for everyone in the tristate area to hear. "I'm almost finished," he'd croon.

"I'll be seeing you soon, so wait for me." That was pretty heady stuff for a high school student.

As handsome as Frankie was, I never felt romantically attracted to him, even after my ardor for Ray cooled off. And though Frankie cultivated a public image as a ladies' man, he was always a gentleman around me, never once making a sexual overture during the year that I knew him. Thinking about him now, I feel nothing but affection. He was like the big brother I never had.

chapter 8

SIMPLE TWIST OF FATE

Teaching myself how to move the fabric
of my homemade dress, age fourteen.
Courtesy of Adelaide Passen.

$\mathcal{M}y$ first brush with high fashion occurred on an ordinary school day.
I was leaving school with Frances, wearing one of my own creations—
a wool black-and-white houndstooth dress with matching leggings, spats
(my mom's idea), and a poplin raincoat. The crosstown bus drivers were
on strike, so the two of us headed for the subway. We were clutching our
books to our chests and walking fast to catch the train when Frances,
who had an adorable Spanish accent, whispered that a lady was following us. I looked over my shoulder, and there she was—pretty, stylishly
dressed, and young (though older than we were).

"Run!" Frances said, and as we did, the lady began to run, too. "Aren't
you afraid?" Frances asked, panting. "She's probably a dyke."

"What's a dyke?" I said. "She doesn't *look* scary." I stopped dead in my
tracks, creating a minor pileup behind me, and swiftly turned to meet

my doom. The lady stuck out her hand and, in a ritzy-sounding English accent, poured on a bucket of compliments about how great my clothes were. "Where do you get them?" she asked.

I told her that my mother and I had sewn them. The lady handed me her business card. In that moment, everything in that stinking, claustrophobic subway station receded. The letters on the card popped out for me to read: V-O-G-U-E. It was my mom's favorite fashion magazine. "Thank you for stopping," the lady said. "I've been running after you since Forty-Second Street and thought I'd lost you. I'd love to write up something about these clothes of yours."

Then, while Frances stood beside me, acting as if I were talking to an alien, I gave the lady my name, address, and phone number. Frances poked me in the ribs and shot me an *Are you crazy?* look.

"I'll send you the piece when it's published," the lady said. Then off she dashed, pastel-colored and pretty, into the heavy, dull crowd of straphangers and commuters, who, next to her, looked like robots dressed in monotones of gray and brown.

I was in the clouds, and I could have floated away entirely, but Frances brought me back down to earth. "She'll probably rob you," she said. "Now hurry up or we'll miss the train!"

Being noticed by *Vogue* seemed to come out of the blue, but this unsought gift was a turning point for me. My mom decided to make the most of it. One sunny fall day, I was sitting at her sketching table, looking at a teen magazine with the ubiquitous, wholesome face of Colleen Corby on the cover. My mom nodded at it and said, "You look just as good as she does."

"*Me?*" I said. Was she nuts? People usually compared me to a giraffe, not a cover girl.

"I'm going to send your pictures to magazines and see if they need models," she said.

Mom decided that I needed professional photos, so she asked her old friend Carl Van Vechten to take them. He was out of town and suggested his friend Adelaide Passen, who had a studio in the building that housed Carnegie Hall. She coached me a little and told me she liked the way I moved and loved my profile. At fourteen, I was thrilled by her words.

A few weeks later, we got the contact sheets, cut out the pictures we liked, and put them in envelopes addressed to editors at *Look*, *Seventeen*, *Glamour*, *Harper's Bazaar*, *Ebony*, and *Jet*. I nearly forgot to mail those envelopes because I stuck them in the bottom of my book bag.

We got some polite rejections, and time passed. Summer turned to fall and then winter, and I'd all but forgotten the attempt to break into modeling. Then, one late spring day when I got home from school, my mom waved a letter at me as if it were a winning lottery ticket. She pushed it into my hand before I even had a chance to shut the door.

Dear Mrs. Cleveland,
  Thank you for bringing your beautiful daughter to our attention. The Johnsons would love to meet you for our upcoming issues of Ebony. *They will be in New York in June. Would you please call us at the Waldorf Astoria on June 15?*

"June fifteenth! That only gives us a week to get ready," Mom said.

Ebony, along with its weekly companion, *Jet* (the first magazine aimed specifically at black people), was owned and published by a visionary couple from Chicago, John H. and Eunice W. Johnson. Mom and I were ecstatic that I might be featured in its pages. When we called the Waldorf Astoria, we were put through to Mrs. Johnson's secretary, who told us that she was looking for models for an upcoming fashion show and would like to meet me.

On the appointed day, Mom had me wear a demure white cotton dress with ruffles around the sleeve and collar. Under my dress, I wore the world's most uncomfortable garter belt to hold up my seamed white stockings. The finishing touches were a white straw hat, three-inch-high white patent-leather shoes with a strap across the arch that closed with a pearl button, and wrist-length white gloves. I looked ready for my first communion.

My hair was pulled straight back in a long ponytail. (Frances had taught me how to iron my hair straight, like all the Puerto Rican girls did.) I also wore black eyeliner, which I practiced putting on while looking in the mirror on top of the fridge. I hated makeup and the sticky way it felt. But Mom said if I didn't wear it, no one would notice me and I'd die an old maid. That scared me into using it.

We were too dressed up for the subway, so Mom splurged on a taxi. We walked into the Waldorf Astoria—which I knew only as the hotel of presidents and diplomats—and I saw huge glittering chandeliers suspended from the high, high ceiling. As we walked through, people sitting in the lobby—all of them white—glanced over. I blushed, feeling admired because we were so nicely dressed. It occurs to me now that perhaps those people thought we didn't belong there. And maybe we looked poor, or like hillbillies, in our homemade clothes.

The man at the desk told us that Mrs. Johnson was in the Presidential Suite. Mom and I clearly looked lost. The man took pity on us and said politely, "That would be on the top floor. Take those elevators to your left."

We got to the elevators, and the doors were opened by an operator wearing a uniform and white gloves. At last, another colored person. "Ladies," he said as he bowed his head slightly and gestured for us to enter.

My mom and I looked at each other with wide eyes. On the ride to the top floor, I noticed the elevator man eyeing me in the mirror. I felt like the virgin sacrifice, dressed in all white, climbing to the top of the mountain to meet Kong, like in the black-and-white jungle movie I'd watched on television.

"Wow," I said to Mom as we got out and started the long trek down the hall to the double doors of the Presidential Suite. "My knees are shaking."

"So are mine," she said.

I looked at her in desperation. I wanted to do anything on earth but walk through those doors. But before I could turn and run for my life, they opened, and out came two stunning, light-chocolate-colored girls. Next to them, fully and beautifully blossomed, I felt like a first-grader.

"They're nice-looking, but you're better," Mom whispered to me.

We stepped into the room. No wonder it was the Presidential Suite: It looked like a wing of the White House (or what I imagined a wing at the White House would look like). Sunlight flooded the place and huge bouquets of flowers, arranged in expensive-looking Chinese vases, were on every surface. There were several pretty ladies sitting around. Models, perhaps? A door at the side of the room opened, and a well-dressed young woman walked straight toward us, extending her hand. "Hello, my name is Sandra," she said. "Let me guess—you're Mrs. Cleveland and her daughter, Patricia." She turned to me. "Mrs. Johnson is eager to meet you."

I froze, unable to utter a word. Mom spoke for me. "Yes, we're so happy to be here."

Sandra urged us to take a seat and to help ourselves to some tea. When Mom and I saw the tea tray with its real silver pot, delicately painted teacups, fruit, marmalade, and coffee cake, we wanted to dig in. In fact, it was all I could do to resist stuffing the food in my purse to take home. Mom said, "Better not eat anything—you might spill."

And thus did I learn my first lesson in suffering for beauty: Never mess up your fancy clothes with crumbs or stains. So I sat, prim and proper, my back straight, legs crossed at the ankles, and hands folded in my lap. Madame Metcalf had taught me well—or maybe I'd just seen one too many Pollyanna movies, in which the girls walked around with books on their heads to develop good posture. I always imitated them, and in that moment I knew all my book-on-the-head practice had paid off.

Sandra came back and said, "Mrs. Johnson will see you now." We walked into the next room, and a woman with a warm smile and kind dark eyes stood up from what I was sure was an inlaid Louis XIV desk just like one I'd seen at the Metropolitan Museum of Art (though hindsight and common sense tell me it was a high-end reproduction). Mrs. Johnson shook our hands. Then she sat back down and said in a lilting Southern accent, "Sandra, ask Miss Cleveland to walk for us."

So Miss Cleveland did just that. And my life as a professional model began.

chapter 9

LOVE WALKED IN

The cover of the 1966 *Ebony* Fashion
Fair program. The photo was taken
on my sixteenth birthday.
Courtesy Johnson Publishing
Company, LLC. All rights reserved.

Eight days later, on June 23, 1966 (my sixteenth birthday), Mom and I reported for duty at *Ebony*'s photo studios.

"Hello, ladies!" said Sandra, greeting us at the door. "Follow me." She picked up our bags and led us through a narrow arched doorway to the dressing room. There were clothes everywhere, hanging on wheeled metal racks. One side of the cramped space was a full wall of mirrors, and the other was a wall-long makeup table, with many small mirrors framed by bright lightbulbs. It was what I'd always imagined the back-stage of a circus would look like.

"We're working with our male model at the moment," Sandra said, putting down our heavy bags. "So make yourselves comfortable. Mrs.

Johnson would like to see you before we shoot, so I'll be back shortly."

Sandra left the area, which wasn't really a room but more of a partitioned-off space separated from the photo area by a row of those overstuffed clothing racks. Mom and I just looked at each other in silence, too dumbfounded to speak. "We made it!" Mom said finally. "We're here!" Quick as a flash, she unzipped one of the big black bags and winked at me. "I thought I'd bring a few tricks from the old days," she said. It was a reference to all those nights when she and Aunt Helen used to get dressed up to go out on the town.

She unpacked several exotic twisted braided hairpieces that she'd made herself (she called these her "masterpieces"); a can of hairspray; foam-rubber bra pads, complete with the shape of the nipple; and her entire makeup kit, because even though her skin was much darker than mine, I didn't have any makeup of my own. For a brief moment, I felt like a show horse about to get saddled up.

I unzipped the other black bag and unpacked a satin corset with tiny whalebones to keep the shape; a brassiere that would need the foam pads because it was too big for me; two ruffled tulle petticoats; and a lady's half-slip, to wear under a dress so you couldn't see through it. Oh yes, we also had natural-colored stockings, long evening gloves in white satin, and Styrofoam wig forms holding a few constructed hairpieces that Mom had stayed up all night creating.

She did my hair while I did my makeup. We were humming away, busy as bumblebees working hard to turn our efforts into honey, which, as Mom liked to say, "Rhymes with money."

"More eyeliner," she said. I followed her command. The more I put on, the older I looked. Within moments, I'd been transformed into a grown-up.

Sandra popped in. "Mrs. Johnson has arrived," she said. "Our photographer wants to start now with you and our male model. It's for a men's hair product." She went to the clothes rack and selected a pale pink evening dress. "Here, put this on." She held the dress up to herself and looked in the standing mirror. "It's Givenchy. Let's see how it fits."

The dress was so exquisite, I almost wept: The fabric and the workmanship were on a whole different level from our homemade clothes. I couldn't even see the stitching, and there were no safety pins holding pieces together, a technique I often used because I couldn't bear sewing for hours before I could wear an outfit. But I just stood there, like a deer in the headlights, holding the dress.

"What's wrong?" Sandra asked.

I didn't know how to tell her that I didn't want to get undressed out in the open.

Sandra caught on instantly. "You can go behind the screen if you like," she offered. I said a silent prayer of gratitude. Intensely shy, I couldn't imagine anything more embarrassing than disrobing in front of a stranger—or even my mom. Little did I know what I'd be in for as a professional model. Undressing in the open is part of the job description.

I ducked behind the screen and pretended I was in the scene from *Gypsy* where Natalie Wood changes behind a screen like that one, throwing her fancy feather costumes over the top. "You okay in there?" Mom asked after a few minutes had passed.

"I'm okay," I said. But I wasn't. The dress was huge on me, and I was afraid to come out, because I thought once Sandra saw how badly it fit, she'd send me home.

"Let's see how you look," Sandra said.

I took a deep breath and ventured out one bare toe at a time. I felt like a little girl playing dress-up in her mommy's gown, eyeliner or no eyeliner. Sandra sized me up and shook her head. Mom looked worried. Sandra left the room and came back carrying a box of industrial-size metal clips. "We'll need lots of these, so hold still," she said. "I'll make this dress fit." She clipped the fabric so tightly that I could hardly breathe. "There, it fits perfectly. No one will know what's going on in back—just don't turn sideways."

Sandra stepped aside, and I got a look in the mirror. There were so many clips running down the back of the dress that it looked like a dinosaur's vertebrae. When Sandra draped a robe over my shoulders, I looked like a hunchback. But when I looked straight into the mirror, I had an epiphany: Sometimes it's what you see up front that counts.

"Ladies," Sandra said, "we have created a wonderful look. Let's go shoot it."

Bright natural daylight was pouring into the studio. The photographer, Sleet, was a tall, light-skinned black man of around forty, wearing glasses and a bow tie that looked like a pinwheel about to start spinning in the breeze. Sandra introduced us, and Sleet asked me to go stand on the no-seam paper. "Is our male model ready?" he sang out.

I heard the smoky voice of a young man coming toward the set, but I couldn't see him yet. "I'm *not* a model. I'm just doing you guys a favor."

"I know, man," Sleet replied.

"Don't insult me by calling me a model," joked the tall young man, who was now striding toward me like a panther. As he came closer, I discovered the most poetically beautiful human being I had ever beheld. (I later found out that his mix of ethnicities was a lot like my mom's: Native American, black, and Irish.) Around twenty, he had dark wavy hair, a neatly trimmed mustache, and skin the color of deep, glowing caramel. My ideal man—until that moment a thirty-foot-by-seventy-foot Warren Beatty in *Splendor in the Grass*—went out the window and was instantly replaced by this guy.

His hazel eyes, flecked with green, bored into me. "I'm sorry to keep you waiting," he said with a slight bow. He gestured toward the stool. "May I?"

I nodded, knowing it was futile even to attempt speech. He sat down just in front of me. I could see Mrs. Johnson whisper something into Sleet's ear.

"Miss Cleveland, I hear it's your birthday," Sleet said. "Happy birthday!"

I croaked out a thank-you.

Then the guy stood up, took my hand in his, and said, "May I be the first to give you a birthday kiss?" He leaned forward, and his lips brushed the top of my hand.

After an endless moment, Sleet's voice broke the spell. "Okay, Kenneth, that's enough. We've got pictures to take. She'll be on the tour with you, right?" he asked, looking at me. I didn't know what to say, but Mrs. Johnson and Mom chimed in together, "Yes!"

Kenneth looked into my eyes again, and I felt something profound move in my sixteen-year-old soul.

"This will be a kind of birthday portrait, so let's get started before it's your next birthday." Sleet stood behind his camera, mounted on a tripod. "If you'd both look this way for a moment. Now, Miss Cleveland, touch Kenneth's shoulder."

I put out my hand and felt his strong body beneath his shirt. Sleet took the picture. I saw Sandra whisper something in his ear. I still had my hand on Kenneth's shoulder. I wanted to keep it there forever.

"Sorry, we have to wait on this one," Sleet announced. "A few of the dresses have to go back to the designers immediately, so we'll do the fashion shots first and get back to the ad afterward."

"Too bad," Kenneth said. "I was just enjoying sitting here with Miss Cleveland." I removed my hand, and he stood up and said, "See you in a while."

I held on to that promise as I went back to the dressing room to try on the clothes, each piece more beautiful than the last. I posed in several outfits, listening carefully to Sleet's directions, sometimes waiting for the flash to work, and showing off the dresses as best as I could. My mom and I changed my hairdo for each of the outfits.

"That's great, Miss Cleveland, just great," Sleet said. "This is the last shot, then we'll get back to the shot with Kenneth."

"You'll wear the pink Givenchy again," Sandra said.

I felt as though it were mine now, forever. I still get that feeling sometimes; once you're photographed in a dress, seen in it, it's as if it belongs to you.

Back on the set, Kenneth was waiting. "So you're going with the show, too?"

I still didn't know what the show was, but I didn't care as long as we were both going. I opened my mouth to say something, but Sleet called out, "Okay, you two, take the same positions." I settled my hand on Kenneth's shoulder as if it had never left. "Miss Cleveland, you need to look at Kenneth in an adoring way in this shot," Sleet explained, "as though you are in love with him because his hair is so well groomed." It most definitely was. I put all I had into loving Kenneth's hair, never once thinking about the photo or the product we were supposed to be endorsing.

Sleet took a few shots and reloaded his camera to take more. Back in 1966, there were only six to twelve shots on a roll of film. "Great work," he said. And we were done.

Mom and I went back to the dressing room. "I'm so happy," I told her, twirling around to accentuate my point. "This is so much fun."

"I guess *so*," she agreed. "Getting to wear these beautiful clothes!" She was busy packing our bags.

"Mom, I don't ever want this feeling to end."

On the way out, we passed Kenneth washing his hair over the sink, shirtless. "Excuse me, ladies," he said. "Don't mean to be rude, but I've got to get this gook out. Does anybody actually *use* this stuff?"

He stood upright, and as he did, I saw his half-nude body, the shampoo suds trickling down his bare chest. My heartbeat accelerated, and all at once I was in the middle of a scene from *Splendor in the Grass* with a darker-skinned, half-dressed Warren Beatty. Kenneth was drying his hair roughly with the big towel, and as he moved, the muscles flexed in his manly arms. He was as toned as an athlete.

Sandra and Mom had gone ahead, but I couldn't move. Kenneth flashed that glittering smile and said, "Hope to see you again soon." That was enough to send me out the door on a cloud.

In the hall, Sandra told Mom and me about the next photo shoot. She said she'd call with the details about the upcoming *Ebony* Fashion Fair. This was "the show" that Kenneth had alluded to—*Ebony* magazine's revolutionary traveling fashion tour. Started by Mrs. Johnson in 1958 as a fund-raiser for a hospital in New Orleans, the show brought all the newest clothing trends directly to black women around the country via a bus filled with girls like me who modeled the clothes on temporary runways set up in hotels, convention centers, auditoriums, and theaters. At the time, it was the best (actually, pretty much the *only*) chance for middle-class black women to experience high fashion or for unknown black designers to gain recognition. The idea of being part of such an historic and important milestone in the lives of African-American women was exciting. Then, too, there was the not insignificant fact that Kenneth would be along for the ride.

Sandra said goodbye and Mom started walking. I dawdled, unwilling to leave this magical place. Everything felt different now that I'd been struck by Cupid's arrow.

"Are you okay?" Mom asked. She dropped her bag and put her hand to my forehead. "You feel warm," she said. "Are you tired?"

"No, Mom." I paused, then decided to just spit it out. "I'm in love!"

"You're what?"

"I'm in love."

"*Really?* Who's the lucky guy?" Mom seemed amused.

"Kenneth."

"But you just met him."

I was in a dreamy mood. "This must be love at first sight. That's what makes it so special."

Mom laughed. "Oh, isn't that cute—puppy love," she said, picking up her bag. "You'll see him again, but for now, let's go home."

chapter 10

TICKET TO RIDE

This Greyhound bus—a.k.a. "The Hound"—was
my home from September till December 1966.

$\mathcal{M}y$ teachers weren't thrilled that I'd be gone for most of the fall semester, but the Fashion Fair was a big deal. I was able to get all my assignments in advance; I'd keep up with my schoolwork on the bus. Because of my age, I couldn't make the trip without a chaperone, so Mom was taking time off work to accompany me. I felt so lucky that I would have her to myself for a few months. Not only would it be a new adventure for us, but she would also be getting a break from Sonny. She never said so, but I'm sure she was as happy about that as I was.

Finally, the big day arrived. On a Sunday at six in the morning, with the streets of New York nearly deserted, Mom and I made our way to Rockefeller Center. We each carried one personal bag and one big suitcase—all we were allowed, since the clothes for the show were travel-ing with us and took up most of the space in the bus's luggage compartment. My case was a hot-pink Samsonite, which had busted our budget, but Mom wanted me to have the best. She thought of it as an investment.

We boarded the brand-new silver Greyhound (henceforth known as "the Hound") and claimed two seats near the front, stuffing personal items into the overhead racks. I looked out the bus window and noticed a group of seven gorgeous girls in varying shades of brown, coming out of 1270 Avenue of the Americas. I realized they were the other models on the tour. Quickly, they boarded, and we made our introductions. There were eight of us in all: Gertrude, Allene, Joanna, Diane, Theresa, Irma (from Trinidad), and Peggy (from Italy). And me, of course.

There were also, among others, our art director, Herbert Temple, and, bless their hearts, the wardrobe ladies, Cooper, Lily, and Virginia—older women who sat in the back between the hatboxes and extra hanging bags and kept the clothes in good shape with their sewing, ironing, and packing talents.

Now I just had to wait for the most important person to arrive: Kenneth. Everyone was really friendly with each other; most of the girls had been at the *Ebony* offices since earlier that morning. Except for Theresa, who was nineteen, they were all in their late twenties and stuck together the way single women of that age tend to do.

We were just getting settled when the stage/road manager, Albert—a small black man with a booming voice—got up and announced, "Ladies, we're going to have a great time together, so let's have a cheer!"

We all clapped and shouted.

"Before you get too excited, I have to let you know that I'm also the bad guy," he said with a smile. "I'm the one who'll be behind you like a sheepdog. So, ladies, here are the rules of the road. Rule one: Don't miss the wake-up calls. Rule two: Don't miss the bus, because we won't wait for you, and you won't get paid your weekly allowance. Oh yes, and rule three: I'm the one who gives you that check at the end of the week, so don't make any mistakes. Be nice to me no matter what happens." We all laughed, acknowledging the good humor with which he delivered the rules. "I'm not kidding," he added in a serious tone. He seemed so stern that we shut up like birds in a cage with the cover thrown on top. Then he laughed, which broke the ice, and he walked through the bus like an inspector.

"Who'd be afraid of him?" Mom whispered to me. "He's so little!"

True, Albert was small in stature, but we'd discover that he was courageous and had a huge heart.

Next up was Ben, our bus driver. He climbed on board, took his seat behind the large steering wheel, and spoke into a mike that was connected to loudspeakers. "Good morning, ladies. I want you to know that I've driven buses for fifteen years, so you're safe with me. And I pack a pistol, so if there's trouble, I'll take care of it." He adjusted the mirrors. "Don't be afraid to come up here and keep me company so I won't fall asleep when it gets late." Right then and there, I knew what my number one job was: to keep Ben awake.

I looked around the bus and didn't see Kenneth anywhere. Perhaps he'd boarded through the back door and I hadn't noticed amid all the commotion. But no, everything in the back was closed up tight. Albert started to count heads, and I started to worry. "Mom, where's Kenneth?" I asked. Just then I looked out the bus window and saw him running toward the bus. He climbed the steps and stood in the center aisle. My entire body heaved with relief.

"Hey, man, what are you doing here?" Albert said.

"I just came to say goodbye to the ladies."

Goodbye? He was kidding. He had to be kidding.

"Hey, girls, have a good trip," he said. All of them (except for me) waved as he stepped off the bus. I heard one say, "Did you know he's Billy Eckstine's son?" That got my attention, because Billy Eckstine was one of the singers Mom had known back when she was part of the Harlem jazz scene.

Ben closed the bus doors behind Kenneth and started up the motor. "We're all here, Ben," Albert said. "Full speed ahead."

"What about Kenneth?" I nearly wailed, knowing how pathetic I sounded, like a small child who's lost her blankie and can't bear the thought of leaving home without it.

"He's not coming, sugar. He's off the list."

My face fell. No Kenneth? He was my main reason for wanting to go on this tour. It would be so romantic! Four months on the bus together, getting to know each other, gazing into each other's eyes . . . Well, so much for that little daydream. I felt as if I'd been putting my pennies into the wrong piggy bank. I curled up in my seat and pouted while everyone else let out a whoop as Ben wheeled the big Greyhound into the traffic.

Peering out the window, I kept my eye on Kenneth as long as I could. Then we turned the corner and headed off to our first show, which was in Staten Island, New York. *Goodbye, love,* I thought. And *Hello, Color-balloo,* which was the theme of this, *Ebony's* ninth annual fashion show. My mood lifted as I thought about what a privilege it was to be part of the cutting edge of black culture.

The first show was in some sort of meeting hall with a makeshift runway that looked as though it had been constructed on top of a bunch of tables, and one large spotlight. The tickets were around fifty dollars a head, and the proceeds were going to one of the American Negro college funds. The backstage was so narrow, there was almost no room for the clothes. But we girls were pros now, and we dressed quickly in our show clothes, which Mrs. Johnson had purchased on her shopping trips to the finest couture houses in Italy and France, as well as in New York. The designers included Balenciaga, Ungaro, Pierre Cardin, Madame Grès, Marc Bohan for Christian Dior, Yves Saint Laurent, Roberto Capucci, Jacques Heim, Chanel, Nina Ricci, Jean Patou, Jeanne Lanvin, Givenchy (my personal favorite, simply because he'd been my first), Ken Scott, Emilio Pucci, Valentino, Jacques Tiffeau, Geoffrey Beene, Donald Brooks, John Kloss, Anne Klein, Norman Norell, Bill Blass, and Chester Weinberg. Mrs. Johnson was the only African-American to attend the couture shows in Europe, so she never had to worry that her audiences would see similar clothes elsewhere.

Dave Rivera, our bandleader, started rehearsing with the jazz quartet he'd put together that day (he used local musicians on every stop of the tour), and backstage, all of us girls started singing to the live music while we put on our makeup. It was hard for the girls with darker complexions to find makeup that matched, so they had to create their own. This was an art in itself; they'd mix various shades of brown eye shadow into foundation to get the right shade. This was back when skin-tone foundations for women of color were not widely available, and crayons labeled "flesh" were a pinkish-peach color. My own skin definitely was not that flesh color, but it was much lighter than that of the other girls in the show.

Mom caught a lucky break before the first show even began. After doing my hair—she always used wigs so my actual hair wouldn't be destroyed during the tour—she helped me dress and then started helping the wardrobe ladies. She decided to put herself forward for the job of dresser and wardrobe lady, and Mrs. Johnson agreed to the deal. It was all arranged very quickly, and before we left Staten Island, Mom was on staff, making money. It was a good thing, too, since she'd taken a leave from her regular job to come with me, and without that income, Sonny would have had a hard time paying the rent and other expenses back home.

My first time onstage as a model was disorienting. As the curtain parted, Dave started up the music. The band played an accented beat whenever a new girl was to appear onstage, and Carole DiPasalegne, the commentator, would describe the outfit the girl was wearing. Carole's voice was so velvety, and she made everything sound so good, that her commentary became my favorite part of the show.

When I stepped into the spotlight for the first time, I had no idea the light would be so strong. I couldn't see a thing; I had to literally feel my way down the narrow platform by walking extra carefully so as not to fall off. It was my first lesson of the runway: Think with your feet. To make matters worse, the stage was on a slant, so I anchored my hands on my hips to keep my balance and distract the audience from what was going on with my feet.

And so it went for the next two hours, back and forth to the dressing room, tearing off the clothes at breakneck speed, pulling on stockings and boots, juggling and almost suffocating as the tight dresses were pulled over my head, which my mom covered with a cheesecloth bag so my makeup wouldn't smear all over the fabric. Out I'd go again, turning and spinning and flying the chiffon, as I like to say.

The frenzy didn't matter, because the audience was so enthusiastic. The joyful spirit in that place was contagious, full of soul. These were folks who genuinely *loved fashion,* and they looked it, too, all dressed up in their finest hats, long satin gloves, and fur stoles reminiscent of the fifties.

As the show progressed, the jazz got better and better, and so did the applause. And before I knew it, I was in my last dress of the evening—a bridal gown—for the finale. The male model who'd replaced Kenneth,

Jorge Ben Hur, was about thirty, South American, and so handsome that the women in the audience swooned whenever he appeared. The show's climax was the moment when Jorge lifted my bridal veil to kiss me, or at least that was what he was supposed to do. I was not expecting it and was caught off guard. Remember, I had never kissed a guy. Not once. I saw Jorge's face zooming into mine, and while he wasn't bad-looking, and he was also nice, he wasn't Kenneth. I wasn't sure I could go through with it. He leaned in, and I turned my cheek toward him. I continued to stall as Dave the Jazzman kept giving me the musical cue to do the deed already. Jorge came in again for the kiss, and I squinted and finally conjured up Kenneth's face in place of Jorge's. Smack, he landed one right on my lips, and I puckered up and kissed him back.

The audience erupted. I guess those women in the audience were living vicariously through me, fantasizing about being a young bride and locking lips with a Latin lover just like Jorge. I had no such fantasies, but there it was: From that evening on, every show on the tour ended with Jorge Ben Hur kissing me and the women going wild. I felt nothing; it was my job. My mother, of course, kept a sharp eye on him, especially since our dressing racks were close together during the whole trip. But he was a perfect gentleman, and he stayed on his side and I on mine.

chapter 11

MAN OF THE HOUR

Muhammad Ali and me in Miami, 1966.

Our Fashion Fair tour bus spiraled its way around the Northeast from New York to New Jersey, Long Island to Connecticut, Boston to Baltimore, Washington, DC, to Philadelphia. As we passed through Virginia—Roanoke, Newport, Richmond—everyone on the bus slept all day. Except for me. I had schoolwork to do; my seat on the Hound was my classroom. As I studied my American history textbook, I looked out the window and saw the very land I was reading about. It was a great feeling to experience my lessons firsthand.

In Winston-Salem, North Carolina, we were overjoyed to be invited to a private dinner party at the home of a prominent black surgeon, his gracious wife, and their handsome teenage son (who was too young to interest any of the other girls, so I had him all to myself that evening). We were grateful to have a home-cooked meal—our first in a month and a half. Often dinners consisted of whatever leftovers from motel breakfasts we'd managed to stuff into our pockets. We rarely had time to stop because we had to get from one city—or one state—to the next in time to put on the show. So we'd wrap pieces of fruit and bread in paper napkins and picnic on the bus. Another lesson from the road: Always have food in your bag, but watch out for bananas; they get squashed. Oh, and be careful what you eat. The trips were long, and the bus had only one restroom, which was usually broken or packed up with hatboxes. More often than not, we had to answer nature's call by the side of the road, which I despised.

The day after Winston-Salem, we headed for Miami, where we had one last show before getting a three-day break. Finally, some time off! We had been in thirty-four cities, done some fifty shows, and were beginning to look the worse for wear. Even so, we knew how lucky we were to be on the tour. Whenever Albert chided us for being even a minute late, he'd say, "Someone else could have taken your place," and we knew he was right. We also knew that if we broke the rules, we could be replaced *like that*. That's why there were basically no problems among us girls. We were buddies, at least for the time being.

Miami wasn't quite what we'd expected. It was autumn up north, and there weren't many people around except for the elderly. The hotels seemed deserted, a bit like movie sets that had shut down for the day. Still, there was sunshine and a beach, and I was starved for both. Our hotel, the Seville, was right on the ocean, and the scent of sea air rejuvenated my spirits.

The clerk at the reception desk told my mom that our room wasn't ready yet, so Albert suggested that the two of us wait in the bar. "Don't forget, showtime is at eight o'clock," he added. "That means be backstage at six." He tapped his watch and disappeared with the rest of the girls into the elevator. That left Mom and me alone, sipping our sodas and admiring the view.

A huge man approached our table. "Excuse me, ladies, I'm here with the Champ," he said, nodding in the direction of a group of men standing at the far side of the lobby. "He was wondering what you beautiful ladies were doing here at the hotel."

Mom craned her neck, trying to see whom the man was referring to, and within seconds, her face changed as from day to night. Her jaw dropped and her eyes grew wide, as if she'd seen a giant. She didn't say anything, so I answered: "Yes, ummmmm . . . *sir*. We're here to do tonight's fashion show, and I'm one of the girls in it."

Mom didn't speak. I'd never seen her tongue-tied like this. Usually, I was the silent one—seen but not heard, like a good child. Suddenly, she regained her voice. "That's really the Champ?"

"Yup, that's him. He's my boss. We're down here training for the next fight."

"Maybe you'd like to come to the show," Mom said. "It's here at the hotel, tonight at eight."

"We just might, 'cause we're off tonight. The boss is taking a little break."

"We can leave tickets for you," Mom said, almost too eagerly.

"That's a great idea," the man said. He pulled a calling card out of his pocket and wrote his room number on the back. "I hope it's not too much to ask, but we'll need five tickets."

"I'm sure it won't be a problem when they find out who's coming," Mom said.

"It's a date! See you ladies tonight."

Mom took the card, and we watched the man rejoin his group. The man known as the Champ was extremely young-looking; in fact, he was just twenty-four at the time. He shot a look in our direction as the other men hurried him into the nearby elevators.

Mom had a smile kind of frozen on her face. "Do you realize who you just invited to the show?" she asked.

"I didn't—"

"You sure picked a big one."

"—invite him. You did."

That night's show seemed to end before it began, and a sea of people poured out of the main ballroom into the hotel's mezzanine lobby. I thought the crowd was for us, but in the middle of the throng, I saw the world-famous Champ. Worshipers crowded all around him, and he was signing autographs while his bodyguards tried to keep the multitudes under control.

Mom and I were attempting to go to our room, but all we could do was move with the flow in the general direction of the elevators. Somehow, as we were swept along, I found myself shoulder to shoulder with the heavyweight champion of the world. (Though he had legally changed his name to Muhammad Ali by then, most people still called him Cassius Clay.) I tried to keep a polite distance between us, but it was no use; we were practically fused. He didn't seem to mind and stayed close as several of us, including his bodyguards and a few other hotel guests, squeezed onto the elevator. Then he turned to face me. He was even better-looking in person than in photographs.

"I enjoyed seeing you in the show," he said.

"Thank you," I said, elated. "It was fun tonight. The audience was really lively."

"Yeah, I like a good crowd," he said. "When they scream for more, you know you're giving them what they want."

"I know what you mean." I laughed, thinking, *Wow, this is almost normal, like a regular conversation between the two youngest people in this elevator.* Half of me was oblivious to everyone around us; the other half was all too aware that we were being watched not only by bodyguards but by my mom. I felt embarrassed.

The elevator stopped and several people had to get off. They were clearly excited to be near the Champ, but the bodyguards made sure they didn't touch him as they eased out. "You're the greatest, Champ!" they said.

The Champ replied, "When you bet on me / You bet on the best / That ain't no mess." When the elevator doors closed, he said, "I love those people." Then he winked at me.

Somehow Mom and I missed our floor, and she said, "Oh no, we forgot to push our button."

Everyone was silent for a moment, and then the Champ spoke. "In that case, you should come up to my place. We're having a little party, and I know everyone would like to meet you and some of your model friends."

The elevator stopped. "This is us, boss," said one of the bodyguards.

The doors parted, and the Champ said, "Are you coming?"

I looked to Mom for the answer. She nodded, and in that split second before the doors closed again, I said, "Yes."

And so it came to pass that on a Sunday night in October 1966, I walked out of the elevator on the top floor of the Hotel Seville in Miami Beach, Florida, on the arm of perhaps the most famous man on the planet, who to me seemed like a sweet Southern boy next door. Mom and I called the other models and told them that Cassius Clay was having a party. They arrived in the blink of an eye. There was lots of picture-taking of them with the Champ, but I just watched.

Then the Champ said, "I want a picture of me and this pretty lady." He gestured for me to sit beside him. "Buzz," he said to his bodyguard, "let her mom take the picture. I don't want you to take it, 'cause your face is so ugly, man, I might make an ugly face just from looking at you."

"I'm with you on that, Champ. They're a lot prettier than me—*and* you."

"Yeah, but between the two of us, Buzz, I am the prettiest, the greatest, the smartest, the best." They both laughed uproariously as Buzz handed the camera to Mom. "I want twenty copies of this one," the Champ said.

I could see that the other girls were a bit envious of all the attention I was getting. When I went over to the bar for a ginger ale, I overheard one of them say, "There she goes again, hogging the spotlight."

"Nothing wrong with that," the other girl said.

"That's the problem," said the first girl. "If she weren't so innocent, he'd be paying more attention to us. We're closer to his age. You know what I heard? She lied about her age to do the tour. She's just fifteen!"

"So? Who cares?"

"She's a baby. Nobody seriously wants someone that young. And guess who's looking for a wife?"

"Let me guess—the Champ?"

"*Bingo.* Whoever gets him is sitting pretty for life. Somebody has to, and it might as well be me."

Just then the Champ came over and asked me to tour Miami with him the next day. I was excited about that but also exhausted, physically and emotionally. So I said good night, left the party, and went to bed.

The next day, I woke at sunrise, put on my new bikini, grabbed a big towel, wrote a note for Mom (who was still sleeping), and headed for the beach. How I loved to be on my own, in nature, with no one telling me what to do. What a heavenly sensation—just sand and water for miles and miles, all for me, the lifeguard, and a few early-morning surfers. I went for a swim in the shallow surf and felt small salty waves tickle my body. I danced with the handful of seagulls and sang with my eyes closed, spinning round and round with joy.

Then, out of the corner of one eye, I saw a man running toward me. As he got closer, I recognized the Champ, without his bodyguards for once. He picked up my towel off the sand and said, "You need this. You shouldn't be out here in that bikini. I don't want other men to see you."

Assuming he was joking, I laughed, and he laughed. Still, he wrapped the towel tightly around me. "If you're gonna be my girl, you can't be running around like that," he said.

What is he talking about? I thought. *Men love women in bikinis!*

Then he said, "My wife has to be covered up."

His wife? I laughed again and didn't say a word, but he looked at me sternly. Then he decided to change the subject. "Hey, you're an early bird like me. Wanna have breakfast?"

His room was humming with activity. "Hey, man, where you been?" his manager said when we walked in. "You gave us the slip again!" The trainer and bodyguards were there, too, naturally.

"You expect to go everywhere with me?" the Champ said. "I know where I go / And when I go, I go / 'Cause I am the show." The men looked offended, prompting the Champ to say, "You guys are so serious, I can't even joke with you! No wonder I have to get away sometimes." He asked them to find me a robe to wear.

I called my mom to let her know where I was, and the guys ordered enough food for an army. The Champ and I shared a stack of blueberry pancakes, and he ate a steak with home fries, and fruit, and raw eggs mixed into a glass of orange juice. "I'm going into training, so I have to eat a lot," he explained. "Right now I could eat a horse. I might even eat you." He pretended to take a bite out of me. His physical presence was so overwhelming that I actually got kind of scared. I think he picked up on my fear, because he said, "Want to see what it's like to stand in front of my fist when I throw a punch?"

He placed me at arm's length and jabbed out his fist, which looked like the front of a locomotive barreling into the station. It stopped about one inch from my nose. "Did you know my fists are registered as weapons?" he asked.

"That's understandable," I said weakly, my knees buckling. I actually thought I might collapse, but he caught hold of me in the nick of time.

"I'm sorry, I'm sorry," the Champ said, looking stricken. "I didn't mean to scare you. I'd never hit you."

I relaxed, and we joked and chatted with each other. He talked about his idol, Sugar Ray Robinson, and I told him that Sugar Ray's son went to my school (I didn't mention my crush, as I figured the Champ might be jealous). He even confided some of his doubts about the way his career was going. "Sometimes I feel like my life is not my own," he said. "It's like I'm owned by these guys who manage me. I get so sick of always looking at their bulldog faces." He also told me I was different from other girls. "Maybe it's because you're so young, like me, but I get a really good feeling around you."

The Champ's manager brought in the latest newspapers, all of which featured articles about him ("This town loves me," he said). He asked me to read them aloud because he liked my "little-girl voice." He put his big arms around me, and I read to him like it was story time.

That evening the Champ, his crew, and I explored the city from the Champ's car—a Cadillac convertible, with the top down. It was a sparkling Florida evening, and in the open air I felt on top of the world. People noticed us from the side of the road and waved, and I giggled and waved back. "If you think these people love me," the Champ said, "I'll take you to a place where they *really* love me." He leaned forward and said to the driver, "Take me to my people."

We drove into the poorest part of the city and pulled into some sort of plaza where a bunch of young black men were hanging out. They looked at the car with curiosity, wondering what such an expensive car was doing in their neighborhood. When they saw the Champ in the backseat, they came running. Children and old people and everyone in between, even stray dogs, poured out of every building, street corner, and alleyway just to get a better look. "This is the heart of what I'm fighting for," the Champ said. "And the people love me for it. And I love them. Watch—I'll show you."

He asked the driver to stop. The car was surrounded by fans, like a swarm of bees materializing out of nowhere, covering a hive. He stood up on the backseat, lifted his arms into the air, and started flexing his muscles. Thrusting fists to the sky, he yelled out, "Who's the greatest?" As if in a chorus, the crowd roared back, "You're the greatest!"

He bellowed back, "No, *you're* the greatest!" He was about to get out of the car to hug his fans, but his bodyguard practically tackled him to stop him. The Champ started to beat his chest like Tarzan; the crowd jumped for joy and started to clap. Then he sat down in the car, and the driver started the engine, and we drove slowly through the crowd, the top of the convertible still down.

The people just kept following the car, whistling. The Champ shouted, "Have no fear / 'Cause the Champion is near / And I'm gonna win / And knock that fool out of the ring / 'Cause I float like a butterfly / And I sting like a bee!"

With those last two lines, the crowd started chanting, "Float like a butterfly / Sting like a bee" again and again. The Champ looked at me and said, "I love this stuff." We slowly rolled out of that place, and I grasped what a profoundly powerful person I was sitting next to. He was like a combination of Little Richard and Martin Luther King, Jr.

We finally got to our destination: the training camp. The Champ jumped out of the car and said, "No woman has ever walked past that door." He pointed to the entrance of what looked to me like a broken-down, totally ordinary one-story wood building. "This is where Sugar Ray trained, and now it's my turn." He thanked me for coming with him, and I told him I'd had a great time. He asked to see me the next day, but I was leaving. He said we'd see each other before I left and instructed the driver to take good care of me. Then all at once Cassius Clay/Muhammad Ali was surrounded by a bunch of big guys who threw a white satin robe over his shoulders. As he walked away, I saw "The Champ" stitched on the back in red. He shot me one final look before being swallowed up in the world of boxing.

The next morning we got a seven o'clock wake-up call from Albert. The show clothes were already on the bus, as well as the wardrobe ladies and our personal luggage. A few of the models were still giving me looks, but most of them were too tired to care; they'd spent their night off out on the town. We all settled in our seats and Albert began roll call. Allene had just said, "Present," when one of the girls in the back shrieked, "Look! Out the window! It's him!"

"He's coming to see me," one of the girls said.

"No," said another, "he's coming to see *me*."

The Champ was running alongside the Hound and banging on it, signaling to Ben to open the doors. Ben couldn't believe his eyes; he'd missed all the hullabaloo because he'd been away for the break and had just arrived back in Miami. He opened the door, and the Champ climbed on board. Girls screamed and sat up straighter in their seats. I sank down as low as I could. I didn't want him to see me because I looked awful. He spotted me anyway and plopped into the seat next to mine. Looking pleased with himself, he said, "I told you I'd see you today. You almost got away from me." He squirmed in the seat; it was too small for him. "This bus is uncomfortable," he said, stretching his huge arms.

"It's not that bad," I said.

"Where are you going? I can take you there. I have a break, and we can have fun together. Stay with me."

Ben was watching us in the mirror with his mouth open, and I could hear the shuffle of the other girls working their way to where the Champ and I were sitting.

"I can't," I said. "I might miss the show."

Ben's voice boomed out over the loudspeaker. "Whoever is *with* the tour stays on the bus. Whoever is *not* with the tour, it's time to say good-bye. We've got a long drive today."

The clock was ticking; already we were two hours behind schedule. I could see Albert in the front, mustering the courage to ask the Champ to leave. Sweating visibly, he took the mike in his hand and said, "Ladies, gentlemen, Champ. We're glad to have you with the tour—"

Ben loudly revved the motor. Meanwhile, Mom rushed up with her camera and said, "Smile!" That was the last thing I could do. I was in the middle of an existential crisis, with no idea what was going on or what to do. The Champ could see he was getting nowhere with me, so he asked my mom if I could spend the day in Miami. She made a kind of clicking noise and went to the front to check with Albert. That's when the other models decided to make their move. They asked to be photographed with him, trying to take my seat. But he wouldn't let them have it.

Finally, Albert came over and said, "I *love* the idea that you would *love* to take our star here out for the day, as her mother just told me. But please understand, I've got a show to put on, and we've got to be on our way. So I ask you, please, whatever else you do, don't take away our star, or else I'll lose my job." I blushed at that. I wasn't the star; I was just part of the ensemble. The only special role I played was that of the bride in the finale, but that was because I was the only one the dress fit. Then again, Albert always liked to exaggerate. He was also, I see now, a master manipulator. He knew that the Champ would never want to be responsible for someone's job loss.

Albert turned and went back to Ben, who revved the motor even more. The Champ said, "I understand. That's show business." He took my hand and kissed it. "We have a lot in common," he said. "I'll be watching you."

"I'll be watching you, too," I said in the barest whisper. Then the Champ got up and walked off the bus.

chapter 12

ON THE ROAD AGAIN

This shot of me appeared on
the cover of *Jet*; it was taken
backstage during the first show
of the 1966 *Ebony* Fashion Fair.
Courtesy Johnson Publishing
Company, LLC. All rights reserved.

From Miami we went to St. Petersburg. When we got to our hotel,
there was a message from the Champ saying that he'd come to take me
back to Miami, then bring me to wherever I needed to be next. After the
show that night, I received another message saying that he couldn't come
after all because he had to train. He was as tied up with his work as I was
with mine. Talk about a two-career couple! We were ahead of our time.

The next day, we left Florida and ventured into the Deep South,
starting with New Orleans. Mom and I spent the whole day together,
seeing the sights and eating shrimp gumbo. My purple miniskirt seemed
to attract quite a bit of attention from the menfolk, not all of it positive.

The style, which was all the rage up north, evidently hadn't made it to Louisiana just yet.

That night, after the show, all the other girls went out to the jazz clubs, but I was underage and had to stay back at the hotel. So I just stood on the balcony of our room, which faced Bourbon Street, basking in the muggy night air and soaking up all the sounds that drifted up from the streets below. I was close enough that it was the next best thing to listening to the musicians in person. The following morning, from that same balcony, I watched a funeral pass by, with its wagon pulling a casket covered in multicolored flowers, trailed by a parade of trumpet players and mourners swinging to the beat. *Dancing at a funeral?* I thought. *What kind of crazy town is this?* I would have liked to stay longer, but Baton Rouge was next on our crowded docket, and then it was on to Jackson, Mississippi. I loved that word: M-i-s-s-i-s-s-i-p-p-i; I used to jump rope to it.

The Fashion Fair was weighted toward the Southern states: We went to nine in all and skipped most of the central states. We were often traveling through the night in the most rural parts of Alabama, Georgia, South Carolina, Tennessee, and Arkansas, en route to our shows in Montgomery, Columbus, Greenville, Chattanooga, and Little Rock. I asked Mom if she was happy to be back in the land where she grew up, but she just shrugged. I got the feeling there wasn't a lot of love lost between her and the South.

One night in the middle of God knows where, the girls were all asleep on the Hound, some stretched out across the seats, some sitting straight up and nodding, others leaning on each other, drooling. In the back, the wardrobe ladies were snoring heavily. In truth, we resembled nothing so much as hamsters sleeping in a cage, huddled in between the blankets, newspapers, magazines, and crumpled potato-chip bags. We ate a *lot* of potato chips on that tour.

Light gradually broke, and Ben greeted us with his perky, wide-awake voice. "Good morning, ladies. Time for breakfast." He pulled into an almost hidden, shabby-looking diner off the detour dirt road we'd been traveling on.

Ben, Albert, and a few of the girls practically sleepwalked their way out of the bus. Mom told me to go ahead with Joanna and Peggy while she tried to wake up the wardrobe ladies. All three of us needed to use the ladies' room, so we followed the signs and walked around to the side of the diner. We found a small, dirty wooden shack with a padlock on the rotten door. I pulled on the handle, but the door wouldn't budge.

Just then a big, lumpish man with blotchy red skin appeared out of nowhere and stuck his huge tattooed arm across the shack's entrance. He pointed to a hand-lettered sign over the door, half hidden by overgrown weeds, that read "Whites Only."

Peggy, whose skin was a pale olive color, was from Italy and was relatively new to America, so it took her a moment to figure out what the sign meant. She sounded it out in her cute Italian accent: "It . . . says . . . 'W-w-w-whites . . . Only.' What does this mean?"

The big guy said, "Just what it says. Your nigger friend here has to go 'round to the outhouse. We don't want no coloreds filthying up our toilets."

This place is an outhouse, I thought. *And it's the filthiest one I've ever seen.*

Peggy didn't absorb what the man was telling us at first, but when she did, she got really angry. "What are you saying, mister?" she asked, putting her face right up next to his. The girl was fearless!

The man pointed to her and then to me and said, "You two can use the toilet, but your colored friend here goes out back." He gestured to Joanna and then to the bushes, which presumably held an outhouse somewhere among them, though I shuddered to think what it must look like if this dilapidated shack was the "nice" toilet.

Peggy lifted her head, straightened her shoulders, and said haughtily, "If my friend can't go in there, I'm not going, either."

"Suit yourself," he said.

Joanna was yanking on her sleeve as if to say, *Let's just go,* but Peggy got even gutsier and said, "*Excuse me.* I'm going in there, and my friends are coming, too." She locked arms with Joanna and me, but the man just sneered at us, spat on the ground, and stood with his arms crossed, blocking the door. "You didn't hear me. I said: We. Don't. Allow. No. Niggers. In. There."

It was time to get the hell out of there. Never mind that the Civil Rights Act of 1964, signed just two years earlier by President Lyndon

Johnson, had outlawed Jim Crow segregation once and for all. I could smell the alcohol on the guy's breath and could see his decaying teeth, cracked and brown, probably from chewing too much tobacco. He was wearing a hunter's vest loaded up with bullets. Somehow he didn't seem like the type who'd be persuaded by legal arguments.

I looked around and noticed one of the other models running to the bus. I tugged on Joanna's arm, and we started pulling Peggy with us. As we approached the diner, Irma ran up to us and said, "Come on! There's trouble in there. We've got to leave."

We reached the bus and banged on the door. Mom pulled the lever and we all scrambled into our seats. "What's wrong?" she asked, but before anyone could answer, the other models were rapping at the bus door to be let in. I opened it as fast as I could, and as they burst in, they said, "They wouldn't serve us! They told us we had to leave."

"Where's Ben?" Mom asked, her head swerving around. "We have to find him."

"I'll get him," I said.

"*No!*" Mom yelled, then said more gently, "You stay here."

Then we saw Albert and Ben rushing to the Hound from opposite directions. Albert got in, looking distraught and disheveled, and Ben followed a step behind. The wardrobe ladies finally woke up, along with Dave and Jorge. Ben was just about to get off and check to make sure the doors to the luggage compartment were firmly closed when he saw several of the men from the diner marching toward us. Three of them were carrying rifles. Ben quickly changed his mind, hopped into the driver's seat, and closed the doors fast. He started up the motor, but it didn't catch. Ben called out, "Ladies, I believe we've just run into a pack of Ku Klux Klan boys, and I have a pretty bad feeling. So stay seated and *hold on.*"

The girls started to scream as Ben tried again to start the bus. "Don't panic," he said. "Stay in your seats and *pray.*"

There were about ten men now; they seemed to be rising out of the earth itself, what with the early-morning fog and the overgrown, untamed landscape. Two bloodhounds appeared out of the mist. It was exactly like something from a horror movie, except it was real. "Mom, what's happening to us?" I whispered, my voice breaking in fear.

Her face wore an expression I'd never seen before—a rigid mask of ice-cold anger. "This is what happens when you're in the Deep South," she said, "and you run into people who don't like Negroes."

Ben was talking to the bus like it was a horse. "Come on, Nelly. Don't fail me now." He kept pumping his foot on the gas pedal, again and again, trying to get the motor to turn over, trying to force it with the key. "He's going to flood the engine," Mom muttered, sounding desperate.

One of the rednecks decided to pound on the side of the bus. He shouted out, "This is a good catch of niggers!" He got more and more worked up, pounding harder and harder. His posse hooted and shouted stuff like "Yessir, we's gonna have a party with some of this nigger tail here!" One of them pressed his face up against the window, and he looked wild and glassy-eyed. I shuddered.

"Keep your heads down! Do *not* let them see your faces," Ben shouted, sounding scared and really, really angry. "They're like a pack of wolves—hungry wolves."

We scrunched down in our seats, some of us on the floor in the aisle. I didn't dare even lift my head.

The next sound was the sweetest I'd heard in many a moon: that of a motor revving up. I let out a breath I hadn't realized I was holding. As we peeled out of there, I couldn't resist a tiny peek out the window. In the quickly receding distance, I saw a hateful, distorted face screaming something that, thankfully, I could no longer hear.

☙

We figured we'd been through the worst, and for a while it seemed we had, as the Hound rolled on and I got a personal on-the-ground lesson in US geography that was the best possible supplement to my textbook. From Atlanta, we made our way north to Illinois, and in Chicago I went on a shopping spree to end all shopping sprees, buying a fantastic (and fantastically expensive) silver leather coat with a silver dress and silver go-go boots to match. (Ah, it was great to be back in a big Northern city, where wearing a miniskirt did not mark you as an alien.) We rolled through city after city, arriving in Little Rock, Arkansas, just in time for Thanksgiving.

I had no particular preconceptions of Little Rock, though I vaguely remembered being a little girl and watching Mom and Auntie Helen cheer as the newscaster on our tiny black-and-white television talked about the "Little Rock Nine." Mom had explained that they were nine heroic Negro teenagers from that city who'd walked through a mob of angry protesters carrying picket signs just to enroll at an all-white high school. It seemed like a very long time ago. Naive Northerner that I was—and despite our recent near-disaster—I never even considered the possibility that racial animosity could still be a problem in Arkansas.

Our hotel, a Little Rock landmark, looked like something a prosperous plantation owner would have built. The exterior featured immense columns and a spacious porch with high-back wooden rocking chairs lined up in a row; surrounding the mansion on all sides was a perfect flower garden that was still in full bloom. The interior had dark polished wooden floors that creaked when you walked on them, and nineteenth-century-style furniture buffed to a high gloss. I felt I had stepped back in time just being there, but I reminded myself that if I were actually back in that time, my family wouldn't have been living in the big house; more likely we would have been in the slave quarters.

Theresa and I decided to walk into town, which was just down the hill from the hotel. At nineteen, Theresa was the model closest to me in age. Thin yet curvy, with green eyes and sandy-colored hair, she was a dark-skinned knockout. She and I liked to sit in the front seat and joke with Ben or simply watch quietly out the window as America unfolded its gorgeous landscapes. Somewhere between Florida and Kentucky, we'd taken to calling ourselves sisters.

It was a perfect sunny day, with birds chirping and warm air ruffling our skirts. We were both in high spirits because there were only thirteen cities left on the tour—definitely something to be thankful for on this day of giving thanks. We didn't have a show that night and were going to celebrate Thanksgiving with a big dinner back at the hotel. When we got to the main street of downtown, it was deserted; all the stores were closed because of the holiday. Only a few young men stood together on a corner, smoking cigarettes. Theresa and I walked past them silently. They shot us dirty looks but didn't say anything at first. Then one of them started to laugh really loudly as he pointed at us. Before Theresa and I knew what was going on, we had four guys following us and hurling horrible racial slurs.

"Hey you, what kind of colored are you?" one of them said to Theresa.

Another one said, "Why, son, I believe she's some kind of nigger."

The two of us walked bravely on, ignoring them. They wouldn't be deterred. "Don't you hear us talking to you, you half coon or whatever you are?" another shouted as all four of them stepped in front of us, forming a human barricade. One of them leaned in close to me and said, "Hey you! White girl! What you doing with that *colored trash?*"

I stayed calm and tried to figure out an appropriate response. We were clearly outnumbered, and now the guys were circling us. *What kind of people act like this?* I thought. *Why are they so nasty? What can I do to change their minds?* (Did I mention that I was a naive Northerner?) I smiled my nicest smile, but the boys just narrowed their eyes and stared.

Theresa and I exchanged looks and silently agreed that we should go back to the hotel. We turned around, and one of the guys pinched Theresa on the rear, and another picked up a rock. When I saw that, I yelled, "*Run!*"

We took off like lightning as rock after rock sailed through the air, accompanied by such charming phrases as "You no-good nigger whores!" We ran so fast that my vision got blurry, but luckily, we missed getting hit except for one rock that grazed Theresa's arm. By the time we got to the hotel—it seemed so much farther away than it had on the way into town—we were both crying and Theresa's arm was bleeding. We didn't tell anyone what had happened, not even my mother, who was off with the wardrobe ladies in their sewing circle, getting the clothes ready for the next day's show. Maybe we should have said something, considering what happened that night.

I'd never been away from home for Thanksgiving, but Mom was my only real family, so home was wherever she was. And she was with me. The table was decked out with cut flowers, several polished silver candelabras, and an eye-popping spread of classic American food: three enormous roasted turkeys with all the trimmings, from corn bread to collard greens, pecan stuffing, sweet potato pie, and cranberry sauce. For once, the whole crew got dressed up and sat down together at the same table for dinner. We bowed our heads and Albert led us in saying grace.

Our prayers were interrupted by shouts just outside the dining room windows. We paused for a moment—I figured it was some sort of holiday celebration—but we were all too hungry and too excited about our meal to spend much time wondering what the ruckus was. Never have so many people made so much fuss over a lousy turkey drumstick. Then our peaceful evening was shattered—*literally*. A huge rock came crashing through the window of the dining room, sending shards of glass bouncing all over the polished wood floor.

We were speechless. Then we saw flames outside the window. My God, were the *trees* on fire? Our group became very still. Should we try to find out what was happening or ignore it and go on eating our dinner? Then we heard the words "Niggers, go home" boom out as if from a megaphone. It became a chant, a drone that filled the air and seeped through the walls like a toxic gas. One by one, we stood up from the table and cautiously went over to the window to see what was going on.

I was clutching Mom's hand as I pushed the curtain aside and looked out on a sight I had never witnessed before and hope never to witness again. Parked in the garden at the foot of our hotel's entrance was what looked like the entire local chapter of the Ku Klux Klan, holding lit torches and dressed in full Klan regalia—long white robes, pointy white hats, and white masks covering their entire faces except for two eerie dark holes that their eyes peered out of. Their cone heads tilted back as they moved toward the hotel in unison, like a blob of maggots. I was certain they'd be upon us in minutes.

Then, as quickly as they'd appeared, they were gone. It was almost as if we'd hallucinated them. Except they'd left us a little souvenir. Albert picked up the rock, which had a crudely printed note attached to it with a rubber band. He read the note silently, shaking his head, then passed it to one of the wardrobe ladies. "What does it say?" Ben asked. She handed it to him and Ben read it aloud: "'No niggers allowed in our historic buildings. Get out of our town!'" There was a collective gasp from the group.

There was no point in trying to salvage the evening. We were too frazzled to eat and scared that we might be murdered in the night. So we all went back to our rooms and hastily packed our bags. The hotel manager was distraught and tried to talk us into staying. He was a liberal with lofty ideas about changing the world through integration. But the Klan had threatened him, too, and our being there could mean more broken windows . . . or worse. I suspect he was secretly relieved when we insisted on leaving immediately.

After canceling the next day's show, Albert asked Ben to go out and start up the bus. So we boarded our big silver behemoth for yet another all-night ride, this time to Dallas. *Great,* I thought grimly, *that's the place where President Kennedy was shot.* Our grand adventure had taken a gloomy turn.

chapter 13

STARDUST

Backstage in Las Vegas, 1966. Acting
grown-up with Bill Cosby and a few
models from the show (*from left*):
Diane, me, Irma, and Gertrude.

After a week of riding through the desert of the American Southwest in that muggy, un-air-conditioned Greyhound, I woke up one night to white light and neon in every conceivable color and shape, brightening the midnight sky as if it were high noon. Compared to this place, Broadway was a dark alley. We were in Vegas, baby.

We pulled into the Sands, the best hotel on the Strip. The lobby was filled with slot machines and crawling with people playing them.

"I can't wait to try them," one of the models said.

"Yes, think of all the money we can win," said another.

I'm not playing, I thought. *I'm saving my money.*

Albert heard this conversation and, ever the prudent manager, decided to nip it in the bud. "If you think I'm going to let you girls blow your salaries on these machines," he said, "think again. You're not getting paid until we leave."

"Why are you so mean?" said the first model.

"'Cause gambling is a bad habit."

"We just want to try," she said sweetly.

"No way, we've got a big show to do here," he said. "Besides, what kind of friend would I be to let you throw your money away?"

Albert's strategy was backfiring, because now that he was forbidding it, I was getting interested. "Please, can we?" I asked.

Albert looked at me incredulously. "You're too young to even be in here!"

We all pouted and sighed. Finally, Albert gave in and went to get some special coins to put in the slot machines. He gave one coin to each of us. "That's all you get," he said.

I deposited the coin into one of the machines and pulled the lever. I held my breath as the numbers and bars and cherries went spinning round and round in the little window at the top. Then the cherries lined up three in a row and came to a dead stop. Bells went off and coins started cascading out of the machine, so many I couldn't catch them all.

"I won!" I screamed. "I won!" Albert was astonished, and he and the girls helped me gather up the money, which was pouring out onto the floor. That did it for Albert. He went off to get more chips, and when he came back, he handed them to the girls and told them to "go win."

I was tempted to play some more but decided to quit while I was ahead. Money had always been too scarce for me to take any chances on losing it. Besides, even though I was feeling lucky, I knew it was probably beginner's luck. I'm not quite sure where the maturity for that insight came from, given my tender age, but luck is just something I've always known instinctively that a person should never push. And I like to think I never have.

The next night I was backstage, getting ready for the show, when I heard Dave, our bandleader, onstage tinkling at the piano. I sneaked out to listen; Dave was a brilliant musician, and I could get lost in his jazz improvisations. He was wrapped up in his playing, but as he paused for a second, the sound of clapping broke through the silence in the auditorium. Then a voice said, "It's me, you old fool."

Dave stood up from the piano, peered out into the darkness, then saw the speaker walking up to the stage—a middle-aged man of short build with a mustache and close-cropped black hair. "Redd!" Dave blurted out, a big grin spreading over his face. Hearing his name, I knew it must be the famous comedian Redd Foxx.

The two men hugged and started talking a mile a minute. That night Dave told all of us that we were invited to see Redd's act at the Aladdin Hotel. So after we finished our show, we tramped over to see his. The man was funny—I mean, so funny that when he told a joke, I started hiccupping from laughing so hard. His act was rude, raunchy, and sexy, what comedians used to call "blue." I felt a little embarrassed, hearing the jokes with my mom there, but also very grown-up.

After the show we went backstage to Redd's dressing room, and Dave introduced us one by one. When he got to me, Dave said, "This is Pat, the youngest model in our show." Redd kissed my hand and gave me a dirty-old-man smile. Then he turned to the group and said, "So what do a nun and a junkie have in common?"

"What?" we all said together.

"A habit," he said.

We all laughed, but Dave clammed up. "That's not funny," he said. I wasn't sure why he didn't like the joke. I thought it was hilarious.

"Never mind," Redd said. "I was just trying it out, my friend."

We were about to leave when a tall, slim man appeared in the doorway. "Stop," he said. "Nobody leaves until I meet each of you lovely ladies." My view of the guy's face was blocked, but the voice was unmistakable: Bill Cosby.

"Hey, Bill," Redd said, "what're you doing here? I thought you were out in LA."

"I'm filming for a week out here, so I thought I'd take in some sun and fun and see your show, of course." He moved aside in the doorway to let another man come through. "I brought my costar with me."

Wow, now I was seriously starstruck. I adored Robert Culp, and *I Spy* was one of my favorite television shows.

"Hi, everybody," Culp said.

Redd shook Culp's hand and said, "Don't be jealous of all these pretty ladies, Robert. They just like handsome men like me."

Bill laughed and said, "I thought we'd hang out with you tonight."

"Wait a minute," Culp said. "You guys aren't gonna gamble, are you? You said no gambling, Bill."

"Oh, come on, Robert," Bill said.

"Not for me, man. I've got a wife at home."

"Ah, you newlyweds," Bill said. "So, Redd, I guess it's you and me and all these pretty ladies."

"What are you talking about?" Redd said. "You got a wife, too! I'm the only single fox around here."

"All right, I'll call my wife right now. Where's the phone?" While he was on the phone, several of us asked Robert Culp for his autograph. When it was my turn, Bill came up to me and Theresa from behind and put his arms around our shoulders. "Don't ask Robert for his autograph. Ask me."

I noticed he was sticking pretty close to Theresa. Redd noticed, too, because he said, "If you don't stop flirting, I'm telling your wife." He turned to the rest of us. "If you want to go out on the town with me, let's go! I'm paying, and you're all my guests."

So the eight of us plus my mom and the wardrobe ladies followed Redd Foxx and Bill Cosby into the Aladdin's private casino, where the stars went to play. What a spectacle. The glamour girls and high rollers. The blackjack and roulette tables spaced out under vaulted golden ceilings and chandeliers. Card dealers dressed in tuxedos shuffling cards, and gambling tables piled high with stacks of chips. It was like nothing I'd ever seen before.

I was arm in arm with Bill when Redd pulled me away and said, "You're my lucky charm tonight." He placed several stacks of bills on the table and asked the dealer to convert them to gambling chips. Redd was about to throw the dice when he stopped and handed them to me. "Here, honey. Throw your luck."

I'd never done this, but I'd seen a lot of gangster movies, so I figured I could wing it. I put on quite a show, shaking the dice and blowing on them before throwing. I didn't let go of the dice until I had everyone's attention, and when I did, they rolled slowly down the length of the table. When they stopped, the man behind the table said, "Win!"

I was ecstatic—maybe I really *was* a lucky charm—and Redd and Bill both hugged me. "I've got to keep you around," Redd said, and nodded to the table where Mom was sitting with the wardrobe ladies. "I hope your mom over there doesn't mind. Now do that thing again with the blowing." So I did.

Meanwhile, Bill and Theresa were getting awfully cozy. Everyone was buzzing about it, and to help offset the other models' jealousy, Bill invited all of us for dinner at his house in Los Angeles, where we were headed in two days.

When we arrived, Bill got in touch immediately and asked everyone involved with the show to come over. We models sat in the living room and chatted with his beautiful young wife, Camille, who was rocking their baby daughter. When Bill kissed her on the cheek, everyone giggled. You'd have thought we were in high school. (Well, I *was* in high school. But the others should have been a lot smoother.)

Bill went into the kitchen and returned with a tray of steaks. As he was heading out back to the grill, he said to Theresa and me, "Have you guys seen the garden?"

"Not yet," we said, following him outside to the patio. It was a cool night, so everyone else stayed inside. I oohed and aahed at the stars and what I could see of the garden, and Theresa busied herself helping Bill with the steaks.

"Listen," Bill said, turning to me. "Since it's so dark out, I think it's best to show one of you the garden and then come back for the other, because we have a crazy swan out there, and the slope is really steep. And someone has to watch the meat. If it burns, my wife will kill me. So can you keep an eye on the grill while I show Theresa around?"

"Yeah, sure," I said. I stood there for a long time, listening to the steaks sizzle, watching them turn crisp at the edges, until I knew they were ready to be flipped. I thought I'd better let Bill know, so I carefully, slowly, quietly went into the garden, not wanting to scare the crazy swan.

Bill and Theresa were behind a big bush, kissing passionately. Maybe I shouldn't have been shocked, but I was. I thought their behavior was despicable (though in light of the later accusations against Bill, the dalliance he had with Theresa seems almost respectable).

Some crazy swan, all right, I thought. I decided not to say anything and hurried back up to the patio and called out, "It's time to flip the steaks!"

As the two of them walked toward me, Theresa adjusted her skirt and Bill followed a few steps behind. Her lipstick was smudged. She looked at me, and I gave her a dirty look. Cosby tended the meat, oblivious. He handed Theresa the tray and put the steaks on it. "Let's go feed the gang," he said. "We'll see the garden later."

We all ate and talked past two in the morning, at which point Bill's chauffeur took us to our hotel in his limousine. Theresa and I were in the backseat, and Mom was in front with the driver. I was really upset. "I don't like what you did," I said to Theresa.

"What do you mean?"

"With Bill."

"It's none of your business. He likes me."

"He's married."

"Look, I hate to disappoint you . . ." Her voice trailed off.

"We met his wife," I said. "She's really nice."

"Listen, you've got a lot to learn," she said. "You're still young. A girl has to look out for herself. After this tour is over, I have nothing."

"You shouldn't do that to another person." I knew that many of the girls on the tour were hoping to meet men. Back then, the biggest ambition a lot of women had was to find a husband who'd take care of them. Presumably, they wanted a man who didn't already have a wife.

"I'm not hurting anyone," she said. "He likes me, and that's that. He can help with my career. He knows everybody."

"You don't have to take someone's husband to make it. How could you?"

"*How could I?* Next week when we're back in New York, he's coming to see me, and we're going away for a whole weekend. He told his wife he has a business trip."

I had a flashback to my mom sitting in the living room, saying, "I'm so tired. I wish I had a dad for you, someone to help us and love us." I was jarred by this memory. Camille Cosby had a husband and a dad for her two little daughters. And he was cheating on all of them.

I turned away from Theresa and didn't speak to her for the rest of the trip. She and Bill Cosby had destroyed any illusions I had about stars.

The tour wrapped up with shows in Bakersfield, Fresno, and San Jose. Our final event was in San Francisco on December 9. At the end, we stood in a single line across the stage, all nine of us arm in arm like a string of paper dolls, including Jorge, our token male and honorary bridegroom. As Carole, the commentator, walked toward the podium, she called out each of our names and noted, "Our bride, Pat Cleveland, and bridegroom, Jorge Ben Hur, have been married ninety times on-stage." Jorge and I stepped to the center of the stage, and he kissed me for the last time. By now I was an old pro and almost sorry to see our little romantic ritual end. We took our bows, and then someone from the side of the stage handed bouquets of flowers to all of us. I started to cry.

That night in the hotel, I fell apart. I got a fever (most likely brought on by sheer exhaustion) and as I slept, I dreamed that a gang of tough girls was threatening me, saying, "Who do you think you are?" and "You're not black. You're not white. You're *nothing*." Then they grabbed me and started to pummel my head. I ran and ran into the distant horizon. "Leave me alone!" I screamed. "I'm not hurting anybody!"

Then I woke up.

Mom was packing our big pink suitcases. "You were having a bad dream," she said.

"It was those terrible girls at school," I told her. "They were hurting me."

"Don't worry, darling, you were just dreaming," she said. "Anyway, you don't go to that school anymore."

The next day Mom and I were flying over the Rocky Mountains. My previous night's bad dream notwithstanding, I was eager to get back into the swing of my normal life in New York City. Doing the Fashion Fair had been an incredible experience, one that had expanded my head and my heart, but it had been hard work, and there'd been some painful moments that had cost me my innocence. *You've grown like a rose*, I thought. *And now you have a few thorns.*

chapter 14

THE BEAT GOES ON

Me, working toward my dreams,
during a typical day at the High School
of Art & Design, New York City.

$\mathcal{B}ack$ in New York, I felt a bit adrift socially. The kids I'd been hanging out with had all graduated the previous spring and gotten on with their lives. Two of them had even married each other. That's how it was back in 1966: People got married right out of high school. Ray had moved away, and Frankie now had a serious girlfriend who occupied all his free time.

I still loved to dress up and go out dancing. The summer before I left for the Fashion Fair, I'd noticed a new boutique at the entrance to the Cheetah. It was run by a mod British woman and stocked with clothes designed by someone named Tiger Morse. This was the height of the Carnaby Street era in fashion, and anything even remotely British was the rage. The walls were painted in Day-Glo colors and lit with a black light; when you walked in, your face looked purple, and your teeth shone so white they seemed radioactive. Hanging from the ceiling were tents made of Moroccan fabrics accented with little mirrors. It was one hundred percent psychedelic.

I was wild about the boutique from the first moment I walked in wearing my red patent-leather microskirt. I guess the feeling was mutual, because the manager saw what I had on and went nuts for it. She asked where I got my outfit (along with my skirt, I was wearing a feathered boa top), and I told her my mom and I had made it. She asked me if I could make the outfit in different colors for her to sell in the shop—or, for that matter, any other creations Mom and I came up with.

So I was soon producing a line of clothes for the Tiger Morse label! My mom, aunt, and I would stay up late, sewing like mad, watching television, laughing, singing, and talking until we couldn't sew anymore. And on weekends, before I went inside the Cheetah to dance, I'd deliver the clothes to the Tiger Morse boutique, collecting hundreds of dollars for the three or four dresses, tops, and skirts I left there. They were a big hit, and the store wanted more. I was ready and willing to keep supplying them. Mom used to say that sewing was like driving a car—easy on the pedal, don't let the needle run over your fingers, and keep going straight—and the rules worked pretty well for life, too. Making clothes was fun and creatively satisfying. Best of all, I'd found my vocation: I wanted to be a fashion designer.

At Madame Metcalf's urging, I applied for admission to the High School of Art & Design at Fifty-Seventh Street and Second Avenue in Manhattan. (Mom was won over by the fact that it was three blocks from Bloomingdale's, the chic department store where the stars shopped and where she and I loved to look at the mocked-up rooms in the furniture department and fantasize about how we'd decorate our dream house someday.) I prepared a portfolio of drawings on different themes, took a written test, and went for an interview. A few weeks later, a letter arrived offering me a spot at the school.

Since I'd been away during the first semester, I didn't start attending Art & Design until the beginning of the second semester. I took sculpting, photography, painting, art history, and (my favorite) fashion illustration. I really excelled at draping. I found I could easily sculpt fabric on the croquis forms we used in class. Draping was natural for me, because I was already doing it at home.

My goal was to get good grades in order to earn a scholarship to college. I was reaching that goal in all of my classes except one: my draping class, taught by a certain Mrs. P. She was a jealous, bitter woman who constantly sabotaged my work. She'd found out I was a model on the *Ebony* Fashion Fair after seeing my photo on the cover of *Jet*. She'd clearly decided I needed to be taken down a peg or two. Mrs. P.'s hostility got so extreme that she would hide my work. It was outrageous. I mean, how could a five-feet-tall croquis form go missing?

"My form isn't here!" I'd say, incredulous.

"You didn't do your work," she'd reply.

"But I left it in the closet."

"Well, you don't see it there, do you? So you'll have to do it again."

This went on for months, with me getting penalized for incomplete work. Finally, I decided to speak to the school counselor, who reported the situation to the principal. One day a school employee found Mrs. P. in the coat closet, destroying my work. Evidently, there was a lot of back-and-forth between Mrs. P., the administration, and the teachers' union, but ultimately, she was fired for harassing a student.

Do you know how hard it is to fire a tenured teacher at a New York City public school? The teacher has to do something a lot worse than being lousy in the classroom—and she usually has to do it many times. That gives you an idea of just how terrible Mrs. P. was. Thank heaven she was caught red-handed. Believe me, I wasn't the only student who was thrilled to have her gone.

That year I made several good friends, my closest being Jimmy, who sat next to me in illustration class and could paint like Michelangelo. It took me only a day to realize that Jimmy was a genius, so I couldn't understand why he was always so sad. We'd eat lunch together in the cafeteria and go home together after school, and he'd tell me that the world didn't understand him. He was my first gay friend.

Jimmy dressed really well and encouraged me to do the same. School dress codes in those days were strict: Girls had to wear skirts below the knees; no pants allowed. Boys could not wear jeans. Our school was more lenient than most, but miniskirts were still taboo. Naturally, I decided to wear one. The minute I passed through the front door, I was given detention and told to go home and change. I protested, saying that I was a designer and expressed my art through the clothes I wore. The argument went on and on: I was threatened with expulsion, but I held my ground. In the end I prevailed, on the principle that this was, in fact, an art school whose very foundation was creativity. Before I knew it, all the other girls had started wearing minis, too. The times they were a-changin'. Jimmy broke the same barrier for blue jeans, and shortly after that, Art & Design became the first New York City public school to allow both sexes to wear denim.

Jimmy's friend Steven Meisel was a total original, with long straight black hair down to his waist. A girl named Donna Jordan, whose signature was bright red lipstick, had a gang of creative-looking friends who congregated at her lunch table in the cafeteria. Then there was a guy named Val, who wore hats indoors and was already socializing with fashion illustrators and underground artists.

One Saturday night Jimmy and I decided to go dancing at a club called Salvation on Sheridan Square in Greenwich Village. When we got inside, we spotted Donna and Val, sitting with an older guy who had a mustache. Val came over and told Jimmy and me that the guy was a well-known illustrator, and we should come to his studio sometime. Then I saw Donna dancing with a girl who had very dark hair and very white skin, and a man with a pasty-looking complexion and floppy platinum hair. Val said he was a famous artist who also made movies. Val wandered back to his group, and Jimmy and I tried to blend in. We danced a bit and left early because Jimmy had to get the train back to Queens, where he lived. I kept thinking, *Wow, look at the world Donna's in. She's such a sophisticate.* I had no idea who her companions were or the "famous artist" I was nearly introduced to.

The following weekend I went back to the Cheetah, by now the biggest disco in the city, attracting some two thousand people a night. I was wearing a cocoa-colored jersey jumpsuit with cutouts on the side, near my waist. Mom, who'd finished it the night before, said it made me look like a deer, and I played up the doe-eyed Bambi effect by wearing it with three pairs of fake eyelashes.

Line dancing was over; now everyone was doing the jerk. I was jerking away when this tiny fireball of a guy dressed in a suit and tie jumped right in front of me and started making moves like I'd never seen before. Here was a guy who could dance! He was so entertaining and energetic, talking to me while simultaneously looking around to see who was who, and cracking jokes. He introduced himself as Bobby Seligman and told me he was a producer (of what, he didn't say). He asked me if I wanted to go with him to another, better club. My radar told me that he was okay even though I knew he was older than I was (I pegged him for twenty-two or twenty-three but later found out he was thirty), so we caught a cab and sped across town to Sutton Place, where the townhouses cost a fortune.

Our destination was Le Club at 416 East Fifty-Fifth, but there was no name on the awning, just a number. In fact, the only sign that the address was special was the line of limousines, Rolls-Royces, and Jaguars out front. Bobby said, "They'd better not see us getting out of a cab—they'll think we're broke." So we got out down the block and walked to the entrance, a polished wooden door with a tiny square peephole at eye level. Bobby knocked and the little square opened. A voice said, "Password," and Bobby said, "Cha-ka-boom." The door swung open . . . and so did a new chapter in my life.

The first thing I noticed was how elegantly the men were dressed and how elaborately styled the women's hairdos were. Lush floral arrangements dominated the central area of the cozy, dimly lit space, and the strains of Astrud Gilberto singing Burt Bacharach's "The Look of Love" filled the perfumed air. This was clearly a place of abundance, glamour, and power. And here, amid it all, was little old me. *Me!*

Bobby and I sat down at one of the round tables by the small wooden dance floor. He ordered me a mimosa, which he explained was fresh-squeezed orange juice and champagne (the drinking age in New York was eighteen at the time, and I was almost seventeen, but no one asked), and then a filet mignon served by a waiter in white gloves. What a leap in a single night: from Kool-Aid and Velveeta (my usual dinner at home) to mimosas and filet mignon.

I was pretty free to come and go as I pleased, because my mother trusted me. Besides, she had her hands full trying to handle Sonny's moods and the demands of her job at Bellevue Hospital. She'd also taught me well. Unlike Little Red Riding Hood in the bedtime stories she'd read to me, I was aware of the wolves; I'd already met a few and knew what to watch out for.

I began to lead two distinct lives with two distinct sets of friends—my school friends like Jimmy and my out-of-school friends like Bobby. During the week I'd sketch and pose (my teachers liked to use me as a model because they said I had the "perfect fashion body"); on weekends, I'd hang out with Bobby, who was really my best friend now, despite our age difference. He and I had a blast together. He introduced me to high society—the wealthy, famous people of every nationality who flew first-class all over the world in new Boeing airplanes just to attend a party. Bobby's friends included Oleg Cassini—a Russian-born fashion designer who was celebrated for creating the "Jackie look" when Jacqueline Kennedy was first lady—and his brother Igor (whom everybody called "Ghighi"). Both brothers, Bobby told me, were on the board of Le Club and were instrumental in deciding who got in. Ted Kennedy was a regular, and even the Supremes came on certain nights. There were politicians and celebrities, and everyone always wore fabulous clothes. We all mixed and danced together. Bobby would ask me to get the dancing started, so after dinner (and boy, did I grow fond of those mimosas and filets mignons), I'd step onto the dance floor and begin dancing alone. After a few minutes Bobby would join me, and then everybody else. Bobby was an even better dancer than I was and taught me a lot of cool moves. Together, we perfected a kind of routine.

Once everybody was up and dancing, Bobby and I would escape upstairs to the VIP rooms, with their plush wine-colored velvet sofas, where we'd join Ann Turkel, a mind-bogglingly gorgeous model who appeared in almost every issue of *Vogue*, and the actor Richard Harris, who had just played Lancelot in the movie version of *Camelot* and whose song "MacArthur Park" was climbing the pop-music charts. I adored his sexy Irish brogue. Then we'd eat caviar, and they'd all drink champagne. I stuck mostly to tonic water or ginger ale, not because I was underage but because I preferred those beverages. From up there, Bobby and I would choose the music for the club. Having an in-house disc jockey was a brand-new trend, especially for a posh place like this.

Bobby would pick pieces that I would sing along to into the microphone—Burt Bacharach, Sergio Mendez, the Beatles. I'd cover them all. Bobby was determined to turn me into a vocalist, and I was happy to go along. My voice wasn't strong and soaring; it was tiny and more of a whisper. Evidently, it sounded sexy, and that suited the times.

Occasionally, Bobby and I would go to the Copacabana to play cards and backgammon with Omar Sharif (who was just as handsome as he was when, at fifteen, I'd swooned over him in *Doctor Zhivago*). Omar was a world-class bridge player, and when he played with Yul Brynner, I'd hold my tongue because they needed to concentrate. Both of them were charming and surrounded by beautiful women in caftans and eye-popping jewels. Sometimes they'd flirt with me and play at trying to seduce me. But it was just for fun. We all knew I was too young for them.

chapter 15

LIFE IN THE FAST LANE

Me, wearing my first Courrèges
outfit, with Bobby Seligman,
my jet set mentor, 1967.

*W*hen I'd first returned from the Fashion Fair tour, I had signed with the American Girls Agency, which represented only black models. The agency had kept me pretty busy. The German magazine *Stern* had published a four-page article proclaiming that "Negro models are conquering the fashion world" (*Neger Mannequins erobern die Modewelt*); it featured me in a two-page spread dancing at Arthur, the hot nightclub run by Richard Burton's ex-wife and her new husband. There were also local jobs like the New York car show, where I earned the astonishing fee of twenty-five dollars a day to dance around new cars as if I were in love with them. Bobby, who was now my unofficial manager, thought I should be represented by a top agency, and one day he surprised me by getting an appointment for me at Ford Modeling Agency—a huge step up from American Girls.

I was petrified as I walked into Ford's glass-paneled entryway in my new white Courrèges go-go boots and beige minidress. This was the big league: Top models like Maud Adams, Ann Turkel, Ali MacGraw, and Suzy Parker had all walked through this very door. *It's now or never,* I told myself, pressing the buzzer. The door clicked and I pushed it open.

"May I help you?" asked a young woman walking past me. She said it as if I had wandered into the wrong building. Before I could reply, she said, "Wait one moment, please."

I didn't dare move, so I stood just where she left me, by the door, until she returned several minutes later. She asked my name, whether I was sure I had the right address, and who had sent me. When I told her I had an appointment and was working with Bobby Seligman and Oleg Cassini, she escorted me through a narrow hallway to a room in the back of the building. There were tables covered with schedules, and everyone was so busy that no one even looked up. I soon realized it was the booking room.

The young woman told me to sit and wait, so I did. And waited. And waited some more. An hour passed, and no one had uttered so much as a syllable to me. Finally, I spoke up. "Excuse me? Is anyone going to look at my book?"

One female booker glanced over at me and said she didn't know I was waiting to be seen. Hmmm. What did she think I was there for? Was I a parrot that had just flown in and perched itself on a chair? Actually, no, because then they probably would have noticed me.

She gave me the once-over and said briskly, "You must be for the other department." She went back to making phone calls.

Just then a fellow from another room called me in. He was friendly, leafed through my rather meager book of photos, and told me that they were experimenting with "a new department of girls" that I might be good for.

And with this lukewarm declaration of interest, I was signed with the biggest modeling agency in the business.

Before I even had a chance to test out my new agency, Bobby had a new adventure in store. It began with my meeting my first professional choreographer (unless you count Katherine Dunham, and I don't, because I was only five years old): the great JoJo Smith. One Saturday night in June, just before my seventeenth birthday, Bobby insisted I go to a dance studio with him. When we got there, Bobby introduced me to JoJo. "You see this girl here?" he said to her. "She is going to blow your mind. She is *funky*" (that being the cool word of the day). "I tell you, she's funkier than you, she's even funkier than *me!*" Bobby ended this little sales pitch with his trademark thousand-watt smile.

JoJo smiled back and said, "Okay, let's see what she can do." With that, Bobby started snapping his fingers, the way he did when we were dancing, keeping the beat. The music came on and I launched into my routine, giving it all I had. Bobby started dancing with me.

The music stopped and Bobby said to JoJo, "How d'ya like that? She's better than all your other dancers put together, and she's younger, too!" Then Bobby snapped his fingers, took me by the hand, and we left the studio. "This is called 'the art of the exit,' " he told me as we hurried down the stairs.

I didn't realize it, but that was my audition for a part in a television movie that Bobby was producing in Mexico called *The Beautiful People*. The next night I was at JoJo's studio rehearsing with Tamara Dobson, the super-tall star of *Cleopatra Jones*, and Marisa Berenson, a delicate beauty who was likewise super-tall. We were the dancing models whom Bobby wanted for his movie. There in the studio with JoJo, I picked up some terrific new moves with dances like the boogaloo and the funky jerk. *Cha-ka cha-ka boom!* To me, everything sounded and felt just like that magical, door-opening password.

Bobby's plan was to take all of us models to Acapulco during Christmas vacation to make the film. In the end, Tamara and Marisa didn't come, because they were busy doing other movies, but other models joined the cast, including Agneta Frieberg, who would be my roommate in Acapulco. She and I and the cameramen working for Metha Productions (Bobby's film company) arrived together two days after Christmas 1967. I'd just gotten my first passport—Mom had to sign for it, since I was only seventeen—and it was a thrill to get it stamped at customs.

After being picked up at the airport, we made our way down a hill toward the Bay of Acapulco. Laid out before us was paradise. The tropical scent—sea air mixed with the smells of beautiful pink and salmon flowers—made me almost faint, and the glowing sun over the bay bathed everything in a golden light. It was the perfect setting for an international jet set with the Midas touch. I felt like Columbus discovering the New World.

Before long, we were driving up to the rocky residential area of Acapulco and a private bungalow retreat called the Villa Vera. There were few high-rises in Acapulco at the time—just the sea, the white bungalows with their terra-cotta roofs, and one three-story hotel. Most of the VIPs who considered Acapulco their playground stayed in private homes or in the bungalow village. When we arrived at the Villa, society reporters from *El Heraldo de México,* Mexico City's major newspaper, were already there, sniffing around for the who's who of Italy, France, England, and America who might be spending the holidays there.

Agneta and I were bunking at a not-so-VIP hotel down near the water; that was where we'd be filming during the day. Both new to Ford, we got along right away. Although she was twenty-two and I, as always, was the youngest person in any room, Agneta was so shy that we felt like equals. We worked for three days straight and partied every night up at the Villa with the crème de la crème of the international set—though in truth, neither of us really knew who those people were. At one of the parties, Maurice Hogenboom, a young American photographer, kept talking about the musical *Hair,* which had opened off-Broadway in New York and was about to have its Mexican premiere at Acapulco's Teatro Acuario. Maurice told me I should see it. I had met some of the cast members at an earlier party at the Villa, including Jamie Mestizos, a beautiful Mexican boy with dark eyes, curly hair, and a gentle flower-child manner. I told Maurice I'd love to see it. Then I wandered off to get a drink.

I was standing by the bar, ordering my usual ginger ale (which looked like champagne but kept me stone-cold sober while everybody else around me was *borracho*) when I was practically blinded by flashbulbs going off around a man walking in my direction. All I could see was his silhouette—wide shoulders, narrow hips, dressed all in black—but before I knew what was happening, one of the photographers pushed me toward that raven-haired beauty, who turned out to be no older than twenty-three. He put his arm around my waist, and the paparazzi just kept taking pictures. When they finally stopped, his arm stayed put.

This ridiculously handsome young man and I were able to communicate thanks to his bilingual friend who translated every word. Come to find out, he was a famous Mexican matador named Antonio Lomelín; everybody called him Tono for short. Tono stayed at my side the whole night, but he had to leave early because he had a bullfight the next day. He asked if I would come and watch him. Of course I said yes.

The next afternoon Tono sent a car to pick me up and take me to the arena. I entered the dusty tunnel leading to his dressing room, barely able to make out the bullring just beyond. *The light at the end of the tunnel,* I thought as a priest cut in front of me to enter Tono's dressing room. Before I could take another step, Tono's driver stopped me and said I couldn't see him until the fight was over. A *torero* must never see a woman before he fights, because she will drain him of his strength.

I was escorted to the VIP box in the lower bleachers, where the president of Mexico would sit whenever he came. On this day, however, I was the only person in the box. Meanwhile, as the loudspeakers blared out Tono's name, a stadium full of his Mexican fans leaped to their feet, stamping on the wooden planks of the bleachers and roaring out his name at the top of their lungs.

As I looked out at the huge ring, I noticed the bulls behind the gates and the flanks of other men on horseback. Then I saw Tono, all dressed up in his elaborate matador costume, looking tiny in that vast space. He was at center ring and starting to circle it. Now the crowd was deadly silent as he moved in my direction, getting closer and closer until he was standing in front of my box. He held a rose to his heart, kissed the rose, and tossed it to me. I caught it! Then he said in a loud voice, "This bull is for you."

I think that was the moment when I realized what I was about to witness, what a bullfight was all about. *Noooooooooo!* I thought. *Don't do it. Don't kill the bull for me.* My heart was pounding and I was gripped with terror. I was afraid to watch and afraid to leave, because he'd thrown me the rose.

The Mexican national anthem was played, another silence fell, and then he was no longer Tono but some sort of deity acting out an ancient ritual for the crowds. The furious beast behind the gate was released, and Tono, the kindhearted guy whose arm had been so sweetly wrapped around my waist the night before, proceeded to engage in what I can only call an extended act of animal cruelty. He teased the bull, and the crowd cheered, and this went back and forth like an intricate dance for what seemed like forever.

At some point, Tono stuck a pair of banderillas into the attacking bull's back, but heaven help me, it wasn't over yet. He came back, flapping his cape and carrying a sword, which he plunged into the bull to finish off the majestic animal once and for all. My entire body went cold as the crowds erupted.

I left the booth in the middle of the cheers and walked in a daze toward the tunnel and Tono's dressing room. As I approached, I looked outside an opening in the ring and saw a tractor pulling the bull's body, bound in chains, its flesh torn. I was shocked by its massive size. I flashed back to last night's dinner, when we'd all eaten bulls' balls. I had laughed about it then, but there was no laughter in me now.

I walked out of the arena and went back to my hotel without even saying goodbye. Tono phoned that evening, but I hung up on him. I literally could not speak after seeing him slaughter an innocent animal.

chapter 16

SOMEONE TO WATCH OVER ME

With Mexican matador Antonio (Tono)
Lomelín in Alcapulco, 1967.

$\mathscr{I}t$ was strangely peaceful at the Villa during the daytime. I'd been there only at night, when it was packed with raucous party people. Now it was empty, probably because everybody who was anybody was out on a boat. I was sitting by the pool, daydreaming about how much I'd like to come back to Acapulco someday for a real vacation, when Jamie Mestizos, the actor in *Hair,* came over. He was at Villa Vera to meet a friend who worked in the kitchen. Once again, Jamie was gentle and deep, and we talked easily and then just looked at the water in silence for a while. He invited me to the opening-night party that evening. He said we could meet up at the theater.

I was excited about going to an opening night. I asked Agneta if she wanted to come, but she had a headache from too much sun. I smoothed some Bonne Bell After Sun lotion on her back, gave her an aspirin, then met up with some other young people I'd met at the Villa—the ones from the wealthy side of the tracks, you might say—and we all walked to the theater, which wasn't far.

"Premier de Gala/Enero 3 1968/HAIR" was printed on a huge flag strung between two tall trees in front of the theater. The poster, with the sun shining behind an angel in the center and the nude figures of a man and a woman on either side, reminded me of the illustration for the lovers tarot card. Unfortunately, the play was almost over by the time we got there; the people I was with just laughed it off, as VIPs do when they're fashionably late. We sat in the front row next to a very special guest, the daughter of Mexico's president, who looked about seventeen, the same age I was. For the show's finale, we were invited onstage, where my group and I sang and danced like maniacs to the song "Aquarius." Jamie and I danced together, the peace sign around his neck flapping as he moved, and everything was just like the song: "Harmony and understanding / Sympathy and trust abounding." Off we went to the after-party for more of the same, complete with fireworks.

It was close to dawn when I got back to my hotel. My new friends went on to the Villa Vera, and I took the stairs to the third floor. I hummed "I Believe in Love" from *Hair* all the way up. When I reached the room, I noticed the door was ajar. *Agneta must have fallen asleep and forgotten to close it,* I thought. I was desperately tired, but I could hear the sound of someone tossing and turning. The room was dark except for the moonlight coming in through the terrace window. I saw the shadow of a person much too large to be Agneta. My knees went weak. "Agneta," I whispered. No answer, and for a fleeting second I thought I'd imagined the large figure. Then I heard sounds like someone struggling and Agneta's muffled voice. I reached inside the door and switched on the light, and as I did so, I felt a rough hand cover my mouth and a man's voice say, "Don't make a sound." I saw Agneta, wedged underneath two men. One of them pushed Agneta's legs over her head. *Oh my God,* I thought, my heart and mind racing wildly. *He's raping her.* I saw Agneta looking at me in despair, like a gazelle caught by a lion. In that split second, I felt the man whose hand was on my mouth pull me into the bathroom. The bathroom door was near the door I had just come through, which was still slightly open.

I remembered the trick of the mouse, from a children's book my mom used to read me. I didn't squirm or make a sound, though my heart was beating so loudly inside my head, it seemed impossible that no one else could hear it. This man, who reeked of cheap cologne, noticed I was calm and loosened his grip on me enough to grope other parts of my body. Just when he thought he had me, I wrenched out of his grasp, slid out the door, and ran for my life out onto the terrace, down all those flights of stairs, taking them two, three at time, not stopping once to look back.

Then I was on the road, crying like a waterfall, sprinting up the hill in the darkness to the Villa Vera, where Bobby would help me. But once I was there, I couldn't find him anywhere (I'd forgotten that he was spending the night on Ghighi Cassini's boat), and I didn't know where anyone else was staying. Not a soul was around at this hour. Frantic, I ran to the pool to look for someone, *anyone,* who could help Agneta, but that area was empty, too. Feeling defeated, I sank into a lounge chair, where sleep overtook me.

I came to as the sunrise was just lighting up the pool. Then I saw Jamie. At the party, he'd kept asking what I was doing in Mexico with such terrible people—terrible because to him they were rich and superficial, and he valued peace, love, and the soul. Now he rushed over and said, "You look upset." I burst into tears, and he took me in his arms.

"I'm so worried about Agneta," I said, explaining what had happened. "Jamie, can you come with me to check on her?"

"Yes, of course," he said in his sweet Mexican accent.

When we got to my hotel room, there was no trace of Agneta. Her things weren't there, and the maids were cleaning. I asked if they'd seen her, and they said she'd left with her bags. I found my plane ticket and passport and quickly packed. After leaving a note for Agneta in case she came back, Jamie and I hightailed it out of there. I was afraid for my life, but I knew instinctively that I could trust Jamie.

Bobby was still on the boat, so I scribbled a note and left it for him at the Villa Vera's front desk: "Left with the cast of *Hair.* I'm fine. I'll see you in New York."

We threw my suitcase in the back of Jamie's tiny car and took off into the desert, where he said some people involved with the production had a ranch. As we drove, Jamie filled me in on what had happened. The Mexican authorities had shut down the show, on the president's orders. They said it was obscene because of the onstage nudity, and if the cast didn't leave town the next day, they'd be put in jail. They were accused of bringing marijuana into Mexico.

How absurd, I thought. *Isn't it the other way around? Isn't Mexico where the marijuana already is?* Jamie was angry and worried about going to jail. He claimed that what really happened was that the president of Mexico didn't want his daughter getting any crazy hippie ideas from the play.

When we got to the ranch, the sky was ablaze in an incredible desert sunset. I met some of the other cast members, about a dozen in all, who'd arrived earlier by bus; the remaining cast had gone somewhere else to escape arrest. While the others were partying at a long wooden table outside the house, Jamie and I went to one of the bedrooms, which had twin beds, and fell into a much needed sleep. He didn't touch me; he was my friend, beautiful, young, peaceful, and loving.

As it got darker and the stars came out, Jamie and I joined the others. He started playing the guitar, and everyone was laughing, singing, and talking in Spanish. Someone lit candles, and the ranch's owners brought out roast chicken and corn. Then Gerome Ragni and James Rado, the co-authors of *Hair,* arrived. Everyone there was a fugitive, including me, simply by being with them. But I felt great and tried hard to blend in because I didn't want anyone to send me away.

Wine was poured, and joints were lovingly rolled and passed around. I didn't smoke or drink, and neither did Jamie. I felt okay just naturally. I mean, here I was in the desert with the creators of *Hair.* The air was fresh and I felt free. Then the music stopped, no one was chatting, and everyone was staring up at the sky. Jamie and I laughed, and he said, "What is it?"

They pointed up at the sky, and I felt like I was in a science-fiction movie. I'd experienced lights like these once before—round, flat, saucerlike—as a child in New York City during a blackout. There were five of them in a V formation, like geese. And they were hovering, very close and very big.

Jamie grabbed my hand and we ran from the lights and hid under the table. Everyone else fled there, too, except for James and Gerome. I guess they were too stoned to be afraid, and when the shapes zipped away, everyone got out from under the table except me. I'd neither smoked nor drunk a thing, and what I'd seen had looked ominous.

James and Gerome started to sing very loudly, "Come! Come! Flying saucers, come!" I figured it was okay to crawl out from under the table. Within moments, everyone was singing along with James and Gerome, like primitives around the campfire they'd started. "Come! Come! Flying saucers, come!" It was like a chant, and all I could think was: *Will I ever make it home?*

Jamie saw how scared I was, but everyone was having such a good time that I started to relax. After all, there was no such thing as flying saucers—*right?* I kept saying to Jamie, "Did that really happen?" And then the saucers reappeared! They came in closer this time, and bigger. Everything got silent as they zoomed in, then zoomed away. This went on for about fifteen minutes, though I can't say for sure, because time stood still. The entire cast, except for Jamie and me, was jumping around with arms stretched out to the sky, singing, "Come, flying saucers, take me with you!"

All night long, everyone danced in circles, falling down and getting back up—stoned, drunk primitives, waving down those lights until the ships finally left. Everyone except Jamie and me, that is. By now I was flat-out terrified, and he and I huddled under the table, sleeping fitfully until dawn, when we woke to a car speeding up to the house, trailing a huge cloud of dust.

Out jumped a member of the Acapulco cast, screaming in Spanish to the others, who were asleep in the open under blankets. "Let's go! Let's go! The police are after us!"

Jamie was on his feet instantly, and within seconds we had our stuff and were racing off in his little car. From the rearview mirror, I saw the rest of the gang hurrying to get on the bus. James and Gerome were just standing there.

By the time we got to Mexico City, we were nearly out of gas. After Acapulco and then the desert, it felt strange to be in a place with so many cars, people, and traffic lights. I was covered in dust head to toe from the ride and looked like a desert rat. My plane ticket had a date on it, and my only goal was to be at the airport on time. I had lost all contact with Bobby and had no idea where or how to call him. I had no money and no other way home. So Jamie and I carried on, driving to the airport on fumes.

Hordes of newspaper reporters and photographers were waiting for us there. Evidently, we were the hottest scandal in Mexico. Arrest warrants had been issued for the whole cast of *Hair* (I was now considered a member, since James and Gerome had asked me to join the New York production), and as flashbulbs popped, Jamie and I were arrested and held overnight at the airport. The next day's front page carried a story that said we were trying to escape Mexico, but because we had no drugs on us, the authorities ended up dropping the charges.

Jamie was set free, and I was put directly on a flight to New York City. I blew goodbye kisses to him as the police escorted me to the plane. I knew I'd never see him again, but I considered myself lucky to have met him, and to have gotten out of there in one piece.

As for Agneta, I never saw her again in person, but she was an extremely successful model whose image appeared in all the major magazines and on more than a hundred covers. As fate would have it, something even more terrible than rape awaited her: In 1971 she fell (or, it was speculated, was pushed) from the top floor of a hotel in Paris and died in a hospital ten days later. She was twenty-five years old.

chapter 17

HIGH HOPES

Wearing my own design in a test
photo on Park Avenue, 1967.
Courtesy of Rex Joseph.

$\mathcal{T}$*he* wet, slushy cold of New York City made the Mexican desert seem like a distant memory. And if the weather wasn't discouraging enough, I got a call from Eileen Ford almost as soon as I got back. She asked me to come up to the agency because she wanted to speak to me personally about my career.

I waited in the lounge until she arrived, wearing a classic tailored blouse and a straight skirt, along with reading glasses and a rather old-fashioned 1950s hairstyle. "Come in," she said with a tight smile. I felt like a misbehaving schoolgirl who'd been summoned to the principal's office.

The room was dark, like a gentleman's library. I sat in a big leather chair, and she proceeded to ignore me for several minutes. Finally, she removed her glasses and turned in my direction. "Patricia, you realize we have very few colored girls in our agency. And do you know why? I'll tell you why. Because there is no work for colored girls. This is not to say that you don't have good bone structure, and you do have a long neck. But as you may not know, this is the first time I've—" The phone rang. She answered, put the caller on hold, and left the room. I was feeling pretty uneasy with what she'd said so far, and by the time she came back, I was nearly jumping out of my skin.

"Patricia," she continued, "the only reason I took you is because Oleg Cassini recommended you. But what I really think is that you will never make it in the modeling business." She paused. "And that's the truth." She stood up, came over, and peered right into my face. "You see, you don't look like an American. Your face is not pretty. Your nose is strange. The beautiful girls in this agency have smaller noses, like mine—straight noses. If you want to work at all, you should consider shortening it."

I couldn't think of anything to say. Not that words would have come out of my mouth. But after the shock wore off, I felt a bit sorry for her. *You're not perfect, either,* I thought. *You're a human being, and I'm a human being, and this is my heritage. I can be a cup of coffee, and you can be a vanilla milkshake, and it's okay.* Then, more uncharitably: *Besides, you've had a nose job.*

"You can go now," she said, making a shooing gesture, as if I were a pesky cat.

"Thank you," I said. My mother had certainly trained me well.

I left her office with a broken heart, yes, but also with a determination to prove her wrong. And with my own nose, at that!

I walked to the office of the young man who'd signed me. Hurt as I was, I had to tell him what Eileen had said. He was sympathetic and told me that he had a different perspective. He believed that times were changing, along with aesthetic standards, and that I and some other girls he'd signed—not one of us a blond, blue-eyed, all-American type like those Eileen loved—were part of the plan to keep pace with those changes. He asked me to stick it out and said he'd book me as much as he could.

In the meantime, he urged me to volunteer to model for photographers whenever possible, to give them a chance to test their lighting and me a chance to get a variety of fashion shots to fill out my portfolio. Those tear sheets helped the photographers, too, because having their work displayed in a model's portfolio meant it got seen by other photographers, editors, and advertising agencies. It was win-win, one hand washing the other. Or that was the logic, anyway.

From that point on, I was like a worker bee out to get the pollen. In pursuit of the best tear sheets possible for my portfolio, I launched into a near-constant round of what we in the business call go-sees, which are basically, as the name implies, appointments with people who might hire you or help you get hired at some point down the road.

During my final year in high school, I'd leave school, then walk up and down one block after another, all over Manhattan. At night I'd come home and collapse, dead tired with an evening full of homework ahead of me. Mom would be at work, but she'd leave food on the stove for me. I kept going even when my portfolio got really heavy, thanks to the extraordinary test photos I now had from a new breed of up-and-coming black photographers like Hugh Bell, Rex Joseph, Jim Hadley, and Owen Brown.

I went to test with every photographer Ford booked and some they didn't. One day, feeling particularly gutsy, I went on my own to Richard Avedon's studio without an appointment, since Ford refused to send me. He was supposed to be the best, and I wanted to find out why. I walked into the reception area of his studio and took a seat. The secretary was out of the room. When she got back, she said, "What are you doing here? Do you have an appointment?"

"No," I said. "I just want to meet Avedon."

"That's not possible," she said haughtily. "That's not how it's done. Who's your agent?"

I told her. She got on the phone, called Ford, and bawled them out for sending a model without an appointment. She told them never to do it again.

Then she went back to her work. I was mortified but didn't let on. I placed a photograph of myself on her desk as I strode, head held high, toward the door.

☙

Luckily, there was another facet of my life that kept me optimistic about my future in fashion: *Vogue*. Three years after that first encounter in the subway, I received a phone call inquiring about my designs. Before I knew it, I found myself at the *Vogue* offices, dressed in a tightly belted, ankle-length bright periwinkle maxi-coat, and knee-high loden-green zip-up leather boots. If that wasn't a fashion statement, nothing was.

I'd learned to tailor from my mom, and that coat, with its forest-green satin lining, was our masterpiece. We defied any fashion-conscious person not to fall in love with it. Mom had taught me that when it comes to clothes, there's no such thing as timidity. The point is to show yourself off. My mom and my aunt had always done that; now it was my turn. If I could get people to love the clothes I made, then maybe my mom and aunt could have the fashion house they'd always fantasized about, like the ones my aunt saw when she was in Paris. Those were the days before Sonny, when the sisters dreamed together, and my mom would draw her dreams every single day.

Amanda Crider, the young woman who'd stopped me in the subway, led me from the reception area into one of the offices and told me that Carrie would be in to see me shortly. Then off she went, closing the door gently behind her.

One of the office walls was covered with large black-and-white photos of slim, poetic-looking men and long-legged, statuesque women in mod clothing, laughing, hugging, and socializing at parties in exotic places. The photos were marked with X's and arrows pointing to one person's eyes or another's hair. I was shocked that anyone would mark up such beautiful photographs. Corkboards on another wall held swatches of fabric and sketches of clothing pinned between them. I sat down in a stiff-backed chair, just in front of the desk, and waited. On a coffee table, a dark green candle with a subtle woodsy scent flickered in a crystal glass beside a potted live orchid (something I'd never seen before). Both items would soon become familiar to me in the fashion environment as symbols of wealth and elegance.

I waited. No one came. Had I made a mistake and come at the wrong time or on the wrong day? I started to get fidgety and hot in my coat, but I didn't want to take it off; I needed the editor to see it. I was so nervous that I could barely breathe. Then I noticed a door slightly ajar on one side of the room. I heard voices whispering through the crack. I turned my head to get a better look and saw the door close. As I turned my head back around, I sensed that it opened again. The two voices resumed whispering. Whoever it was, they were spying on me, so I sat up extra straight, just in case. Posture is everything, my mother taught me. It makes you look taller and richer, like royalty.

I listened hard and recognized two elegant male voices. One of them said, "But darling . . ."

I looked around again and this time caught sight of their eyes peeking at me from behind the door, which they quickly closed. Finally, the person I'd been waiting for arrived and went straight to her seat at the desk. She was wearing a pale blue turban, large golden ball earrings, and a pale blue cashmere sheath. She had on charm bracelets and gold bangles, which she wore over powder-blue gloves that came up to the middle of her arm to meet the sleeve of her dress. Her face was covered in the largest black-framed round glasses I'd ever seen, and her twinkling blue eyes showed from behind turquoise eye shadow. She looked dead at me.

My heart pounded. This was the magazine's fashion editor Carrie Donovan, who—though I didn't know it then—was a legend.

"Hello, dear," she said, and I stood straight up. Before I could utter a word, a secretary came into the room.

"Excuse me, Miss Donovan. Mrs. Vreeland would like to see you immediately."

Carrie quickly gathered some papers from her desk, said, "Excuse me, dear," and left the room.

Once again I was alone. Once again the people behind the door peeked in, whispered, and then backed away. This peekaboo game went on for several minutes before Carrie came back.

"Where were we?" she said. "Ah, the young designer. Have you brought your sketches?"

"Yes," I said, and dove into my portfolio, pulling out drawings that I'd stayed up all night making for this meeting. Because I wanted to treat the sketches as if they were professional illustrations, I had matted everything, to give the art a frame.

I handed them to Carrie, and she studied them carefully. "Well, these are very good," she said finally. "I'm going to Paris next week, and I'll take these. Givenchy is looking for a student designer from America." Carrie looked at me closely, sizing up what I was wearing. "Did you make what you're wearing today?"

"Yes, I did." I didn't say that my mom had helped me with the lining; maybe Carrie wouldn't like that.

"Well, let's see. Stand up." I stood and showed her the coat and the lining, and she saw that underneath I was wearing my heavy wool forest-green maxi-skirt and my Scottish-plaid jersey top.

"Take off your coat, dear, so I can see the skirt," Carrie said. I did, and I could tell she liked it. "Have a seat, dear."

I sat as gracefully as I could. Then the door behind me popped open, and out came the most gorgeous men I had ever seen: One was tall and blond, the other dark-haired and Asian. "Carrie, darling," the tall one said, pecking Carrie lightly on the cheek.

"Joel, darling." They were like two swans bobbing toward each other in a synchronized routine.

Then the Asian man sat down in the chair against the wall. "Hi, Carrie," he said in an all-American accent.

"Carrie, darling," Joel continued. "I don't know what to do. I have to shoot 'Vogue's Own,' and there's no model. Berry is waiting, and I need a model." The Asian fellow kept smiling at me. Then he winked at Joel, as though to say, Go ahead.

"Carrie, who is this beautiful young thing?" Joel asked.

"This is Patricia, a new young designer," she replied. "We found her in the subway."

Joel looked at the Asian fellow and raised his eyebrows. "Maning, how about Patricia? Can we use her?"

The guy named Maning said, "Yes, definitely!" Now I knew who and what the peekaboos were about.

"Carrie, what do you think? It's your story," said Joel.

"Well," Carrie said, "I don't know, she seems a bit—"

"She's perfect," said Joel. "Just what we need."

I had no idea what was going on. I looked around, and Maning whispered reassuringly, "We *need* you." With these three words, I felt as if my guardian angel had arrived.

Joel handed me my coat, grabbed my hand, and said, "Come on!"

I followed. "My sketches?" I said as we were leaving.

"Don't worry, you can leave them here with Carrie."

I looked at Carrie, who seemed a bit in shock over Joel's quick decision. I looked at Maning, and he gave me a nod. Before I could even gather my thoughts, I was in the elevator with Joel Schumacher, on my way to having my life changed forever.

Joel's limo was outside *Vogue*'s offices. We jumped in the backseat, which was filled with shopping bags and colorful kites. His driver and secretary sat in front with more bags of stuff. "We're going to Central Park," Joel said. "But first we have to pick up our photographer."

Vogue's offices were right next to Grand Central Terminal, in the Graybar Building, so we drove west on Forty-Second Street and uptown on Park Avenue, where we stopped to pick up a young blond girl with bright blue eyes who squeezed into the backseat with us. "Berry, Patricia," Joel said. "Patricia, Berry."

We exchanged hellos and took off for the park. We were all in high spirits, and I felt as though I'd been lifted from street level to the penthouse of the world. Our limousine came to a halt not far from the Metropolitan Museum. The driver opened the car doors, and we piled out and ran up Dog Hill, my favorite spot for sledding when I was a little kid. The secretary and Joel carried the kites, and a coat and hat they wanted me to wear. The secretary handed me a kite.

"Now," said Joel, "all you have to do is fly the kite, and Berry will take the pictures." It was so windy, the kite almost carried me away. "Yes," shouted Joel, "that's perfect!"

We had a splendid time, but even so, I was aware of the dampness and chill in the air, and the slipperiness of the ground, and how desperately I wanted to get in out of the cold. Fortunately, everybody else felt the same way, and before I knew it, the job was done. We rushed back into the warmth of the car, where Joel instructed the driver to take us back to *Vogue*.

Whew! Berry Berenson—the younger sister of Marisa, whom I'd met at JoJo Smith's studio with Bobby—had taken the first pictures of me for *Vogue,* and Joel Schumacher had followed his heart by using me. I was truly grateful. Joel would go on to become a well-known film director who made such blockbusters as *Batman Forever* and *The Phantom of the Opera*. Berry went on to marry the actor Anthony Perkins, have two sons, become a widow, and lose her life aboard American Airlines Flight 11 when it crashed into the North Tower of the World Trade Center on September 11, 2001.

chapter 18

BEAUTIFUL DREAMER

Modeling my own design in Central
Park for a spread in "*Vogue*'s
Own Boutique," 1968.
Courtesy of Berry Berenson.

Later that year, in the spring, I was called back to *Vogue* because Carrie Donovan had returned from Paris, where she'd gone to see the latest collections. She had taken my design sketches with her, and now she'd asked Joel to have me photographed in my own designs, as a young designer. So there I was in Central Park again, sitting on that big rock by the pond, dreaming about my beautiful future. At seventeen, I had my heart set on becoming someone or something, and now, as the flower buds were beginning to pop, and the air still had a touch of that early-spring frostiness, it was happening.

I posed wearing an antique lace shirt that Mom and I had made from strips of sixty-year-old lace, a long skirt, and a big-brimmed floppy hat that Joel had brought. He also added a long chiffon scarf, which made it all very *Vogue*. He loved a romantic look.

After the shoot, we all returned to the magazine's offices. When I went back to see Carrie, she was holding up my drawing. "I've shown your work to Bendel's," she said, like a fairy godmother about to zap me with her magic wand. "I told them how wonderful your designs are, and they'd like to meet with you on Monday. My secretary has made the appointment. Can you do that?"

Can I do that? I thought. *That's what I'm living for.*

Bendel's liked my designs, and I set about making several skirts and blouses for the store. They bought them all, put my name on the label, and sold every last item. But there was a problem. Mom and I had been so busy sewing like mad that, without thinking, we'd made everything in my size. When the store asked me to make things in larger sizes, it got complicated. I had to make darts in the blouses, which I'd never done before. (The whole point of my clothes was that they were for girls with small breasts who couldn't find clothes that fit.) Because I didn't really know how to make the larger sizes, I lost the order. I was so disappointed—not just for me but for Mom, too.

Fortunately, *Vogue* still wanted me. Or, should I say, Maning Obregon, the beautiful Asian man I'd seen on my first visit, wanted me. Maning was *Vogue*'s illustrator, which was an extremely important position, especially since photographers were not allowed at fashion shows in those days.

Born in Brooklyn to Filipino immigrants, Maning had begun his career at sixteen in Paris, as a sketch artist covering the collections for *The New York Times*. He'd moved to *Vogue* to cover the same beat. At the time, illustrators were like a mysterious, revered cult; they had as much mystique as their subjects. Maning was known not just for being the quickest but also the best illustrator of his time—one who could see and capture on paper every seam in a garment as it was moving. He was also adept at conveying the personalities of the people he sketched.

Little did I know then how much influence Maning had at *Vogue*, thanks to his being the pet of Diana Vreeland, *Vogue*'s editor in chief. She was said to adore Maning because of his exotic Asian air. In any case, Maning took a shine to me immediately, and so I was called in just before the *Vogue* Seminars—the hectic month during which the editors analyzed all the designers' looks for the upcoming season, which Maning then frenetically sketched so that they could decide which ones to feature in the magazine. I wouldn't find out until years later that the reason he liked me was that I was a dead ringer (in his eyes, anyway) for his former favorite model—a young man who dressed up in women's clothes to pose for Maning. As this fabulous drag queen was no longer available, I, his doppelgänger, was the next best thing. I was hired on the spot to pose for Maning for fifteen dollars an hour, which felt like a fortune. I couldn't believe my luck. I was going to be part of the *Vogue* Seminars!

The next day I was escorted into the Seminar Room, which was decorated with pale green flowered wallpaper that matched the fabric on the sofas. I ducked behind a screen to put on the little shorts I'd just been given.

"Good morning!" a voice bellowed out. I popped my head over the screen. Maning, dressed in white from head to toe, smiled brightly. "Well, I got what I wanted," he said, pointing to me in an exaggerated, comical way. "And that was you, girl! You're all mine, and you're not getting away till I make you a star."

I hurried to finish, zipping up the shorts and putting on espadrilles that tied up to the knee. Then I put on a boxy, feather jacket and stepped out from behind the screen.

"My, my. Forty-Second Street finally hits *Vogue*," he said saucily. "Don't tell them I said that." I stood there, wondering what the next step was. He snapped his fingers. "You never know how many looks they'll give us. So hit it, girl."

Maning guided me to stand on the table, and up I went; I was used to this sort of posing because I'd done so much of it at school. "My God, you look just like him," he said under his breath as he reached for some sketching paper. Then, "What would they do without me? They're all terrible except for Mrs. Vreeland."

"Who?" I asked.

"Diana Vreeland, darling. She's the empress here. The rest are just slaves, like worker bees in a hive. Don't tell them I said that. Oh, except for Carrie Donovan. The rest of them hate her because she has power over them, but she's the only one finding new people, and they're all jealous."

As if on cue, Carrie Donovan ran into the room, frantically waving her arms. "Maning, darling, commands from the top! The cubby jacket is in, she loves it, *loves* it, I tell you. And just to think, we came up with the idea, and the short shorts with the tights and the feathers. Yes, that's the look. We win." She whirled around to take a breath, then continued her monologue. "Maning, did you see Joel? Are we right? What did Vreeland say? Oh, darling, it's in your hands. So, Maning, do your very best, draw as big as you can, because this *is* big. *Harper's Bazaar* is out to get us, so let's step it up. We have one hundred looks to do today." She turned to the model booker. "Oh, dear! We never know when Diana's going to surprise us, do we?"

"She's faster than fashion," Maning said, agreeing with Carrie.

"Darling, it's in your hands." She blew him a kiss, then hurried out the door. "I'm off. Back in an hour."

A few young men brought in racks of clothes and trays of food. When Maning and I were alone, he said, "We should lock the door before the evil witches bring in more clothes." Then he whispered, "Don't tell them I said that."

For the next six hours, I put on a different outfit every ten minutes. Maning sketched furiously; Carrie paced, thinking of what to put together next. Both of them examined the clothes inside and out, going so far as to rip sleeves off dresses. Assistants ran around tidying up the mess, and there I was in the center, spinning, posing, and changing clothes as I watched the walls fill up with six-foot-tall sketches.

Evening came, and we were still working. Finally, Carrie said, "Stop. Diana has gone to dinner. I must leave, too, but we'll continue tomorrow."

I went home drained but exhilarated, eager to tell Mom every detail.

The next day Maning and I continued to work very well together. For the rest of that week and into the next, we laughed about how everyone was vying for attention from Mrs. Vreeland, who never appeared at the office until late afternoon.

One day, after he'd done a ton of drawings for the Seminars, Maning looked at me and lifted one eyebrow. "I'd love to do a few sketches of you in movement instead of just still," he said. "But first I have to show you a few walking tricks. Go over to that side of the room and watch me. I'll show you how to walk like a real mannequin."

With a twinkle in his eyes, he spun around and came walking toward me, full speed, head held high with a look of haughty daring, as though looking down from Mount Olympus, a god staring at the mortals. He moved his hands like two Chinese fans, and his long legs and shoes, which came to a point at the toe, accentuated the direction of his feet, like those of a dancer about to pirouette. "Now you do it," he said. "Walk across the room with attitude. Let me see you walk like the greatest mannequin in the world."

"The greatest mannequin in the world?"

"Yes! Like Dovima, like the empress of China. It's all in the eyes," he said, lowering his voice and squinting his eyes into a look of seduction. "Be mysterious." He whipped around the room at high speed again. "Do it like this," he said, bending his body back from the waist into an arch, jutting his hipbones forward. "You mustn't look real. They must never see you breathing. In Paris, the models paint their faces many shades lighter to look like they're made of plaster."

That didn't sound particularly appealing, but I watched what he did and then did exactly the same. Again and again, until that walk became mine.

‹›

The more time I spent at *Vogue,* the more comfortable I became. Being a fitting model came naturally to me, and I was used to being sketched. During my breaks, I roamed the office to see how they put the magazine together. In truth, I was more interested in what was going on in the graphics room than in modeling: It looked like a big art classroom at my high school, with everyone working intently on the mock-up of the next issue.

One day as I was just finishing a break, Mrs. Vreeland's secretary came to the Seminar Room and told me to change into a dressing robe. Then she led me to an area of the *Vogue* offices where I'd never been: the editor in chief's quarters.

I stood in complete silence before the lacquered door to *Vogue'*s inner sanctum. The crystal doorknob turned, and the silence was broken by a low hum of voices on the other side of the door. Nervous, I stuffed my hands in the pockets of my robe to keep from shaking. The door was opened by a woman carrying an empty silver tray and dressed like a maid in the classic black dress with a tiny white apron and little white cap. Memories of Marian Anderson's house, all those years earlier, came to mind.

Grace Mirabella, the associate editor and all-purpose helper to the editor in chief, walked by me and said, "Give us a moment." The door shut; when it opened again, Grace invited me to enter. I'm not sure what possessed me, but I leaped into the room like a ballerina and landed right in front of the great Diana Vreeland.

She wasn't even looking my way, so I just stood there on tippy-toes in the baggy dressing gown. The walls were red lacquer, and there were plants everywhere—deep coral amaryllises, white lilies, luscious fuchsia peonies, and (of course) tall delicate orchids. The obligatory Rigaud candles glowed, giving off their faint perfume, and the walls were hung with big black-and-white photographs in heavy black frames. And there *she* was, like some exotic bird in her own jungle paradise.

I couldn't see her face, because her back was turned and she was on the phone. But I could see her shiny raven-black hair and the black tunic and two heavy ivory cuffs she wore. Then she was off the phone, busying herself with lighting a cigarette, which she inserted in a long black-and-white cigarette holder. She lit the cigarette, took a puff, and turned to face me. Her face was powdered white, and her dark, almost onyx eyes twinkled with wisdom, as though she were thinking Delphic thoughts. She blew out the smoke through her crimson-painted lips, and it shrouded her face like a veil. She lifted her head and turned it slightly, and I got an up-close view of that world-famous profile, which reminded me of the cockatoo in one of the paintings behind her desk.

When she spoke, it was to the maid, who was watering the plants. "Tell Grace to have a mineral water sent in." I was still standing there on my toes, wondering what to do. Next to me was a rack of the world's most beautiful clothes, which I assumed I would be trying on. The maid went out but returned almost instantly with the water. D.V. drank it, finished her cigarette, and handed the holder to the maid. I was concentrating on keeping my balance when she crossed her long arms across her upper torso, and said, "Oh, *vous êtes élégante*!" She could tell I didn't understand, so she said, "You are elegant."

I am elegant, I thought, excited.

"But my dear . . ." She stopped speaking as she walked out from behind her black desk and came over to me. She put one hand—I noticed the bright red, perfectly lacquered nails—on my left shoulder and the other hand on my right shoulder and pushed down until I was standing flat on the floor. "To be strong, you must be rooted, like a tree. Stand still and firm like a tree."

She walked back to her desk and pushed a button on her phone. "Grace, come in, please." Grace arrived swiftly, along with two assistants, who began taking clothes off the rack and pinning and fitting them to my body.

As they worked, D.V. spoke, gliding her slender hands through the air in a kind of dance, speaking to all of us. "There was a time when people would say, 'Oh, how elegant you look today.' You would hear the word 'elegance' in the air, everywhere. There is as much elegance today as there has ever been. But it is no longer essential. Some people are elegant to the bone, but if one does not have elegance, it is nothing to regret. It is individual."

She began flipping through the mock-up of the next issue, page after page. She took a black marker and made an X across one of the pages. "Inelegance is unsharpened pencils. Sharpened pencils are elegant." She stopped and cocked her head slightly, as if in contemplation. "I don't think that I have elegance; I have a certain refinement, and I keep my eye on the ball . . . too many balls. *L'élégance c'est le refus.* Elegance is to refuse. To refuse! It is the opposite of overdressing." She clapped her hands, then stretched out her long arms as if to reach for the future. "So let's get started."

I was soaking up every word that flowed from her lips and trying my best to apply it all, right then and there, as I modeled looks that might strike her fancy and make it into the magazine. "Discretion in every movement!" D.V. said. Was I moving with discretion? Were my roots planted deep into the ground? I felt as if I were growing into a mighty oak just by being in her presence.

She stood, straightening out her tunic, which didn't have a single wrinkle in it. Then she opened her compact, peered into the little mirror, and applied her rouge, painting cherry-red dots high upon her cheekbones. She looked exactly as I imagined a Chinese princess in an opera would look. She took a few twenty-dollar bills out of her wallet, handed them to her maid, and said, "Please press these bills; I'll need them for tips." Turning to Grace, she said, "A truly elegant person always has crisp bills."

She even has her money ironed? I thought. *I want to try that.*

"Elegance is a form of intelligence," she went on. "It cannot be connected with stupidity."

Not wanting to seem stupid, I kept quiet.

"It's a mysterious aura that some people have and others don't. Elegance. You use it like a magic wand."

Just then, the assistant dressing me accidentally stuck a straight pin through the dress I was wearing and into my side. I jumped, but I bit my tongue rather than say "Ouch!"

I spent the better part of the next seven days in Diana Vreeland's office, trying on the clothes that would be chosen to go into the magazine and worn by some glamorous model. Sometimes I stood naked before her, waiting anxiously for a dress to arrive from across town; or I'd be in an ornate dress, thinking, *I'm standing like a tree—a Christmas tree.* And D.V. would read my mind: "No, no, you are not a Christmas tree. Eliminate! Eliminate!" She would tell the assistants, "Elegance needs space!" The next thing you knew, they'd be ripping the bows off dresses—*original designer dresses.*

"We must refuse!" D.V. would proclaim. "We must not allow the material world, and material thoughts, to settle on us." She was like the pied piper or a guru, teaching and leading us into her worldview with complete confidence. "The space around the thing is what is beautiful."

Mrs. Vreeland was right about that: The space around me was becoming more and more beautiful, because I was in the presence of greatness. *Vous êtes élégante* became the mantra of my fashion life, a gift from the divine Diana Vreeland.

chapter 19

BEWITCHED, BOTHERED,
AND BEWILDERED

My first great love, Kenneth/Matthew/
Diamond Stone Red Rose, standing
in front of the Dandelion Fountain on
Sixth Avenue, New York City, 1969.

$\mathcal{B}y$ the time I was in my senior year of high school, I felt like I was juggling three radically different identities that never intersected: One was the fashionable, confident young woman who hung out with society and fashion types; another was the dutiful daughter who lived at home with her mom and hateful stepfather (who was always mistreating my mother and making lewd, insulting comments when she wasn't around); and the third was the girlfriend of Kenneth, philosopher-poet extraordinaire. Yes, *that* Kenneth. My sixteenth-birthday crush from the *Ebony* photography studio had come back into my life—in a big way.

Before going off to Mexico to make the movie with Bobby, I'd come home from school one day to be greeted by the sounds of jazz playing on the new stereo Mom had just bought. She was sitting on the sofa chatting with a guest. *Kenneth*. She glanced up and said, "Look who's here." He just smiled and said nothing. "Maybe you two want to be alone," Mom said, and left the room.

As so often happens to me at critical moments in my life, song lyrics popped into my head: *It's a funny thing. I look at you, I get a thrill I never knew.* That's a pretty good description of what happened to me every time I laid eyes on this man. He had changed a lot. The boy from Mrs. Johnson's studio with the slicked-back hair now had a wild, curly Afro. But something about him still mesmerized me and caused my heartbeat to accelerate. As we talked—he had an intimate, euphonious voice, as though his words were coming directly from God (appropriate, since his biological father was a preacher)—he told me a bit about his family, whom he'd just visited out in California, and what it was like to be the adopted son of the great jazz vocalist Billy Eckstine. Kenneth was a poet at heart, and because of his dad (who'd married Kenneth's mom when Kenneth was a baby), he'd grown up around some of the greatest jazz artists of all time. But Kenneth claimed he was the black sheep of his family, a man with a mind of his own whose radical political ideas were becoming increasingly unacceptable to his liberal parents.

Kenneth leaped up from the couch and asked me to come with him to visit a friend of his, a dancer who lived on the Upper West Side near the Hudson River. When we got to her tiny apartment, I felt out of place. The dancer was not only incredibly beautiful, she was also pregnant. Kenneth kept looking at her adoringly, and she looked at him the same way. I was one hundred percent certain she was in love with him—and about ninety percent certain that he felt the same way about her. (I left that little ten percent opening for hope.) I might as well not have been there; the two of them disappeared into the tiny bedroom, leaving me by myself in the living room. I was crushed, but before I had a chance to feel too sorry for myself, the doorbell rang, and they called out for me to answer it.

I peeked through the peephole and saw this very small, very dark man standing there holding an enormous bouquet of tulips. *Ah, someone sent flowers,* I thought. *How nice.* "Special delivery," the man said. So I opened the door and there he stood, dressed in a long black leather coat with silver studs, his huge eyes almost all pupils. This was no delivery guy.

The small man didn't speak. Then Kenneth and the dancer came out of the bedroom, the man gave her the flowers, and they kissed sweetly but in a way that made it clear, even to a clueless seventeen-year-old like me, that they were lovers. Both of them gave Kenneth a look—hers one of deep longing, his one of deep irritation. She said, "We need to be alone." Kenneth got the hint and we left.

Once we were on the street again, I asked Kenneth who the man was. He said, "He thinks he's the daddy of that baby, but it's mine." *What?* I thought. Then he said, "That was Miles, a friend of my dad's. You know, Miles Davis."

"That was *Miles Davis*?" I said, not really grasping what he'd said about the baby. "I thought he was a deliveryman!"

He took me by the arm and said, "Let's go." I didn't ask where; I was simply under his spell and ready to follow him anywhere. The next thing I knew, we were in Harlem at the Apollo Theater, meeting "some friends" of Kenneth's. We went backstage and were sitting on a dirty sofa in one of the dingy dressing rooms when Stevie Wonder came into the room and plopped down next to me. Then Ray Charles came in and sat next to Stevie, followed by Sammy Davis, Jr., whose first words were "Wow, Kenneth, who's the pretty girl?"

It was one of those enchanted nights when I just blended in and soaked up all the genius around me. Stevie Wonder held my hand, and Ray Charles slapped my knee every time he laughed. They chatted about Kenneth's dad (or, as Sammy Davis, Jr., called him, "Mr. B.") and other showbiz stuff that I didn't understand but thoroughly enjoyed. Being there at that Harlem landmark among those legends was like the soul version of the glamorous life Bobby was introducing me to on the East Side of Manhattan. I managed to forget about the dancer who might or might not be pregnant with Kenneth's baby. I had a ball and couldn't wait to tell Mom all about it.

It was early in the morning when Kenneth finally brought me home. He gave me a quick kiss goodbye. It would be another year before I saw him again.

&

It's hard, from the vantage point of adulthood, to dissect Kenneth's appeal to my teenage self, but a big part of it was his air of mystery and his incredible sexual magnetism. He seemed to live in a world of his own—one that I would briefly enter and fall deeply into whenever he'd show up, usually very late at night. Every time I felt as if I'd known him forever and we were finally coming together. His mind moved in all directions, but when it was focused on me, I felt like his one and only "foxy lady," to use the era's highest compliment.

He began arriving at my house with flowers just before midnight. From the start, I wanted to throw my arms around him and kiss him forever. But if my mother happened to be there, he didn't let me kiss him, out of respect. It took many visits before we broke through that wall. Luckily, between my mom's graveyard shifts and my stepfather's odd hours as a taxi driver, Kenneth and I found an opening. Plenty of openings, actually. We were crafty: He'd stay until Mom and Sonny went to work, then leave with them. Then he'd come right back, serenading me from twelve stories below with one of the many flutes he'd started carrying around with him.

It was a chaotic time in America. The Vietnam War had divided the country, and everywhere you looked, there were antiwar protests, black militants, and flower children who just wanted to give peace a chance. Kenneth, a twentysomething with high ideals and an ethical code all his own, was deeply opposed to the Vietnam War, and even though he was of a prime age to be drafted, he had no intention of going into the army. (Decades later, I learned that he'd already served in the military in the early sixties and had been discharged before I met him. So *that* explained why he never got a draft notice, like most able-bodied young men of that era.) He told me he would dodge the draft any way he could, even if it meant moving to Canada or Norway. He asked if I would go with him, and I said yes. It never came to that, of course. In any case, when Mom got wind of the idea, she hid my passport.

On nights when he didn't come to my place, I'd go to his room, usually at the Columbus Hotel on West Forty-Sixth Street. It was a frightening, seedy place in a neighborhood where the only women walking around after midnight were prostitutes. But when I arrived at his room—#76N, just down the filthy hallway—it was always worth the trip. I'd knock lightly and say, "Hello, it's me." He'd open the door, and the scent of incense would envelop me.

We'd make love amid the candlelight and the incense. I'd die a thousand little deaths and leave the material world completely, until it was nearly dawn and time for me to go home. This went on all summer, and no one knew. I visited him wherever he was. Sometimes it was a place on the Bowery, where I'd literally step over bums in the doorway to get to him. I didn't care. I'd have gone to the end of the earth to be with him, and when I got there, the incense, the candles, and the sensual sounds of Ravi Shankar and Indian ragas would take over my senses and blot out everything else. Kenneth was a fantastic lover and teacher, and from him I learned the ancient Indian sexual traditions of tantra and the *Kama Sutra*.

After lovemaking, we'd take midnight walks into Central Park and look up at the stars. He'd tell me about other worlds, other planets; I could have listened to that soft, honey-smooth voice forever. America was firmly in the space age, and Kenneth was my rocket ship, taking me to places I'd never even imagined. With his help, I became an uninhibited, liberated woman. I started wearing bell-bottom jeans and love beads and allowed my hair to go natural, wild and long, because he liked it that way. The two of us truly entered the Age of Aquarius, which I had merely sung about with the cast of *Hair* back in Mexico. We wanted to spread harmony and understanding throughout the world.

And then he disappeared.

I continued to go to high school and to my modeling go-sees, secure in the knowledge that he was somewhere on the planet. Respectful of his freedom, I genuinely had no desire to possess him. In my soul, there was no separation between our time together and our time apart. It was as if we were two drifting galaxies, each in our own rotation—and when we came together, it was the Big Bang all over again.

Eventually, he got back in touch. He told me he was into something that he couldn't talk about because it was too dangerous, and that the

FBI was after him. That something, I'd find out later, was the Black Panthers.

Then he disappeared. *Again.*

The next time he came back, he said he'd been in California. He looked more like Jimi Hendrix than ever, with his hair grown into an enormous ball. I'd never seen anyone so beautiful in my life. His dark eyes had a new light. He was dressed in a T-shirt and bell-bottoms with fringe. He said he'd come back to town to perform his poetry for a dance company.

He unwrapped a goatskin rug and showed me a musical instrument he'd brought back with him. It was a bassoon made of cherrywood that he'd converted into a transverse flute, an instrument that was roughly three feet tall. When he played it for me for the first time, he seemed to go into a trance. The flute had only four keys, but in those four keys he found an infinite variety of sounds; he played as if possessed by a divine energy, moving his body with the music. He was stumbling into a new sound, beyond jazz, what we now call New Age. He was a true pioneer, but at the time, no one understood what he was doing. He would play for strangers under the stars, and then we would go wherever he was staying and make love.

Birth control pills had just become widely available; I made an appointment with a gynecologist and got a prescription. Once I started on the Pill (which, to my pleasant surprise, enhanced my figure), my liberation became complete. I felt as free as any man.

In the meantime, Kenneth changed his name to Matthew, and his outlook grew more biblical. He was determined to heal the world with his music, so at night we'd sit under the little dragon and bear constellations, and I'd listen as he played to his creator, whom he called Jove. I joined Matthew on his path to spiritual fulfillment, soaking up everything he told me about the nature of the mind and reading the poems of Kahlil Gibran. Thanks to Matthew, who gave me a black book to write in, I began keeping a journal, where I recorded drawings, thoughts, dreams, and everything that happened to me (a habit I have continued to this day). We swore off meat and went macrobiotic, eating lots of hippie food and smoking the hashish that Matthew liked, which took us to what we thought were higher and deeply philosophical states of understanding. We listened to Paul Horn and made love to Ravi Shankar and the Doors. I was crazy in love.

Or maybe just crazy? I suppose many people would think so, but to me, it all felt like a form of meditation. As I gazed up at the night sky, my head filled with his music, I truly felt one with the universe, expanded. It was an almost out-of-body experience.

chapter 20

STORMY WEATHER

Me outside Carnegie Hall, where I
celebrated after having just graduated
from high school, June 1969.

J finally graduated from high school in 1969 in a big ceremony at Carnegie Hall; I was almost nineteen. I told Mom I wanted to take the summer off, at least until September, when I would go to college—*maybe*. What I really wanted was to spend every possible minute with Matthew.

He had changed his name again, this time to Diamond Stone Red Rose, and he was now living in a commune on the west side of Manhattan with a friend from MIT, house-sitting for a group of people who spent their summers on Martha's Vineyard. The friend was a brilliant mathematician and violinist who also played tabla, a kind of Indian drum. The two of them would play for me for hours on end. When the friend had to go back to Boston, he invited us to visit. He gave us two plane tickets and a locked suitcase. So the next day Kenneth/Matthew/

Diamond Stone Red Rose, a huge flute, a locked suitcase, and I boarded a flight to Boston's Logan Airport. We went straight from the airport to Cambridge, where his friend had an apartment near the MIT campus.

That night we went to a party, and everyone drank tons of beer. It was a wild college scene, and when we got back to the apartment, his friend opened the suitcase. It was filled to the brim with dozens of plastic bags of marijuana. I actually jumped back when I saw it, aghast that Matthew and I had been tricked into transporting this stuff. I realized that I needed to start being more careful about the people I associated with.

The next day we flew back to New York City, which was hot and stifling. When I got home, my mom wasn't there, so I went into my room to relax and read *Commentaries on Living* by Jiddu Krishnamurti, one of the books of spiritual teachings that Matthew had turned me on to. I was still thinking about Matthew and how much I loved him when Sonny barged into my room without knocking. He'd grown more volatile than usual over the past few months, and I'd stayed out of his way as much as possible. He was territorial and always insisted on being the boss, so my budding career and Matthew's presence infuriated him. Matthew was much stronger and more virile than Sonny, and my stepfather was obviously intimidated by him.

Sonny stood over my bed and told me he wouldn't allow Matthew in our apartment again. I protested and he smacked me across the face. Then he said, "You want to have sex? I'll show you how to have sex." He hit me again and held me down with all his might and proceeded to rape me. It was unspeakably horrible. Though he'd made suggestive and sexually threatening remarks before, I'd never thought he'd attack me and force himself on me. I can't write more about it except to say that I started to scream at the top of my lungs. The gods must have been listening, because by some miracle Matthew came by to say hello, saw that my bedroom door was ajar, and took a running leap and landed on top of my stepfather. Punching and pulling him off me, he yelled, "You leave her alone, old man!"

Sonny left the room, and I thought, *Thank heaven, we won.* But no sooner had I caught my breath than Sonny roared back into my room with his pistol. He pointed it at Matthew and told him to get out of the house and never come back or he'd kill him. I had never seen Sonny look so angry or so insane, and Matthew was understandably scared. He backed off, said he'd return, and then he ran.

My stepfather locked me in my room and said through the door, "If you say one word to your mother, I'll kill your friend."

My shirt was ripped half off, my arm was bloody, and my jeans were torn. But all I could think about was escaping. Jumping out the window was impossible because we lived on the twelfth floor. I considered climbing out the window and up the side of the building to the next floor, but that was too dangerous. Then I heard the front door slam and lock, and I knew he was gone.

Somehow I broke the doorknob off my bedroom door, and without a second thought, I was out of the apartment and up on the roof of my building, hiding, looking out over the city, wondering what to do. It was one of those summer Sundays when it seemed that everyone in New York was out of town. I looked down onto the street, and when I was certain my stepfather wasn't coming back, I ran down fourteen flights of stairs, past people who turned and stared, and across Central Park to the West Side, where I knew Matthew would keep me safe.

When I got to the commune, I was greeted by two lesbian lovers. They calmed me down and gave me tea. It was July 20, 1969, and I'll never forget sitting with them in front of the television watching Neil Armstrong become the first man to walk on the moon. Despite the heat, I was shivering and scared: I'd just run away from home. I hadn't traveled as far as Neil Armstrong, but I felt as if I had. All I could think was: *My poor mother—she'll be so worried.*

Matthew got back later that night with his friend from Boston, and we watched the moon landing over and over again. He comforted me but was afraid and didn't know what to do. I stayed at the commune for three days without going out.

On the third night, Matthew's friend (who, to judge from that suitcase full of weed, knew his way around the drug scene) brought home some LSD. He told us it would expand our minds, so we all took some. At first everything was beautiful and full of light, but the next minute, I felt terrible, as if I were being chased by demons. It went on like that, back and forth, light and dark, all night long. Morning came and we left the commune to join up with friends at the fountain in the middle of Central Park. I was now wearing Matthew's clothes, and we were like one. We danced in the grass barefoot and walked uptown to a theater that was playing the Beatles' animated film, *Yellow Submarine*. The colors saturated my mind, and I ran out of the theater barefoot, onto the cement of New York City, singing, "All you need is love." We returned to the park, where we watched the sun set and then rise again. Time moved ever so fast.

All the flower power seeped into my head, and the world became one colorful, psychedelic love-in. We walked downtown toward the towering glass skyscrapers where people dressed in suits, and we danced among them in our love beads, fringes, dirty ripped bell-bottoms, and flowered T-shirts. We sat on the steps of the subway at Fiftieth Street and Sixth Avenue and watched the people moving like robots, going up and down.

By the time we'd been on the streets for at least three days, I started to wake up. I saw what it would be like to live as a street person and realized it wasn't for me. I didn't want to have alien voices speak through me. I didn't want to do drugs that took me to dark places, and I didn't want to sit on the ground and watch a parade of heels click by. There are few things as dehumanizing as watching people walk by and refuse to meet your eyes.

The next day we all started to make our way back uptown via Madison Avenue, and that was where my journey ended. Without warning, a police car drove up beside us, and out jumped two Blue Meanies, just like in the Beatles film. They pushed Matthew up against the wall of the building and handcuffed him. They took me aside and told me they were taking me home. I'd been missing for two weeks, and my mom had called the police, even though I'd phoned her to tell her I was okay (but refused to say where I was). The cops made Matthew get into one car and me into another; he was driven away, and I was taken home. There was nothing I could do.

We pulled up to the door of our building, and any relief I had upon seeing my mother evaporated when I saw Sonny standing beside her, smiling as though he'd done nothing.

There was no word from Matthew. I hoped he wasn't in jail. Or maybe he was too afraid to come around; my stepfather was not someone whose threats you took lightly. I was used to Matthew's mysterious absences; still, every day without him broke my heart a little more. I did know one thing for sure: I never wanted to live on the streets with no money. I was done with drugs and scrounging for food and all of that. And when you know what you don't want, you choose what you want.

For me, that was fashion, and I rededicated myself to my career. I started to dress up again, making myself look as good as I could with the raw material (and makeup kit) that I had.

chapter 21

SHATTERED

During a dark and tumultuous
period in my life, I often struggled
not to show emotion when I posed
for portfolio photographs.
Courtesy of Sean Kernan.

$\mathcal{D}$*espite* my constant efforts, I wasn't getting any paid modeling jobs. And now that I was no longer a student, that was a problem, both for me and for Ford. The agency told me that if I didn't make more money, they'd be forced to drop me. Shortly after that conversation, they booked me for my first catalog job. They probably thought I'd balk—catalogs were for people who couldn't get high-fashion editorial work—but as far as I was concerned, nothing was beneath a working professional. (Remember, this was long before the era of the so-called supermodel.)

The job was in downtown Manhattan near Houston Street, and the shoot was in the factory where the clothes were made. When I arrived promptly at eight in the morning, some of the models were already on the set. I soon learned that this kind of work was an art in itself. You had to hold your hand in a certain way to accentuate—or fake—the cut of the garment. The lighting flattered the clothing, not the model. And the stillness allowed me to practice rooting myself like a tree, just as Mrs. Vreeland had counseled.

After several weeks of catalog bookings, I'd earned a good amount of money but little satisfaction. Finally, Ford told me that I was doing well enough that they were considering sending me to some top photographers. One was Patrick Lichfield—officially, Thomas Patrick John Anson, fifth Earl of Lichfield. He was Queen Elizabeth II's first cousin once removed and a very "in" photographer, discovered by none other than Diana Vreeland. Dressed in high heels and perfectly coiffed, I arrived at the building—an old factory in the East Twenties—and entered a dark hallway, thick with the smell of urine and lit by a single dangling light bulb. I felt my way past doorways until I found a freight elevator with a retractable iron gate. I pushed the button and could hear the elevator squeaking and rumbling toward the ground floor; it seemed to take forever to crawl down the heavy cables. It arrived on the ground floor with a thud. I almost didn't step in, but I'd come this far and didn't want to be late. So I slid back the iron gate and got on.

The elevator was dark inside. I pulled a small chain, and a light came on. The car was like a small cage; when I pushed the button for the sixth floor, the gate closed, and a bump signified that the ascent had begun. Then the car stopped between floors. It started up again and jerked its way to the sixth floor and came to a halt. I opened the gate, found the office, and knocked on the door. Nothing. After a few more unanswered knocks, I pushed the door open and saw a man standing at a desk by a large window, speaking to a pretty blonde. The man—handsome and tall, with wavy blond hair—was wearing an open-at-the-collar white silk shirt that revealed his upper chest and a gold chain around his neck. He looked casually aristocratic.

I walked to the desk with my portfolio. The man stared at me and stepped aside, as if I had cooties.

"May I help you?" said the pretty blonde. She seemed to have no idea what I was doing there.

I introduced myself, and she said, "Who sent you?"

"Ford," I said.

She looked at the man and said, "There must be some mistake." The two of them laughed merrily, as if at some private joke.

The man said, "Are you sure your agency gave you the right address?"

"Yes," I said, realizing from his accent that this man was Patrick Lichfield. I was briefly awestruck until he spoke again.

"Tell that agency not to be ridiculous," he said. "This is not the type of girl I want to photograph." He looked straight at me, turned on his heel, and left the room in a huff.

The elevator was still there when the girl handed back my portfolio. With tears welling up in my eyes, I thanked her, retreated, closed the iron gate behind me, and quickly pushed the down button. When the door closed, the tears came streaming down my face until my eyes were so flooded that I didn't notice the elevator had skipped the ground floor and gone all the way to the basement, where it stopped abruptly and the light went out.

There I was, in the dark, in the basement, feeling devastated as well as dizzy from the ride and the dank, dirty smell of dust and mildew. The only source of light was a narrow shaft from a basement door leading outdoors. *Pull yourself together,* I thought, wiping away my tears and willing myself to calm down. The elevator gate closed and the machine started whirring on its own. *Good,* I thought, *that's good.* I pushed the button for the ground floor, barely able to see the button, and waited to move. That was when I noticed a large man standing on the other side of the gate. He yanked it open and got in. I smiled and asked for his floor, but he didn't answer. He just closed the gate behind him, and the elevator started to move.

The light went out again and the man spoke. "Don't be afraid," he said. I felt his hairy arm brush past me to reach the elevator buttons, and then I felt his big body move nearer. *Please stop standing so close,* I thought, my anxiety mounting. *There's space.* Then he grabbed me and put his hand over my mouth. His dirty fingers touched my lips, smearing my lipstick. Then he rubbed his heavy body against me, pushing me against the elevator wall, where the metal bars poked into my back.

I reached for the buttons to make the elevator move, but he knocked my hand away. He stank horribly of urine and his clothes scratched against my face. He put his hand on my head and pushed it hard against his lower body. I tried to scream, but the sound was stifled by his pants, his private parts against my face. I tried to squirm away, but his grip was like a vise, and my head was throbbing. My knees hit the floor, and I could feel my stockings rip on the rough wood beneath me.

The elevator started up. He pushed another button, and the elevator stopped. I was being crushed in the corner of that cage. I tried to reach the emergency bell on the floorboard, but he grabbed my hand, forcing it into his pants. He didn't say a word, just kept breathing hard. Then, somehow, the elevator rumbled up to the ground floor.

He kicked me aside, opened the gate, and scuttled out of the elevator like a roach. I fell on the floor, bruised, cut, and trembling all over, but glad to be alive. I picked up my portfolio and made a mad dash for the street, nearly knocking over a delivery boy. I kept looking behind me to see if the wicked man was following me, but he was gone, having vanished into thin air.

I jumped into a line of people waiting to board a bus. As I rummaged in my purse for the fare, I noticed the other riders looking at my bloody knees. Even amid that crowd, I was afraid the horrible man was nearby. When I got home, I didn't tell my mother what had happened. I didn't want to scare her, even though I was sick to death of having the same thing happen again and again just because I was a girl. I didn't have a dad to measure other men by, or an older brother or even an uncle who lived nearby, so for years I'd thought that maybe all men were good, like my only role models—Santa Claus or Jesus or Warren Beatty in *Splendor in the Grass*. In other words, made-up men. I knew better now. There was my stepdad, the men in Mexico, this horrible pervert in the elevator. All over the world, men would hold you hostage and threaten you and force you down the drain into a dark world. I started to build a shell around myself that men couldn't penetrate—not even Matthew, who had a pure soul but couldn't be counted on to be there when I needed him. (It had been weeks since I'd heard from him, and I had no idea where he was.) Still, I tried to hold on to a tiny hope of something better. Surely there was a good man—a real, live man, not just a fictional one—out there for me somewhere.

Grandma Nancy Edwards, 1910.

Grandpa Albert Cleveland, 1914.

My father, Johnny Johnston, 1948.

My mom, Lady Bird Cleveland, 1948.

Aunt Helen dancing onboard the *Queen Mary,* en route to Europe, 1950. Mom was supposed to go but gave her ticket to her sister when she got pregnant with me.

Living in Muskegon, Michigan, with my uncle Randolph, aunt Emily, and cousin Gregory, 1953.

Mom posing for Carl Van Vechten with her self-portrait, New York, 1953.
Courtesy of Carl Van Vechten

Me, age four, at home, watching the yellow birdie and posing for my first professional photo.

Mom and Henriette Metcalf in Madame Metcalf's garden in Connecticut, 1954.

Carl Van Vechten shot this photograph of me and Mom, 1957.
Courtesy of Carl Van Vechten

My school photo in second grade, 1957.

My mother painted this watercolor of me at age eleven.
Courtesy of Lady Bird Cleveland

The champ Muhammad Ali and me, on the *Ebony* Fashion Fair bus, early morning, Miami, 1966.

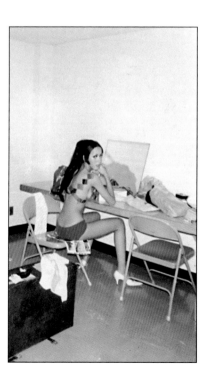

Backstage at the *Ebony* Fashion Fair 1966, getting ready for the bathing-suit number.

My first appearance in *Vogue*.
I am wearing my own design.
Courtesy of Berry Berenson

Stephen Burrows, 1970; I'm
wearing his "lettuce dress."
Courtesy of Charles Tracy

Who wouldn't feel glamorous
in this Stephen Burrows dress
with a train, 1970?
Courtesy of Charles Tracy

My first editorial for *Harper's Bazaar,* 1969.
Courtesy of Neil Barr

Working with Antonio Lopez in
the green room at *Vogue*, 1969.
Courtesy of Juan Ramos

My first photo shoot with the great Irving Penn for *Vogue,* 1971.
Courtesy of © Condé Nast, photograph by Irving Penn

This photo was shot by Norman
Eales for a photo book he put
together. London, 1971.
Courtesy of Norman Eales

Wearing Dior for my first
European magazine cover,
L'Officiel, Paris, 1971.
Courtesy of Guégan

Me in a studio pool in Milan, for a shoot for *Linea Italia*. I used Vaseline to keep my makeup from getting washed away.
Courtesy of Gian Paolo Barbieri

Vanity Fair cover, London, 1971.
Courtesy of David Montgomery

Here I'm posing as a Vargas Girl, London, 1971.
Courtesy of Hans Feurer

This shot for British *Vogue* was styled in London by Grace Coddington, 1971.
Courtesy of Norman Parkinson, Ltd.

I had no paid work for the next two weeks, which turned out to be a blessing, because it took that long for my knees to heal, even if my emotions didn't.

But my streak of bad luck wasn't over just yet. Back in my cycle of go-sees, I went to the studio of the photographer Hugh Bell. I'd met Hugh, who was known for his brilliant portraits of jazz musicians, back in the Fashion Fair days, and he'd always been a booster of mine. He took many wonderful photos of me and always told me not to give up, because I'd be a big star someday.

I dragged my suitcase full of clothes up to his large, light-filled studio near Union Square. While I got dressed and made up my eyes with lots of black pencil, Hugh constructed a set for me to pose in. When I saw what he'd done—he'd attached a hammock to beams suspended high in the ceiling—I thought, *Hmmm, that doesn't look too safe.* Before I could say a word, Hugh said, "Don't worry, I'd never put you in harm's way." He helped me into the hammock and backed away to start shooting. I posed carefully as the hammock started to sway. He said, "Now throw your leg over the edge."

"Like this?" I said.

"Yes, like that."

I felt proud of how well I could take direction, and as Hugh looked through the camera, I thought, *I'm a good model.* And that was when it happened. The beam holding the hammock slipped loose. Bam! My back landed hard on the floor, and the heavy beam crashed on top of me. I heard Hugh shouting, a camera dropping, and feet pounding the floor. I couldn't speak because I was crushed right down the middle, and I certainly couldn't move. I could hardly breathe.

The beam was so heavy that Hugh couldn't move it off me. He put his face next to mine to see if I was breathing, then went to the phone to call someone. I yelled, "I'm all right," but it came out as a tiny whimper. He rushed over, relieved. In reality, I wasn't all right at all, but I didn't want to tell him. He gave me aspirins and eventually got me out from under the beam and onto his sofa so I could rest. All I kept thinking was: *I'm a good model.*

"Do you want me to call a hospital?" Hugh said.

"No, I just want to do the pictures," I said, worried that I'd get in trouble with my agency.

He said we should probably stop for the day, which was a relief. I was in agony. He called a cab for me, and somehow I made it home and into bed. Several hours later, when my mom got home, I couldn't move at all. The pain was so excruciating that I blacked out, and when I woke up, I was in the hospital in a strange slinglike contraption that stretched my arms in one direction and my legs in another. The doctors told my mom there was something dangerously wrong with my back. She also said the agency had called to find out why I hadn't shown up for the other go-sees scheduled that day. When they found out what had happened, they suggested that I sue the photographer. Hugh was my friend; I never considered it.

The doctors told my mother that I needed an operation, but the chances of full recovery were slim. I flat-out refused. No way was I going to let them muck around with my spine. If something went wrong— even something small—I could end up paralyzed for the rest of my life. Instead, I spent the next six months of my life in the hospital in one of two places: my bed (where I was usually hooked up to that contraption, known as traction) or my wheelchair. Every day I'd watch other people who were in the same boat summon every ounce of strength they had in an effort to regain movement in their limbs.

The first day I tried to take a step out of the wheelchair, I fell and wouldn't let anyone pick me up. Two boys about my age with whom I'd become friendly—they were both paralyzed and would never walk again—saw me crying and wheeled over and said, "You can do it, you have a chance." All I remember is looking at their legs from my position on the floor and seeing them smile at me. That motivated me to pull myself up by my arms onto nearby exercise bars. I mustered all my strength to bring my legs along, but they felt like deadweights. Ten steps might as well have been ten miles. All I could do was sob. When I realized that my sobbing was holding me back, sapping my strength, I concentrated all my energy into a ball inside my head—my head actually ached from the effort—and pictured myself walking. My body started to feel lighter and lighter, and I heard the two boys cheering me on. By the time I managed to pull myself to the end of that length of carpet, I knew that I would walk someday. But I didn't know how or when.

Over my many months in the hospital, I got to know other patients; all of us acted as one another's pep squad. Eventually, I could take a few steps with the help of a cane. What a gift, simply to be able to walk a few tiny steps! I kept refusing the operation, and when I left the hospital and returned home, my cousin, a Jehovah's Witness, gave me the name of her chiropractor, whom she swore by. This was in the days when everyone thought chiropractors were quacks, but I'm forever grateful to this one. The adjustments he did on my back worked wonders.

Slowly, I got stronger and straighter. And then there I was again, walking around the living room with a book on my head, just as I had as a kid. Next, I tried a few tentative dance moves. Within three months, I was actually dancing—very carefully, back brace firmly in place—around the apartment. I wasn't pain-free, not by a long shot. It would be years before I could say that, and even after the pain was mostly gone, it would occasionally return out of nowhere—on the runway, in the shower, at a fitting—and I'd be sidelined temporarily.

But I knew I was healed.

chapter 22

OVER THE RAINBOW

Getting dressed with the help of the
master of color, Stephen Burrows, at his
apartment on East Seventh Street, 1970.
Courtesy of Charles Tracy.

$\mathcal{M}$*ostly* recovered, I went back to go-sees. Now, at least, I'd graduated
to some A-list photographers, thanks to my relationship with *Vogue* and
Diana Vreeland. Ford got me an official go-see with Avedon, though
they did it reluctantly. So there I sat, in the same reception room from
which I'd been ejected, in front of a different receptionist, who quickly
but politely flipped through my portfolio and said she'd keep my name
on file. Off I went to my next appointment, with Irving Penn. The same
thing happened there. On to Bert Stern's studio and the same thing. I'd
leave feeling pleased, a name checked off my list with a note to follow
up in the next week. Only in the evenings did I give in to feeling hungry,
demoralized, and beat.

One of the photographers I went to see was a protégé of Hugh Bell's named Anthony Barboza. Tony was a hip guy who loved Rasta music, had lots of opinions, and was all about black power. His studio was hung with his photographs of exotic-looking black women like Pat Evans, who became known for her clean-shaven head, Joyce Walker, Arlene Hawkins, Barbara Cheeseborough, and Carol Hobbs. And now he wanted to photograph me! I went to see him several times because he wasn't sure I was right for the work he was doing. Tony was helping develop a new magazine called *Essence*—it was going to be the first glossy fashion, beauty, and lifestyle publication for black women—and he wanted it to make a strong statement. He wasn't convinced that I fit in with its mission. He would kid around, saying, "I only photograph *black* girls" or "You're not *black* enough." That hurt my feelings. I just wanted to be photographed no matter what color I was, though I understood what he was getting at. I'd worked for *Ebony* and *Jet,* the only successful magazines for black people at the time. But I also came from *Vogue.* These represented two different cultures; they were like different sides of the railroad tracks, and I kept crossing over from one to the other. In the end, Tony didn't use me.

My career was my first priority now, even though Matthew had come back to town and wanted to see me as much as possible. I'd book him for late Saturday or Sunday afternoon, when all good people in the American fashion world were off having fabulous weekends in the country. I longed to do the same but was stuck in the city. (Believe it or not, New York in those days was a quiet town on Sundays.) When Monday came around, I was back pounding the pavement in single-minded pursuit of my goal. Nothing mattered but modeling.

Then, through a relatively minor mistake, I got a lucky break that would change the course of my entire career. I was booked to do a *Vogue* run-through from five-thirty to six-thirty P.M. After a day of go-sees, I went to the Graybar Building. Just being at *Vogue's* offices did me a world of good; I mean, what could be better than beautiful clothes and smart people who call you "darling" and "dearest"? And when Mrs. Vreeland liked a look I was modeling, it was like oxygen itself.

I bumped into Carrie Donovan as I was leaving that day. She was still busy finding new talents for her "*Vogue's* Own" pages, and her scouts were always on the lookout. The mix-up came when one of her scouts thought I was someone else and scheduled me to meet a new designer at Henri Bendel's studio who needed a fitting model.

When I got to Bendel's, I took the elevator to the eighth floor, and it opened onto an enormous cutting room with scores of men cutting layers and layers of cloth on large tables. I'd never seen such a big cutting room; I could have stood there for hours, watching those guys snip fabric around the paper patterns, imagining the dresses they were making.

A slightly built guy wearing a T-shirt with phallus-shaped appliqués of orange, pink, red, green, and turquoise approached me. "Are you looking for Mr. Burrows?"

"I am," I said.

"You've come to the right place," he said. "My name is Bobby Breslow; come on, I'll take you to Stephen." In a musical sort of cartoon voice, he yelled, "Steve! Someone's here to see ya!" We walked toward a closed metal door. "Steve!" Bobby yelled again.

I heard nothing beyond the whirring of the machines. Then: "Go away for a minute. I'm not ready."

"Steve! It's just me. There's a young lady to see you." We waited for a few minutes, and Bobby rapped on the door again. It opened, and out poured a cloud of smoke and the sounds of Motown and R&B. The room was dark, with brightly colored drawings covering the walls. And there, amid a cluster of hanging flowering plants, he stood: Mr. Stephen Burrows, a beautiful African-American man of medium height whom I guessed to be around twenty-six, wearing fringed leather pants, an appliquéd T-shirt similar to Bobby's, and silver mirrored sunglasses, something I'd never seen. He had a mustache and was smoking a very tiny rolled cigarette.

"Bobby! Close the door!" he said, as if he had state secrets inside that had to be kept safe. "I don't want the smoke to get out," he said to me by way of explanation. "They don't like the smoke here."

So I just stood, enveloped in smoke and incense, feeling as if I'd fallen into the den of a great wizard. "Are you Norma Jean?" Mr. Burrows asked.

"No," I said. "My name is Patricia Cleveland."

Mr. Burrows hesitated, and that was when I knew there'd been a mix-up. He took a last puff on his cigarette, then buried the tip in a pile of sand. "Well, Miss Cleveland," he said politely, "do you have time to try something on?"

"Of course," I said.

His voice changed when he spoke to Bobby. "Let's put Miss Cleveland in the lettuce," he said sweetly, almost whispering.

The lettuce? I thought. *I have to wear lettuce?*

I remained quiet as Bobby, who seemed to be Mr. Burrows's assistant, got a dress off the hanger for me to try on. "Here you go, Miss Cleveland," he said, handing me a silk jersey dress with a hemline that looked like the round, feathery edges of several heads of lettuce. I'd never seen a hem so fine or delicate, and trust me, I'd sewn a lot of hems.

"Show Miss Cleveland the screen, Bobby," Mr. Burrows said.

No one's ever called me Miss Cleveland before, I thought as I went behind the screen to change. *They must really think I'm a grown-up!* I could hear them whispering: "She's not the girl Carrie said she was sending. There must be some mistake. But she looks good, don't you think, Hector?"

A new voice, tinged with a Puerto Rican accent, piped up. "Right on, Steve, why not?"

"You think we should use her today?" Bobby asked.

"We should use her today," said Stephen.

I finished dressing and came out from behind the screen, and they stopped talking. The new guy, who must have been Hector, looked at me, put his hand over his heart, and said, "Oh my Gawd," as if he'd seen an apparition. They all looked at me, dead silent. Then, simultaneously, they all said, "Oh my God!" and screamed with delight.

"Look how she looks in that dress!" Mr. Burrows said. "It's perfect! *Perfect!*" He picked up his cigarette and happily relit it.

"Okay," said Hector. "We've got our girl."

"We'd better get over there," Mr. Burrows said, while I wondered where they had to get over to. "No, wait! Let's put her in one more thing."

Bobby handed me a bright chartreuse top and a midi-skirt decorated with yellow appliqués and bands of suede in different colors. These two pieces felt so good on my body, it was as though I had found a perfect second skin.

Mr. Burrows began winding a long ribbon of fabric snugly around my waist, and as he wrapped, the scent of his musk oil sent me into ecstasy. I think I was falling in love with this man. As he was finishing off the knot, I took a long look at his sketches. They were minimal, with thin, almost cartoonlike figures; they reminded me of my own drawings. (He must have felt something similar, because years later, he described meeting me as "having one of my sketches come off the page and walk straight toward me.") I knew then that I'd found my master designer and that I'd never again have to design or sew another stitch of clothing, because he was doing it for me—flawlessly.

"Steve, we gotta go," said Bobby. "They're in the park, waiting for us."

There I was, dressed in that skintight kelly-green midi-skirt with bands of color in buckskin and suede, and the chartreuse top. A couple of models I'd run into on go-sees entered the room, already dressed in Mr. Burrows's creations—a girl named Deanna who was as white as porcelain and had the highest cheekbones I'd ever seen, and a boy named Bobby Rovetta. They were accompanied by a photographer named Charles Tracy (everyone called him by his last name), who was also dressed in Mr. Burrows's designs. I'd never seen anything like it—this chic bunch of people, dressed in the best-looking clothes I'd ever seen. And I was part of it.

We all walked out the front door of Bendel's, past Buster the doorman, who, I was told, was seventy-eight years old and had been working at the store since he was sixteen, when horse-drawn carriages pulled up to the door and Fifty-Seventh Street was a residential area with townhouses. We walked to Central Park, and a passerby asked Tracy if we were with a circus. "No," he said, "we're from Stephen's World." It was true—that was actually the name of Mr. Burrows's new boutique at Bendel's, and we were wearing pieces from his first collection.

We marched past the majestic Plaza Hotel and down a grassy green hill, over the little stone bridge that crossed the pond, toward a colorful new universe filled with young, beautiful people. It was as though I'd walked into a rainbow or the Land of Oz. I felt as if I'd finally arrived at my true home, the place I was really meant to be in. I was coming to life, and I felt beautiful for the first time. That was the effect Mr. Burrows's clothes had on me. I'd put them on and feel like dancing.

I met another of his friends, Renaud White, and then we posed under the tall trees, and Tracy snapped away—for *Vogue*! After the shoot in the park, we went back to Bendel's studio, where Mr. Burrows dressed me in a few more outfits. When we finished, he gave me a jersey jacket to keep, and even took me to the store's shoe department to pick out a pair he wanted me to wear—brown patent-leather wedges, a sort of variation on Buster Browns, with candy-striped shoelaces. The brand was Goody Two Shoes, and they were so tall that I got dizzy when I first walked in them because the floor seemed so far away. I strapped on those platforms and once again felt like Dorothy from *The Wizard of Oz*.

The next day I went up to Bendel's again, and Mr. Burrows hired me as his fitting model. That meant he'd be making the clothes on me while I was wearing them. I felt like the luckiest girl in New York. From then on, I started going to his studio regularly. Stephen (we soon graduated to first names, though he still enjoyed calling me Miss Cleveland) was a master of color. When I watched the vibrantly hued cloth fly back and forth as he draped those jersey fabrics on the bias, it was like witnessing a magician at work.

Stephen was unusually sensitive and respectful. I especially liked the way he'd apologize if he thought he'd stuck me with a pin, or the way he'd ask, "How does that feel?" when he was draping something on me. The studio was such a lively, happy place, with a constant "cookin' up something in the kitchen" quality that happens when creative people come together. The week the studio opened, friends constantly popped in to visit, including Norma Jean Darden, the original (very lovely) girl whose name Carrie had given Stephen, and Carrie herself, with none other than Cher in tow (they were preparing for a *Vogue* shoot).

Bobby Breslow and Hector Torres, the two guys I'd met that first day, were Stephen's two assistants. Hector was sort of Stephen's right hand, a homey type who took time with the older ladies who came into the studio; Bobby was tiny, animated, and enthusiastic about almost everything Stephen did. He cracked us up with his constant one-liners. Then there was Don Fendley, who handled the music for Stephen's shows. He knew about trends before they hit the mainstream, and brought soul music to the fashion world. Don came up with the idea of deejaying for fashion shows and immediately cornered the market. People loved the fantastic selection of soul music he put together for Stephen so much that all the other designers wanted it for their shows, too.

And there was Tony, who ran the flower shop at Bendel's, also on the top floor. Sometimes I'd go there after lunch just to spend a little time in that heavenly hothouse high above the city. Tony kept the studio supplied with paradise flowers and jungle ferns, including plenty of fuchsia flowers, Stephen's favorite: He said they looked like little ballerinas wearing petals. I loved that image. Stephen's unique way of seeing things always inspired and pleased me. *No more running around to studios,* I decided. I just wanted to work for Stephen.

His fanciful imagination, along with his playful, color-saturated designs, brought to mind the brilliant animation of Walt Disney; indeed, Mr. Burrows reminded me of a latter-day Mr. Disney as he sat in quiet concentration at his drawing board (he rarely spoke until he was finished with a design) and puffed not on a pipe but on his exotic tiny cigarette. Wearing his trademark mirrored wire-rims, he'd dress in multicolored leather pants and what he called "muscle shirts"—very tight tees with the sleeves turned up to just the right place to show off the wearer's biceps.

Just watching him made me almost giddy with happiness. Becoming a member of Stephen's World was a turning point for me. It lifted my career—my whole life—from black and white to Technicolor.

chapter 23

HOT FUN IN THE SUMMERTIME

First day on Fire Island, feeling free in
a design by Stephen Burrows, 1970.
Courtesy of Charles Tracy.

One of the benefits of knowing Stephen was that my social life kicked into high gear. And that was a good thing, because once again Matthew had taken off for California without telling me. He left the day after my birthday. Now I was twenty and single.

I did Stephen's first show at Bendel's a couple of months later, in the middle of August. It was held in his boutique on the third floor, Stephen's World, which was light-years ahead of its time and looked absolutely spectacular: shiny black vinyl walls creating a mirrored effect; recessed lighting above the clothing racks (which had silver studded borders); and lacquered black ceilings and floors. The effect was of a su-per-slick nightclub or a trendy piano bar. The show was such a hot ticket that helpers had to keep extending the show space out into the hallways, bringing out folding chairs for the extra people until seats reached all the way to the elevators. Some editors arriving late found themselves, as they got off the elevator, walking along with the models in the middle of the runway until they located their assigned seats among the small gold chairs lined up against the walls. Geraldine Stutz, president of Henri Bendel, was the official host, and tastemakers like the newspaper columnist Eugenia Sheppard and the publicist Eleanor Lambert, who founded the Coty Awards and the Council of Fashion Designers of America, were scribbling away enthusiastically in their notepads.

That night after the show, I went to my first party with Stephen. When we got there, the festivities were well under way, and I didn't know a soul. Then I noticed my high school friend Donna Jordan. She came dancing into the room, holding up her wide fifties-style petticoated skirt like a cancan dancer. She was with a girl who had very black hair and a face painted so white that it looked almost like a Japanese mask; her tiny lips were bright red. The two of them went to sit with a guy with a mop of very white hair; it was the same person—the "famous artist"—I'd seen her with at the club in Sheridan Square when we were in high school. I was about to go over to say hello when a tall, very handsome man dressed entirely in black walked in and sat near us. He kept looking at me, so I asked Stephen who he was. "His name is Halston," Stephen said. "He's a designer, too."

I eventually caught up with Donna, who introduced me to the girl with the white face—Jane Forth—and her other friend, Andy Warhol, who smiled at me with twinkling eyes and then gave me a heavy-duty once-over, twice. Donna pulled me aside and whispered, "He's a filmmaker, and I'm making a movie with him. How about that?"

Making movies? Not bad, I thought. Then another guy—a small, tanned South American with a Spanish accent, dressed flamboyantly in feathers and fringe—came over and started complimenting me. His name was Giorgio di Sant'Angelo—he dramatically rolled the R in "Giorgio"—and he asked me if I would do his show. I told him to get in touch with me through Stephen. I really didn't know who he or anybody else was, partly because at that time there wasn't a big who's who in the fashion world. We were all just starting out and trying to make our mark.

The next day, at half past six in the morning, I was in the greenroom at *Vogue*, being sketched by Maning. We worked all day—though it never really felt like work, because Maning would talk so entertainingly about fashion history or his travels with Mrs. Vreeland or his love for the legendary couturier Madame Grès—and then I was off to another party with Stephen, this time at the photographer Berry Berenson's apartment, a beautiful floor-through with all-white walls; it was the first example I'd seen of a new type of living space called a loft. That evening Stephen invited me to spend the weekend with him and his friends on Fire Island. I was over the moon. Finally, a weekend away from the city! And to a place I'd always wanted to visit.

We were leaving on Friday afternoon. I spent that morning doing publicity shots with Stephen and another model, a Brazilian hippie named Ramona Sanchez, for *Women's Wear Daily*. Afterward, Stephen decided to give us a tutorial in walking in his style of clothing. Bobby and Hector were there to help with the critique.

"Bobby," Stephen said. "Show them how the walk goes."

Bobby, who was about four feet tall, was standing next to Ramona, who was six feet tall. As he demonstrated how to do the walk, with Stephen directing, we all cracked up. We laughed so hard we could barely breathe, much less walk.

That walk, "a modern couture walk but with a twist," according to Stephen (who invented it), reminded me of the one Maning had taught me, but even more extreme. In other words, it was an exaggerated version of an already exaggerated form. I had to jut my hip bones forward as far as possible, then lean back with one leg forward and my tailbone tucked in. The idea was to get a straight line from my neck to my knee, so it looked as though I was leaning back on something, the way you would lean on a bar. But I had to be in forward motion as I leaned. Ramona and I practiced until we got it right.

"So," Stephen said, "that's the walk you'll do in the next show." He didn't teach anyone else how to do it. It was our secret. And that walk, combined with the moves Maning taught me and a few dancelike flourishes of my own that I improvised along the way, would become my trademark on the runway.

⁓

Before we left Stephen's studio, he dressed me in a multicolored jump-suit and topped it off with a pair of silver mirrored sunglasses just like the ones he wore. We looked like space aliens, but it was great fun to see people and not have them see your eyes.

Friday afternoons at Bendel's were highly anticipated. Sometimes photographers would be waiting to snap pictures of celebrities going in or out of the store. That was where I saw Bill Cunningham, the beloved *New York Times* "On the Street" photographer who then worked for *Women's Wear Daily*. "Smile, you kids!" he said, and *flash!* I felt like a movie star as Stephen, Hector, Bobby, and I quickly dashed into the waiting limo and dove into the backseat.

We were catching the last ferry, and when we arrived at the dock, I looked around and saw nothing but boys! boys! boys! And more boys, with an occasional stylish, interesting-looking female sprinkled in here and there for visual relief. Sometimes I couldn't tell who were the boys and who were the girls, but what the heck, it didn't matter. Fun belonged to everyone, and it was there to be had.

We stood in the ticket line, catching bits and pieces of all the different social groups and plans around us:

"Yes, well, we have to redecorate for the party tomorrow."

"Okay. You bring the food and I'll bring the boys."

"Look at Miss Thing over there. Looks like she's been out for weeks."

"Oh! Don't let her see you, she'll want to come, too."

"Pull your hat down, honey, she might not recognize you."

Then there it was, pulling up to the dock, the five o'clock ferry. As we boarded, I noticed how many people were carrying little dogs in their arms. Some of these dogs were so well groomed that they looked better than I did. Onto the boat we all went—dogs, bags, boys, and girls with jewels and summer looks. As we sat on the wooden benches, the mainland disappeared. I was so excited; I couldn't wait to step foot on "The Island." All my cares blew away with the wind.

The island appeared as if out of a dream. There was a small hotel by the dock called the Botel, and the sundeck was swarming with people. It looked like a late-afternoon dance in full swing. As the ferry's ropes were thrown out to the dock, everyone on both sides started waving.

The sun was still high enough in the sky to give the evening that warm, late-day summer feeling.

Because the island was so tiny, everyone was immediately friends with everyone else. Fire Island was a sort of utopia built on having fun and being creative, and all doors were unlocked. It seemed like everyone there was connected with the business of art, as a designer, an interior decorator, a painter, a chef, a writer. Even the playwright Tennessee Williams was there. We were staying at the home of Paul McGregor, who was known as "the hairstylist to the stars." Paul had sent someone to greet us at the dock with a little red wagon for our luggage. I was charmed by that; I'd never been in a place that allowed no automobiles whatsoever. We set off for Paul's house—one of the first to be built on the island, and pretty isolated from the rest—and stopped on the way at a small grocery to pick up a few provisions. I was shocked to see people milling around in bathing suits, chatting and shopping for food.

We walked up a long wooden boardwalk between a grove of pine trees and bunches of wild rosebushes. The sea air hit me. The combined scents of pine and salt water and the musk oil worn by the boys was intoxicating. As we made our way along the path with our wagon, we were greeted left and right by other islanders welcoming us and inviting us to parties. I was proud to be with Stephen and the boys, because when people saw us, they just lit up.

Paul's house was large and modern, a wood-and-glass structure he'd designed himself. Stephen had told me that virtually everyone on the island had a custom-designed house because he was either a famous architect or was good friends with one. Two heads peeked out from an upper level: Tracy the photographer, who'd arrived earlier, and Stephen's best friend, Roz, who came outside in a sheer white caftan, beautiful brown hair cascading over her shoulders. She took care of the business side of Stephen's World and was one of those rare people who are naturally beautiful, both inside and out. She greeted me with a warm hug, like a sister. I put my bags in the room Roz was using, then went upstairs to the huge living space, with its high-beamed ceiling shaped into a pyramid, wooden verandas, floor-to-ceiling glass walls, and white hammocks strung around the room. Roz was relaxing in one of them by the open kitchen; she'd already prepared appetizers for us.

Tracy was here to work, though. He wasted no time preparing to take photos. Stephen, Bobby, and Hector dressed and painted me, and as the sun began to descend, I posed with wet hair, veiled only in a sheer flowery silk scarf over my naked body. I heard the waves crash behind me and felt as though I'd struck my best pose yet, with Tracy and Stephen directing me.

We changed clothes and sets until the last rays of natural sunlight were gone. The boys created a room out of red chiffon and silk, then put me in a leather-fringed dress as the breeze blew through the windows and ruffled the fringe. I could tell exactly when they got the shot they wanted. Everything felt so sensuous; this was truly what photographers called "making love through the lens." Now I felt fully ensconced in Stephen's world, with a new family of the most inspired people I'd ever met in my life.

Roz cooked dinner, and then it was time to party. The house had only one bathroom, the site of its sole mirror, and we all rushed to use it. The girls went first. In addition to Roz, me, and a girl named Daryl, there was Pat Ast, another of Stephen's pals. Weighing around two hundred pounds, she was one of the first plus-size models; she was also sarcastic, aggressive, pushy, stylish, and a drama queen on her way to becoming a big star. For some reason, she had a grudge against me from the word go. Every time I saw her, she'd tell me I had no charisma. It was like having a wicked queen constantly trying to cast an evil spell on me.

When it came time to dress, we would don whatever outfit we had packed, only to have Stephen re-dress everyone. He'd pull something out of his seemingly bottomless duffel—yet another aspect of Stephen's genius was that he designed clothes that could fold up so small you could fit a hundred dresses into a tiny bag—and fling it across the room to someone, and he or she would put it on. At some point, Stephen ran out of stuff, but he still wanted to dress me, so he gave me his own clothes to wear. So there I was, dressed like a boy, in a pair of Goody Two Shoes platform wedges.

Shooting stars and a bass sound guided us to the Botel. We went arm in arm, talking and laughing and being free, passing blunts from person to person. As we walked along, people greeted us and stared at me. Well, not at *me*, exactly, but at the way I was *dressed*. Stephen was already known as the designers' designer, and people got a lot of ideas and inspiration from him. If Stephen conceived it, it was bound to pop up soon in someone's collection.

Heads turned like magnets to metal when we arrived at the Botel. The music was so loud we couldn't really converse, so we drank instead. I stuck to fruit punch and put the little paper umbrella in my hair for decoration. From then on, that was where my paper umbrellas usually ended up. The place was packed with beautiful guys and a few girls whom everyone seemed to be calling "hags." The primary mode of socializing was to dance as hard and as fast and as much as you could. People always wonder how models stay in shape. Here's the secret: They test-drive their clothes on the dance floor. And in those days, I was one of the best test pilots around.

Our fashion tribe squeezed its way through the mass of dancing until we reached our post. Everyone wanted to be near Stephen; he had incredible energy and effervescence. The new dance that summer was a saucy Latin creation called the bump—fresh in more than one sense of the word—that was like a wacky tango emanating from the legs and hips. It felt really sexy to "bump" against someone in that way. Stephen was unquestionably the "it" boy that summer, and everyone was falling for him, even the other designers. I knew exactly how they felt: They all wanted to leave their gray-by-contrast world and join Stephen's free-spirited, rainbow-colored world.

The weekend flew by in a blur of colors and bodies and music, and before I knew it, we were on the ferry again, heading back to reality.

chapter 24

OUR DAY WILL COME

The *Essence* shoot, 1970. Me
(*center*) playing volleyball with
Norma Jean Darden (*left*) and
Ramona Saunders (*far right*).
Courtesy of Kourkin Pakchanian.

At last, one of my go-sees had paid off! Just before leaving for Fire Island, I'd had a rather rushed meeting with Gordon Parks, the celebrated
composer, poet, novelist, film director, and, in case that wasn't enough,
now the editorial director of *Essence,* the new magazine for black women.
Though it had been an honor to meet him, I'd been a bit distracted by
the impending trip to Fire Island. So imagine my surprise and excitement when he ended up picking me to appear in the premier issue. Best
of all, we were shooting in a bucolic setting in upstate New York, which
meant another weekend away from the city.

I went to the address where the van was being loaded and was met
by three cultured, beautiful women of color who introduced themselves

as Susan Taylor, the primary stylist, and Iona and Sandra, her assistants. There was a sense of soulfulness about them—a spiritual depth—that was vital, since they were in charge of making the first issue a success.

"How does that look?" Susan asked, holding up a pair of shoes next to a dress. She had creamy caramel-colored skin and wore her hair in African-styled braids, but what I loved most about her were her sparkling almond-shaped eyes.

Iona snapped her fingers and said, "Tell me 'bout it, sister," meaning it looked great. Iona laughed and smiled with such radiance that I just wanted to keep looking at her. She was a churchgoing, soft-spoken girl who said things like "God knows what you're doing" and "God knows what's in your heart."

Sandra, the tallest of the three, said, "It looks fly, don't you think?" She liked to crack jokes and said "don't you think?" at the end of each sentence, and the funny thing was, you actually *would* have to think.

These women were the essence of *Essence:* young, black, proud, and eager to share that pride with everyone. They were the first black fashion editors I'd met since *Ebony,* and it was inspiring to watch them meet the challenges of the times. They were spearheading a new trend in black culture, and I was definitely in on it, even though I was constantly aware that I was half-Viking.

So while blacks were often denied opportunities because of their skin color—and believe me, I lost plenty of jobs because I didn't have the conventional all-American looks that higher-ups at fashion magazines considered pretty—I also got passed over for jobs that went to models who were a deeper shade of brown. (I admit I found some satisfaction in the fact that I'd be appearing in the first issue of *Essence,* the very magazine that Anthony Barboza had refused to photograph me for because I wasn't "black enough.") As it turned out, *Essence* was inclusive enough to want someone like me in its pages.

It was a terrific shoot. Four of us had been tapped to be featured in that first issue, including Carol Hobbs; Norma Jean Darden (the girl Stephen had been expecting that day I walked in); Ramona Saunders, who would become a good friend; and me. It was a clear August day when we piled into the van and headed upstate. After riding through miles and miles of farmland, we stopped in front of a grand, romantic-looking turn-of-the-century mansion, which functioned as both our stage set and our hotel.

Over two gorgeous days, we shot several photos. One particularly memorable picture was of all four of us playing volleyball in long taffeta skirts with beautiful calico underskirts that made us look like schoolgirls of that pre–World War I era. In another shot, we posed between the garden doors and the pillars in the conservatory and on the veranda. The experience was like stepping out of time. Everyone on the shoot, from the models to the editors to the photographer and crew, bonded because we knew we were participating in something beautiful and important.

If all my jobs had been as pleasant and solid as that one, I wouldn't have had a complaint in the world. But I was frustrated with Ford's representation. The *Essence* job had been the result of a go-see that Ford had booked, but on the whole I felt the agency wasn't doing enough to steer my career in the right direction, and the most likely reason for that was because Eileen Ford didn't believe in me. At the end of the day, she just didn't think I was pretty enough to be a truly successful model.

In fact, my primary income stemmed from three sources that Ford had nothing to do with. There was my work at *Vogue,* being fitted in outfits and sketched by Maning; there was being Stephen's fitting model, which was the direct result of my work at *Vogue;* and then there was the regular gig I'd been doing on Seventh Avenue as a fitting model for the wonderful French émigré designer Jacques Tiffeau, which had materialized through the recommendation of Mrs. Johnson from *Ebony.* At that time, the French designers were the most important in the world of fashion, but America was an exciting frontier. The possibilities were limitless, and the fiercely independent Monsieur Tiffeau was eager to push the limits. We worked well together, and photographs of me wearing his clothes appeared regularly in the *Daily News.*

Meanwhile, Ford would often book me for jobs like one that involved standing in front of a bank on the corner of Fifty-Ninth Street and Lexington Avenue handing out fliers, dressed as a huge yellow chicken. Or another weeklong assignment where I had to remain motionless in a store window like a mannequin for an entire afternoon, moving only slightly to startle passersby. By the end of the week, I had a crowd at the window, and I rather enjoyed putting on a show, especially for kids, but this was *not* the career I had in mind.

I tried to concentrate on the money I was making—I'd hum the popular song "Takin' It to the Bank" every time I deposited a check—but I was getting impatient. I wanted more, which was why, on a sunny day in September at eight-thirty in the morning, I found myself in the office of Wilhelmina Models, a relatively new agency founded by the stunning Dutch model Wilhelmina and her husband, Bruce Cooper. I'd heard that Wilhelmina had a broader, more modern concept of beauty—one that maybe, just maybe, was modern and broad enough to include me.

chapter 25

THINGS ARE LOOKING UP

Pat Cleveland

Height: 5' 9½"
Dress: 8-10
Bust: 32
Waist: 22
Hips: 35
Shoe: 8
Glove: 7½
Hat: 22
Hair: Dk. Brown
Eyes: Brown

Wilhelmina
9 EAST 37 STREET
NEW YORK CITY 10016

PRINT: 532-6800
TV: 532-7141

John Bishop

My model card for Wilhelmina, 1970.

The beautiful Indian summer day put me in such an optimistic frame of mind that I decided to splurge on a cab. Before getting in, I double-checked my wallet to make sure I had enough money for the fare. The cabbie flicked on his meter, and I held my breath. Just by stepping inside, I'd already depleted a quarter of my stash.

We stopped in front of a very tall building and I got out, scraping together the fare. I entered and then hesitated before pressing the elevator button. I asked myself why I was going to a new agency when I was already with the best in the country. But Tracy, Hector, Bobby, and Stephen were always telling me that I should be higher up on Ford's list. And I knew I could trust them because they were doing so well themselves.

Wilhelmina—or Willy, as she was known in the industry—was a shot at something different. Her agency was having an open model call, which meant any young man or woman seeking representation could show up out of the blue, without an appointment.

I pushed the button and went up to the twelfth floor. The elevator opened directly into a small white room, and as I got off, two luscious male models got on, giving me a smile and a wink. Nice-looking guys! I liked what I saw so far. Then I shook my head, distressed that I'd lost myself in a reflexive boy-crazy moment instead of focusing on my mission. Before I could gather myself fully, a perky, fresh-faced young woman passed me in the hallway and asked, "Are you looking for someone?"

"I'm here for the model call," I said.

"You're really early; we don't see anyone before ten," she said. "But you're welcome to stay." She gestured to a nearby room.

Walking toward what I assumed was the waiting room, I noticed a photo of a beautiful woman and then many more, all of the same woman. Indeed, the walls were lined with pictures of her on the cover of *Vogue*. I started counting: twenty-seven. My eyes widened, and my mouth dropped. Twenty-seven *Vogue* covers! Amazing. Who *was* this woman? The answer, of course, was Wilhelmina.

Her face was perfect, with beautiful brown eyes and lashes, lashes, lashes. Her neck was long, slender, pale, and smooth. I remembered that my mom had done a few illustrations of her when I was a child. She'd seemed otherworldly back then, and she still did, as if she'd been sculpted by a master. I stared for at least ten minutes at one photo, in which she was the face of a Revlon campaign for a new lipstick and nail polish color called Fire and Ice. She looked cool and poised, with her slender hands showing off the nail color next to her pouting fire-engine-red lips. No one was wearing that color anymore except me. Stephen had told me I looked good in it, and I'd worn it from then on. That very day, I was wearing the most vivid crimson lipstick I'd ever owned.

Studying the picture, I wondered idly if I could ever be a Revlon girl. Could I look sufficiently aristocratic or classic? Did Wilhelmina suck in her cheeks to get that high-cheekbone look? Did she deliberately pout to get her lips to look so luscious? What tricks did she use to appear so perfect? I started to suck in my cheeks, trying to feel my cheekbones, until the inside of my mouth hurt. Then I attempted to pout, puffing out my lips slightly, until I wondered if they looked too big, since thin lips were the preferred look at the time.

It was now a quarter to ten, and I was getting anxious, because I had a go-see to squeeze in before my work with M. Tiffeau. I decided to speak up. As I headed toward the front hallway, I saw a gracefully thin woman walk across the back hall, followed by three girls carrying portfolios, so I ran back to my seat. The girls came in and sat near me; we talked for a bit, and then they were called into another room. *That's not fair,* I thought. *I was here first.* But I kept waiting. Finally, it was my turn. The perky-faced woman called me over, introduced herself as Fran, and escorted me to the door of Wilhelmina's office. "You can go inside. She'll be here in a moment."

Wilhelmina's office was modern in decor, with a wall of windows that looked out onto the Empire State Building. I was so caught up in the view that I didn't notice Wilhelmina herself walking in, taking a deep drag on a cigarette. She looked utterly divine: sleek and thin, dressed in a black pencil skirt and a white satin blouse, and dripping with loops of pearls. Her long-limbed body seemed to have a life of its own. I couldn't believe I was sitting in her presence, but before I could say a word, a tall blond man entered the room and blurted out, "That shit! I say we fire him, Willy!" Then he left.

Wilhelmina dropped her cigarette on the floor, rubbed it out with her foot, bent to pick it up, placed it in an ashtray, reached into her pack for a new one, and lit it. As she did this, the man came into the room again, walked over to her, and pulled the cigarette out of her mouth. "And I told you to stop smoking."

She grabbed the cigarette back. "*You* make me smoke." Then they looked at me and seemed to become aware of my presence. But not for long. "Hello," they both said, trying to cool down before quickly going at it again. "You're drunk, Bruce. How about you stop drinking at ten in the morning, then I'll stop smoking," Willy said, puffing harder on her cigarette.

"How do you like that?" he said, turning to me. "I'm telling her something that's good for her." He left the room again. I have never wished so hard to be invisible.

"You see how men are," she said, looking straight at me. "This is *my* business. He has the Carson show, and I have this." She picked up her telephone. "Can you please tell Bruce to bring me a tomato juice?"

She hung up the phone, took a couple more drags on her cigarette, and snuffed it out in her ashtray, which was overflowing with cigarette butts. Bruce—I'd figured out that he was her husband—came in and handed her the tomato juice. "I settled it," he said. "I just fired him." His wife shot him a dirty look, and then he was gone.

Wilhelmina started flipping quickly through my portfolio. Then she slowed down and started to scrutinize every photo. "Well," she said, "I really like the way you look."

Ding! Did she, the great Wilhelmina, say she liked the way I looked?

"You'll have to excuse me," Wilhelmina said, "but I'm not feeling well. Can you come back tomorrow, and we'll go over everything together? I know who you are, Patricia. One of my favorite male models, Renaud White, told me about you. I'd love to have you in my agency." She closed my book and left the room, calling out, "*Bruce!*"

I sat there, flummoxed. Should I take my portfolio or leave it? Thankfully, Fran came into the room, wrote my name and the time for my appointment the following day on a card, and handed me my portfolio.

Descending in the elevator, I felt as though I were ascending instead. Wilhelmina wanted to sign me! But there was no time to savor my triumph; I was running late, and without enough money in my pocket for a cab, I had to fast-walk in high heels. My first stop was a go-see with Claude Picasso, the photographer son of *the* Picasso, an artist whose cubist works I had adored when my mom had taken me to the Museum of Modern Art as a kid; I'd also studied them in great depth in my high school art classes.

Claude didn't seem particularly interested in me, but I think a bit of his father's magic rubbed off on me, because later that day I did some of my best work ever for Jacques Tiffeau as I modeled for the buyers. I held my most elegant posture and moved as gracefully as I could to showcase his designs. "You worked very well today, Patricia," M. Tiffeau said approvingly. I told him that I'd just met Picasso's son, and he gushed to me about meeting Claude's mother, Françoise Gilot, in Paris. "She is a beautiful woman," he said in his adorable French accent, "and a painter, too." *It's a small world after all,* I thought, the Disney song reverberating in my head.

At nine sharp the next morning, I returned to Wilhelmina's agency.

This time, when I entered her office, she was sitting tall behind her desk, drinking a big cup of coffee. I hadn't eaten breakfast, because I didn't want to be late, and the aroma soothed my senses.

"Patricia," Wilhelmina said, standing up from her desk. "You're prompt, which is very professional. I'm glad I didn't scare you off yesterday. Please, sit down." She sat. "Bruce, my husband, whom you saw yesterday, had a lot to do, and one of our partners was not on board . . . Anyway, I understand you're with Ford."

Oh no, I thought, *she doesn't want me because I already have an agent.*

"I used to be with Eileen. How's she treating you?"

I had no idea how to answer.

"You know, if you sign with us, I'll get you a better rate. My girls start at sixty an hour."

Sixty an hour! My head rang a series of dollar signs, as in a slot machine. I started fantasizing about my bank account. She continued, "We have a whole new look and lots of work for girls like you. But first let's get down to business. Do you want to be with my agency?"

"Yes!" came out of me so fast, I didn't even hear it myself.

"Good." Wilhelmina moved gracefully to the door of the office, like a calm breeze. "Fran!" she called out mildly, not as she had the day before. Fran came in immediately with papers for me to fill out. When I finished, Wilhelmina flipped through my portfolio and selected a recent photo that I'd added the night before. "We can use this on the head sheet," she said, referring to a collection of head shots of all the models represented by the agency, which includes photos, names, sizes, and hourly rates. *My,* I thought, *this is going really well.*

Willy sat in the chair behind her desk and poured herself another cup of coffee—her third since I'd been there. She cast those beautiful brown eyes on me, and a pensive look passed over her face. Abruptly, she sat forward and said, "Pat! Just Pat. Do you mind?"

Mind? What mind? She was my mind now, and whatever she said, I agreed with.

"I want to abbreviate your name. I couldn't use my full name, you know; they call me Willy. You can be Pat. It's easier to remember, and it suits the times, what with the world being so unisex. It could go either way, boy or girl."

I could see the logic in what she was getting at, though no one called me Pat. If it wasn't Patricia, it was Patty, or Patsy, or Trish.

Her eyes took on a faraway look. "It's a shame how men try to rule the world," she said, taking another sip of coffee. Then she started rifling around in her desk drawers. "Just a moment." She left the office and came back with a new pack of Lucky Strikes. Then she put the pack down and whispered, "No, not today. I'm trying to quit." She turned back to me. "Pat, you have a very poetic look. We won't have a problem with that. But to make it here in America, you'll have to travel to Europe first." This was something I'd never heard before. Europe? "The world will love you, Pat, but let's get you on that head sheet and do what we can while you're here. I'll arrange for you to go to one of our agencies over there, and when you come back, you'll have so many magazine shoots and tear sheets that they'll speak for you. Does that make sense? You can go into the bookers' room now. Fran will introduce you to everyone and get you started. Maybe we can get a few editorials in before you fly over there. Oh, and if you need anything, please call me. Here's my number at home. I'm always here for you unless I am with my children." As I walked out of Willy's office, another girl with big dreams walked in.

Everyone welcomed me into the agency and called me by my new name, Pat. "PAT C." was immediately written on my booking chart, and I was given a voucher book with "Wilhelmina Model Agency Inc." printed on the cover.

Pat. I'm Pat. I'm Pat Cleveland! I felt invincible. I left Wilhelmina's office and went to the French Institute on East Sixtieth Street and signed up for French lessons. I'd need to know another language if I ended up in Europe. Then I dropped by the drugstore to pick up my new pack of birth control pills. I had a date that night with Matthew, who had just returned from California. The game was on. And with my new name, my new agency, and my sexual freedom, I felt poised to win.

chapter 26

A STAR IS BORN

Anne Klein show at the Plaza
Hotel. They said, "Do what
you feel," and so I did.
Courtesy of Roxanne Lowitt.

 $\mathcal{T}he$ Coty Awards, which were sponsored by Coty Fragrances and
recognized the work of American designers, were the Academy Awards
of fashion. Eleanor Lambert, the fashion publicist who created the Best-
Dressed List (which was pretty much the goal of anyone who cared passionately about clothes), was the force behind the awards. The girls who
usually worked the ceremony were a group known as "Seventh Avenue
models." These were models who worked mostly for designers in their
showrooms, as opposed to the glamour-girl photography models who
made their living by appearing in glossy magazine spreads. Except for
maybe Twiggy or Jean Shrimpton, there were still no supermodels who
moved easily between these two very different spheres.

The Seventh Avenue models were the real workhorses of the industry; if they'd been dancers, they would have been the chorus girls. These girls were pros through and through, and I liked them immensely and was always eager to learn the tricks of the trade from them, whether it was how to stuff my bra, or keep my shoes from falling off, or just how to be patient and respectful. (They were so nice that I was shocked when, later in the business, I met a lot of models who were out for themselves and didn't care whom they hurt.) I wasn't really aligned with either camp, but Eleanor Lambert suggested to a few of the top designers that they use me for the 1970 awards ceremony. She was very high on Stephen Burrows, as were most of the New York designers who knew of his work, and she wanted to help him and his gang in any way she could. It was a huge break for me.

With a few exceptions (such as my wonderful Jacques Tiffeau), the French thought that Americans had no taste. Consequently, most of the elegant women in the social elite went to Paris to buy their clothes from the established couturiers there. Here in the United States, designers like Donald Brooks, Geoffrey Beene, Chester Weinberg, and Bill Blass (who was himself on the International Best-Dressed List and whose name was already on products ranging from car upholstery to sheets and perfume) were beginning to put this country on the fashion map. And these were the designers for whom Coty and Eleanor Lambert created the awards.

So off I went to meet Bill Blass at 550 Seventh Avenue. I had to wait for him, of course, and when he finally did show up, he seemed to appear out of nowhere, through one of the farthest doorways of his showroom. He was a tanned, ruggedly handsome man dressed in a tweedy English country-style sports jacket with a silk ascot around his neck, like someone from a fifties movie. He held a cigarette in one hand, and its long curls of white smoke danced around his face, which wore a "seen it all" expression. I noticed that he had a lot of laugh lines around his eyes, even though he wasn't laughing. I looked straight into his deep-set green eyes and waited for his verdict. I was nervous because he was very conservative-looking. Actually, I was afraid of him in general, because he was known for dressing Happy Rockefeller, the wife of New York's governor, Nelson Rockefeller, who was one of the richest men in the world.

Mr. Blass looked me up and down—I could have been cattle—then he laughed and said, "You're awfully skinny." He called his assistant, who came running. "We'll give you a try," he said, winking at me. Then he turned and left without another word.

I stood there wondering what to do next, but his assistant led me into a small room with a large three-way mirror. I stayed there all afternoon, trying on dress after dress. I felt almost like one of Mr. Blass's wealthy clients. The workmanship of the dresses was remarkable—I always checked out the seams of anything I tried on (once a design student, always a design student)—but they seemed more appropriate for older women or politicians' wives like Mrs. Rockefeller than for a twenty-year-old like me. Still, I did my best to look as sophisticated as I could, even though the clothes were two sizes too big for me. I guess I pulled it off, because before I left, several dresses had been chosen for me to wear.

Two days later, I went to Alice Tully Hall at Lincoln Center, the grand New York City performing arts complex that had opened the year before, where the Coty Awards would be held. Eleanor Lambert had set up (through Wilhelmina) an appointment for me to meet the designer Kasper, whose designs I would also be modeling. Alice Tully Hall was spectacular—a shrine to classical music awash in polished white marble (I thought it worthy of the ancient Greeks)—and I was overjoyed to be there.

When I arrived, a rehearsal was going on. An assistant came up and asked whom I was working for, and I said, "Kasper." Right away, I was taken to a dressing area, fitted into a bathing suit, and told to go to the stage area, where I was introduced to the choreographer. It was easily the most glamorous place I'd ever worked.

I had to line up with fourteen other girls and go on stage. The choreographer asked us all to do our own movements, as if we were swimming. I really got into it and started to "swim" like Esther Williams in all those old movies I used to watch. Next thing I knew, the choreographer pointed to me and said, "Girls, I want you to do what she's doing." Then she pulled me out of the line of girls. "What's your name?" she asked.

"Pat," I answered. It was the first time I'd identified myself that way professionally.

She put me up front of the line. "Okay, girls, I want you all to follow Pat out onto the stage and copy her movements." *My, my, this is an interesting turn of events,* I thought. (Who would have guessed then how irritated I would eventually become every time I'd invent some interesting or unique move and the person in charge would tell the other girls, "Okay, do what she just did." I always want to say, "Do you have any idea how long I worked to come up with that? Why don't they do their own thing instead of copying mine?")

The next evening at the awards ceremony, I led the pack onstage at Alice Tully Hall in doing something memorable and outrageous on the runway. In truth, I felt as though those fourteen girls were a boat I was pulling behind me: They were ever so slow, and as usual, I wanted to move fast, fast, fast. But I couldn't, lest I lose one of them along the way. So I just swam upstream across that stage, trailed by my cargo of fourteen mermaids, until I got to the other side. And the audience ate it up.

The Bill Blass number followed. Bill, who was inducted into the Hall of Fame that night, was in the audience watching and (he told me later) loving what he saw. Afterward, all the models and designers went to the Coty Awards party at a grand mansion on Madison Avenue. I went back to Stephen's place on East Seventh Street to get ready. He, Bobby, Hector, and Tracy all wore black tie in Stephen's style, with studded jackets and pants, and I wore a black silk jersey wrap dress. We all danced like crazy at the party, and Bill Cunningham, as per usual, was there, camera in hand, to document the occasion.

chapter 27

I LIKE IT LIKE THAT

When I let my hair go free—and
fuzzy—what was once a flaw
became an asset, 1970.
Courtesy of Charles Tracy.

$\mathcal{W}hile$ I was in rehearsal for the Kasper number at the Coty Awards,
I received a hand-delivered message from my agent to call Halston.
I vaguely remembered the name as belonging to the tall, handsome
designer Stephen had pointed out at the party after his first show at
Bendel's. It tells you a lot about those antediluvian pre–cell phone days
that I actually was not able to return Halston's call for three days.

I couldn't call the first day because the rehearsal didn't end until
midnight. The next day I was doing the awards show onstage. On the
third day, Wilhelmina called and said she'd scheduled a fitting for me
with Halston that very morning. So I rushed over to East Sixty-Eighth
Street, which was farther uptown than a typical fashion address. I looked

for number 33, a five-story redbrick building, and found a nondescript entrance at the side.

The wood-paneled two-person elevator moved so slowly, I could have taken the stairs and gotten there faster, but finally, the door opened. I looked out onto a small alcove heavily draped with batik-print curtains, beyond which was a larger square room with the same fabric covering the walls. Oversize palm plants gave the room even more of a jungle effect. The look was a trend: a jungle for city folks.

A large arrangement of orchids in every color sat on a big round table in the middle of the room covered in the same matching fabric. The scent of orchids evoked Mrs. Vreeland's office at *Vogue,* and I felt right at home. It was the scent of fashion; it was the scent of the expensive Rigaud candle I had seen recently at Bendel's and been tempted to buy, but I simply couldn't burn my money like that, literally.

Out from behind this jungle-print curtain, far to my left, emerged a man not much older than I was, dressed head to toe in black. "I'm so glad you're here," he said with the hint of a Southern accent. "I'm Ed. Come on back with me, honey."

He put his arm around me and, without another word, guided me through the curtained doorway through a tight little hall, past a bathroom, and into a stark white room. There was an oversize cutting table in the middle of the space, immense three-way mirrors against a wall, and racks of clothes covering them. Leaning against the other walls were long storyboards covered by six fashion figures, drawn on stationery in felt-tipped pen and thumb-tacked up. They hung there, still in their poses, cartoons in black and white.

"How nice," I said to Ed, looking around.

"Oh, those are the clothes for the show," he said shyly. "I only did the drawings."

I walked over to the drawings and started to read the notes on the sides until I felt someone coming into the room behind me. I turned around to look.

He was taller than I was, even though I had on my highest heels, and he had a slim, nicely proportioned physique. His wheat-colored shoulder-length hair shone in the studio light, and without even seeing his face, I could tell he was knockout handsome, dressed (like Ed) in all black, with a silver Navajo belt woven through with black leather accenting his waist. I could have climbed up him like a cat, but I reminded myself to behave like a lady.

He was talking to someone behind him on the other side of the curtain, and then he turned and looked dead at me, his blue eyes glistening and kaleidoscoping into a frosty green. It was like a romantic dream, and if the daze had stretched a second longer, I might have fallen madly in love with him then and there, but my professionalism asserted itself. This was Halston, one of the hottest fashion designers in America.

"Hello," he said politely.

"I'm Pat," I said, stumbling over my still relatively unfamiliar name.

"I've seen you before." He paused and looked past me at the dresses on the rack. "I bet you can't guess where." He looked pleased that I seemed puzzled. "I saw you in a *wonderful* show," he said, smiling. Then he shouted, "Ed! Where's the other dress?" He stood completely still, as though lost in thought. "The Fashion Fair," he finally said. "You were there . . . it was you." He looked at me directly. "I watched you move to the music." He snapped back to attention. "How about we get something on her, Ed?" he said, adding impatiently, "How about *now?*"

Ed was rolling in a rack of clothes, but Halston said, "No time for standing around." He waved Ed off to the back room. When Ed returned, he quickly moved out two or three other garment racks to make room for the fitting. The cutting table in the center of the floor was so large, it took up all the space. It was a cramped place to change clothes, but at least there was a changing screen.

"Let's see," Halston said, pausing to look at me. He seemed to be standing almost in a pose, with one of his arms crossed over his chest and his other hand up to his mouth with his fingers rubbing lightly over his lower lip, as if pondering momentous matters. Then he came over to me and encircled my waist between his two hands. "Ed, she has the smallest waist. *Ed!* Bring the tape measure."

Ed flew around me like a hummingbird. "Thirty, twenty, thirty-two."

"She's the smallest one," Halston said, looking happy about my size. His attention shifted swiftly back to the clothes. "Are the pieces finished yet?"

"N-n-not yet," Ed said. A stutter had surfaced.

Halston frowned. "You'll have to come in before the show. Go give them the measurements." Ed retreated. "We'll just sew you up in them if they don't fit," Halston said, and smiled again. He picked up a silver box off the worktable, flicked it open, took out a cigarette, and lit it with a silver lighter that materialized from his pocket. He took a long, slow drag and slowly exhaled, looking upward as though contemplating the cosmos.

"Actually," he said, returning to Planet Earth, "if they don't fit, we'll have to fire Ed." He winked at me. "I'm just joking," he said in a low voice, "but don't let him know that. The workers perform better if I shake them up a bit." With that, Halston said, "Okay, we're finished."

Then he walked away.

Did I get the job? I wondered. I really wasn't sure. But as he was going through the door, he looked over his shoulder, eyes sparkling. "We'll see you for the show. Wear your hair exactly the way it is. I like it like that. And don't be late."

I stood still, not quite taking it all in. *Halston just hired me.* (That was how it was done back then; the designer hired you in person.) Now there were two popular designers in my corner, which was a really big deal. I still wasn't confident about my looks, but the red lipstick was doing wonders. I knew I'd never have Grace Kelly's little nose or Rita Hayworth's figure, but I could have bright red lips, lots of hair, and a job with Halston.

With a new spring in my step, I exited the building, lifted my face to the sun, and met the warm orange glow with a red-painted smile. The weather was so nice, I decided to walk. I headed uptown on Madison Avenue toward Seventy-First Street, and there, I noticed a new clothing store with the name Yves Saint Laurent printed in large gold letters over the door. I didn't have an Upper East Side income, but I was feeling really good and looking really good, so I figured why not go in?

The shop was wall-to-wall with exquisite things, and the salesladies treated me as if I were the most important person in it. I overheard some of them speaking French to one another, which lent a flavor of Paris to the atmosphere, or at least what I imagined Paris to be like. I browsed through the clothes, and sure enough, I couldn't afford anything. But I was too embarrassed to leave without buying something, so I purchased my first French designer dress—a silk dress in a rust color with tiny covered buttons up the front, a little bow tie, and a thin belt—and shoes of the same color, with the highest heels and the highest arch I'd ever owned. Was I becoming materialistic? Maybe, but beautiful design and workmanship had always given me pleasure. Besides, given how much I was working every day, I felt I deserved them.

I left the store with an oversize shopping bag that had "Yves Saint Laurent" printed on the side. Having spent my last paycheck and every cent I had in my pocket on that outfit, I knew a taxi was not in the cards. But I didn't care: I walked the rest of the way home, swinging my bag, feeling like the queen of the world.

When I got home, Mom was heading out to work—she was still a nurse's aide on the graveyard shift in the mental ward at Bellevue Hospital—but as always, she found a minute for me, sharing my jubilation at being hired by Halston, inspecting the workmanship on my new dress and finding it impeccable. She was always tired, a far cry from the glittering young woman throwing parties and going to jazz clubs with her sister—two high-spirited "bachelor girls," as they called themselves, who loved being out on the town. Now, with a tyrant for a husband and a job that exhausted her, Mom had no freedom, no social life, no time for the movies we'd always loved. She was the most creative person I'd ever known, and yet she had stopped painting; she'd even stopped making clothes. The only artworks she created now were sketches of the patients at the mental ward or, during the holidays, Christmas murals on the hospital walls to cheer the place up.

The job was draining in every way. One morning Mom came home really shaken. She told me she had been in the solitary confinement area, face-to-face with a killer who was on his way to death row. For some reason, he had been brought to her hospital ward. While my mom was with him, she had sketched his portrait. He told her it was the nicest thing that anyone had ever done for him, and he took my mom's drawing with him to the electric chair. I couldn't sleep after she told me this story. She was living in a very dark world, and I could see her suffering.

She had made so many sacrifices for me, and she'd married someone she didn't love just to have a steady income. In "settling," she had been forced to abandon her own artistic gifts and stifle her need for self-expression. I understood why and didn't blame her, but I vowed never to let it happen to me. No matter how desperate things got, I would never marry for money. I and I alone would be responsible for me.

chapter 28

SECRET LOVE

In the dressing room of Halston's
Sixty-Eighth Street studio, before
my first show with Halston, 1970.
From left: Pat Ast, Shirley Ferro,
Anjelica Huston, Halston, and me.

The story of my life was unfolding on a split screen, and as if to demonstrate its schizoid nature, Matthew called the night before my first show with Halston. I hadn't heard from him in several weeks and had no idea where he'd been. I was half convinced that this time he really had received his draft notice and moved to Norway or Canada to avoid induction.

As usual, I was instantly spellbound by his voice. "Do you know what time it is?" he asked. "It's time for me to see you. Where have you been?"

I could ask the same of you, I thought. "Modeling," I said.

"Are you selling out?" This was a constant refrain. As his politics had grown more and more radical and his worldview more occult, he'd become intolerant of anyone who sought traditional success or cared about frivolous things like clothes or possessions. All that mattered was one's inner spiritual life.

"Why would you say that?"

"Those people you've been hanging out with . . ."

"I'm working . . ."

"They're the enemy," he said. "They're superficial and enrich the capitalists who distort our world."

"They're not the enemy—they're artists, too."

"They're not real."

"They are to me."

"It'll be too late when you realize what you've given in to. Come where I am, the place in Brooklyn. I'll wait for you."

"I can't tonight," I said weakly. "Maybe tomorrow." I hung up, puzzling over whether I should get on the train to Brooklyn to see him. Instead, sanity prevailed, and I decided to put together my things for the next morning. *Let's see, here's my voucher book, my makeup . . .* This was my before-bed ritual, to get everything ready for the next day, like a Girl Scout, always prepared.

I arrived at Halston's promptly at ten in the morning. The small back cutting room had been transformed into a dressing room, and several models were sitting at a long table in front of the mirrors, applying makeup. One of them was Naomi Sims, an onyx-colored, structurally perfect icon who was so high-fashion she could have been mistaken for one of Halston's customers. Next to Naomi was a girl named Marina Schiano, a *Vogue* model who looked as if she'd just stepped out of the magazine's pages. Then there was Elsa Peretti, whose low-chignoned head was turned to reveal an aristocratic Italian profile. All of these girls were much bigger than I was, both professionally and in terms of their polished looks. In the silent room, each was focusing on her reflection so intently that you could have heard an eyelash drop.

My presence did nothing to break their concentration. So I sat down beside them at the makeup mirror and tried to do what they were doing. I noticed that Marina and Naomi had spidery eyelashes on both upper and lower lids, and Naomi highlighted her cheekbones with a shiny cream bronzer. Marina wore very white powder all over her olive skin and put on lots of eyeliner, which came to a fine point at the corner of each eye. Elsa, who was the oddest-looking of these three, applied lots of kohl around her eyes as she puffed away on a cigarette in a holder that hung loosely from her lips.

I observed all of this surreptitiously, because whenever one of the models caught me watching her, it was if I'd pushed a pause button, a freeze hold, that kept me from seeing the next trick she was going to use on her face. *Ah.* Evidently a model's makeup routine was a carefully guarded secret. I didn't know if I could keep up with these big-time girls, so I just did my usual thing, concentrating on my red lips.

At eleven o'clock sharp—showtime—we were dressed by Halston's assistants, all of whom were dressed in black, just like their boss. It was the Halston uniform, a way of dressing that would later be identified with New York City but at the time was new and very odd to me.

In model jargon, there is a name for every movement—before the show, backstage, during the show, onstage. The "Indian file," for example, is the (admittedly politically incorrect) term for the single-file lineup of models waiting to go onstage. That's when the designer walks by each model to see if the look is pulled together in exactly the right way, with the clothes and accessories just so. A single hairpin pushed in at the wrong angle is as bad as a hanging hemline.

As I stood in the Indian file, I kept looking in the mirror at my silhouette, trying to figure out if I should emphasize the left side of the outfit I was wearing more than the right, and wondering where the pockets were, and whether I should put my hands in them in order to show off the clothes. What I finally figured out—it was something of an epiphany for me—is a concept known as "working with the clothes." By treating them as though they belong to you, they become part of you, and both you and they look fully alive, displayed to full advantage. And *that*, I realized, is what fashion is all about.

At the last minute, a girl with straight black hair arrived. She was as thin as I was, but her very broad shoulders made her look twice as tall. Because she came in late, there was a big rush to get her dressed, and when she was ready, she was gently wedged in line just behind me. I didn't mind; she was wearing an intoxicating scent and a friendly smile. "Hi, I'm Anjelica Huston," she said. I didn't know who she was, and would not know for years because she was so normal and unspoiled, with no attitude whatsoever.

Just before we were to go onstage, Halston stood before us and cleared his throat. "You're the best-looking girls in the world, or else you wouldn't be here," he said. "So be divine and go out there and kill 'em." Then he came up to each of us and whispered something into our ear. To me, he said, "Be better than the rest, because you are." *The best?* I thought. *He really means that I am the best?* I found out later that he'd told all of us the same thing.

The competition was on, with each girl standing at her full height, which made me want to stand taller and be as graceful as I could be. We were like racehorses at the starting gate, ready to take off. Needless to say, I was racked with doubt because the other girls were so confident and experienced.

Both the morning and afternoon shows went really well. Editors from all the best magazines, such as *Vogue* and *Harper's Bazaar*, were in the audience, seated across the aisle from one another, pretending they'd never met. I saw Joel Schumacher and Carrie Donovan seated together in the *Vogue* section; they were family at this point, and I did my best to make them proud as I passed by in the cashmere capes and silk crepe Halston designs, which were so modern, sculpted, and ladylike. With some of the outfits, we carried a number, so the society ladies would know what dress to order. It was a bit old-couture in terms of showing style, but also very au courant, with the smooth jazz accompaniment and all these models from glossy print publications.

I was struck by the elegance of everything and everyone out front. Halston had given us a rundown of some of the VIPs in attendance: Babe Paley, the wife of William Paley, the chairman of CBS; Patricia Kennedy Lawford, President Kennedy's sister; and Jane Murchison, the wife of Clint Murchison, a Texas oil heir and owner of the Dallas Cowboys. All of these women were fixtures at the fashion shows (and on Eleanor Lambert's Best-Dressed List) and spent hundreds of thousands of dollars a year on their wardrobes.

For some reason, doing the Halston show and being near all those top models and society ladies lit a fire within me. My love of clothes deepened, because I saw where they could take you, almost like a magic carpet. Being beautiful definitely involves how you feel about yourself inside (witness the way I talked myself into thinking I was as nice-looking as the other girls and how much better I felt when I was dressed in Halston's dazzling designs). It also means taking care of the outside of yourself. That is no hocus-pocus, just fact. I wanted to have *allure,* and all that the word implied, just like the beautiful, well-dressed women I was encountering in high fashion. And I was determined to get it.

As my external life became more and more glamorous, Matthew was always in the back of my mind, cautioning me against being a sell-out and letting me know there was a higher internal path—a spiritual path—above and beyond the one that, in his opinion, I was being "se-duced" into taking.

After the show, I saw Naomi leave with a handsome, well-dressed, wealthy-looking young man. Me, I got on the subway to Brooklyn. Rationally, I knew that Matthew (as I still thought of him, though he no longer answered to that name) wasn't good for me, that he was undependable and growing weirder and weirder, but I couldn't seem to resist him. In retrospect, I think my hormones were simply trumping my common sense. At the time, no matter how busy I was, he was al-ways on my mind. I persisted in thinking of him as my personal pied piper—a poet whose flute, Arch-Admiral-Ramtree-Rose-Ann, produced an almost hypnotic sound that made me want to follow him anywhere.

I would sometimes walk with Matthew before dawn—in the sacred hours, as he called them, because that is when everything is quiet—and he would tell me that there was the Mother Earth, and the heavens, and that he spoke to the angels as he played his music to the moonlight, the Milky Way, and to Jove, the god of the sky. He gave me a two-thousand-page book to read called the *Urantia Book* ("Urantia" is another name for Earth), in order to cure me of the "nearsightedness of a creature of time." The book, he said, was written (or "revealed") by celestial beings offering a new interpretation of the teachings of Jesus Christ and a unique way to unify science, philosophy, and religion. The book was very difficult, he allowed, but the key to enlightenment. I lugged it around with me everywhere, arousing curiosity in all my fashion friends.

Matthew now described himself as a "celestial vagabond," and I had to admit that the latter word seemed to fit. He had no permanent home that I could discern, but simply crashed here and there for short periods and spent most nights playing his flute in the park, disappearing, as daylight broke, into the crowd of the city. The address he gave me in Brooklyn was somewhere near the Brooklyn Museum of Art. Back in 1970, this neighborhood was very different from the hip, thriving community it is today, and I felt strange and afraid wandering around there alone. In late afternoon, the streets were deserted, unlike in Manhattan, where they were always filled with people and the kinetic energy among them. I even started to worry, as I walked past rows of brick and limestone buildings that all looked alike, whether I'd be able to find my way back to the subway station, and I told myself to pay attention to exactly where I was going.

When I finally found the address Matthew had given me, the building—a nice-looking brownstone—appeared empty. I glanced up, and on the third floor I saw an open window. I approached the main door, which was unlocked, went in, and climbed the stairs to the third floor. There didn't seem to be a soul in the place. I shuddered, thinking that I wouldn't want to live there. I also thought that as long as I could see Matthew, nothing else really mattered. The door of Apartment 3C was slightly ajar, and I thought, *That's nice, he's left it open for me.* I knocked, and when no one answered, I pushed the door all the way open and walked in.

The room, a kitchen, was brightly lit and pleasant but had no furniture. To my right was another room, also free of furniture. But there were white curtains on the open window I'd glimpsed from the street, and they were fluttering in the breeze. "Hello?" I said in a whisper. I noticed a second door to my right. "Hello?" I repeated. Silence. I was certain I'd come to the right address, unless I'd misunderstood Matthew. I was equally certain he'd said Apartment 3C.

The bare wood floor creaked as I walked on it. The sound echoed off the walls; it was so quiet, I could hear my own breathing. I thought it was strange that someone would leave the window open when it was so cold outside. The room felt frozen. I was about to leave but thought, *Why not look in the other room, since I've come all this way?*

I opened the door to one of the most terrifying sights I have ever witnessed. Sprawled facedown on a grimy mattress in the middle of the floor was a young man in a white T-shirt and jeans pulled down around his ankles. A syringe was stuck into his arm, and in the fading afternoon light, motes of sunlight danced around his blue-tinged, lifeless body. It was the first time I'd seen a dead person outside the confines of a funeral home. I suppressed a scream as a rush of adrenaline surged through my body, propelling me over the creaking wooden floor, out the apartment door, down the stairs, and into the street. I ran as fast as I could, not pausing until I was in the subway, on the train. Even then, I felt like I was still in that barren room with the dead man.

I was horribly upset and confused. Why would Matthew send me there? Was this man a friend of his? Was Matthew heavily involved with drugs? By the time I got home, it was dark, and I went straight to my room. A couple of hours later, Matthew called and asked where I was. He told me I'd gone to the wrong address. I wasn't sure I believed him, but I let him talk me into meeting him and his friends at an African restaurant in the West Village. My mom and stepdad were both working, and I sneaked him into the apartment, where he stayed until sunrise. Passion doesn't care what time of day it is.

chapter 29

I HEAR A SYMPHONY

In the green room at *Vogue*
with Antonio Lopez on
the day we met, 1970.
Courtesy of Juan Ramos.

At Vogue, there was change afoot, as I discovered when I was booked for another round of *Vogue* Seminars. I had no idea that Mrs. Vreeland was on her way out and would be unceremoniously fired in a few short weeks. But I was surprised to hear, when I got to the greenroom, that Maning Obregon was in Europe with Carrie Donovan and that I would be working with a new illustrator, Antonio Lopez.

I was wearing my red Danskin tights under a new coatdress, with snaps down the front, that Stephen had just given me, and those chocolate-brown, patent-leather wedgies with candy-striped shoestrings. I had just sat down and was writing in my journal when in walked a handsome young Latin guy with curly hair, a mustache, and a playful grin that reminded me of a cat about to play with a ball of string. "Are you the model?" he asked, scrunching up his face in mock confusion.

I looked at him and scrunched up my face in the same way, like, *Isn't it obvious?*

"I'm joking," he said. "I know you're the model." He extended his hand. "Hi, I'm Antonio. Now I'm going to draw you. What have you got on under there?" He gestured to my dress, winked, and said, "Take it off."

My jaw dropped. *Is he crazy?* I thought. *We're at* Vogue.

"I'm *joking!*" he said again, flashing a boyish grin that made my heart lurch. From the beginning, there was a kind of light around Antonio that I found irresistible. Meeting him felt like a symphony had come to play in my heart. I knew immediately that this guy was going to be a keeper.

A smaller man dressed in tweed trousers, a tightly buttoned vest, a crisp white shirt, and a little bow tie entered the room. Antonio introduced him as Juan Ramos; he was Antonio's right-hand man or, perhaps more accurately, his cat's paw. Both of them conveyed the impression that they were on their way to someplace more important and had just stopped by *Vogue* for a visit. As they conferred with Emmy Lou, the booker—Antonio seemed to charm her, too—I tried to figure out why he looked so familiar. Then it dawned on me: He was the "well-known illustrator" who was sitting with Donna Jordan at the club in Sheridan Square where I'd first seen her with Andy Warhol. I tried to stay calm as my mind raced off into a fantasy about Antonio. I just wanted to wrap myself around him like a cape and fly off to paradise.

Before I could get too carried away, we got to work on the Seminar. Antonio sat at a small table with pencils in hand while I stood on the tabletop in the center of the room, dressed in a pair of flesh-colored tights and dance leotards. I couldn't wait to see what he was busy drawing, because I could feel his concentration and the way he was truly taking me in. I would soon learn all about Antonio's outsize reputation—he was *the* reigning god of fashion illustration—but I could sense the magnitude of his talent simply from watching the way he worked.

At the end of the day, Antonio invited me to work with him at his private studio in the Carnegie Hall building. As I stood in the elevator,

I thought back to when I was fourteen and my mom brought me there to be photographed by Carl Van Vechten's friend Adelaide Passen. Carl Van Vechten himself had kept a studio there.

Juan, neatly dressed in his perky bow tie and ready for business, let me into the studio and shouted, "Antonio!" in an exaggerated sing-song voice. I was surprised that someone who seemed so serious one moment could be so funny the next. He led me through the hallway, and I noticed several magnificent black-and-white photos of the same girl; she looked like a glass-faced Pagliacci doll, with dark brown eyes that suggested great emotional depth. I recognized her as the model for Danskin dance clothes, which automatically made her an icon in my book.

"You like her?" Juan asked. "That's Cathee Dahmen. She's been Antonio's model since he started illustrating."

We walked farther down the narrow hallway, which opened into a bright duplex. At the far end of the main room was a floor-to-ceiling arched window surrounded by white space. In front of it, on a sleek black settee—"a Corbusier," Juan told me, "made just for Antonio"—sat Mr. Lopez himself, with his drawing board on his knees, charcoal in one hand, colored pencils in the other. With every breath, he shifted positions, holding the board differently. He was concentrating just as fiercely as he had at *Vogue,* but here in his own environment, he looked like a deity, with his hands moving back and forth, creating a swish against the paper as he passed over it with each stroke of charcoal.

Juan pointed, and I squinted into the room and saw, just behind a pillar, Cathee Dahmen, the girl in the photos. She looked like a child, with the palest skin, prettiest eyes, and absolutely no makeup. She was a rare argument for natural beauty.

With a sweep of his arm, Antonio stopped. Without even checking his work, he set the drawing board aside; he looked completely drained, as if he'd been riding a wild horse and had just let go of the reins. It seemed to take him a minute to come out of his trance. "Hey! You made it," he said, registering me for the first time. Then he switched to his jokey mode. "What's that on your shirt?" he said, pointing as though he saw poop on me. When I looked down, he said, "April Fool's! I made you look!" I had completely forgotten until then that it was April 1, and

I gave him a feeble smile. Meanwhile, Antonio laughed hysterically, with his hand on his stomach, almost as if he couldn't stop. Eventually, he said, "You know Cathee?"

I turned and waved at her. She was just getting out of her pose. "She's my sister," Antonio said. Cathee walked over to him and he hugged her affectionately, squeezing her cheeks together until she looked like she had fish lips. "Don't we look alike?"

"You wish," said Juan.

"Shut up, Tweety!" Antonio teased back. "Don't you think he looks like Tweety Bird? The shape of his head?"

We all laughed except Juan, who looked all business. "Look what you did," he said to Antonio, pointing to the sketches. "You drew outside the lines again. I told you not to."

"So?" Antonio replied. "That's what happens with charcoal."

"How am I going to line up the color if you can't even stay inside the lines? Jeez, it's like you're in kindergarten."

"Don't be sore—just erase it," Antonio said. Juan shot Antonio a wicked look, took the drawing gently by the top corners, and went to the table in the center of the room and began furiously erasing stuff off the paper.

"Back to the old drawing board, Wile E.," Antonio said. "He's that silly coyote," he added to Cathee and me.

"I know what to do, wise guy." Juan seemed to be getting really pissed off. I didn't know it yet, but this was a regular routine of theirs. Like many longtime collaborators, they were always sparring with each other, but in the end, their squabbles were like performance art that they enacted to amuse themselves and others.

There were Magic Markers and colored inks at Antonio's feet. He stayed seated when Cathee jumped up, kissed him on the forehead, and gave him a big hug. Then she said goodbye to us all and left.

"She'll be back," Antonio said to me. "She can't live without me."

I was sitting there, unsure what to do, when Antonio gestured to the pillar where Cathee had been. "Sit there, girl," he said. I was thrilled to inhabit the space she'd just left and hoped the ghost of her presence would inspire me. "Hold that pose."

As I sat there, Antonio tilted his head sideways to the left, then to the right; he slightly crossed his eyes and extended his hand with a pencil in it, as though measuring me with his thumb. He gathered his charcoal together and directed me to take off my jacket and unbutton my shirt. "Show one of your shoulders. No, better yet, take off your shirt and tie it loosely around your neck."

I turned my back to him, shyly, because I was wearing nothing under my shirt.

He waited patiently. "More shoulders," he said. "That's good. Now sit with one hand on your thigh, like this." Antonio went into the pose himself, and I mirrored what he did until my body was twisted into the same shape as his. It was like a tango: He was me, and I was him, and as soon as we replicated each other, he flexed his long fingers like a piano player and began to draw, as if some rhythmic force had taken over his body and soul and right hand.

I flashed back to the experience of posing for my mom at Madame Metcalf's home in Connecticut. As with her, I adored watching Antonio work, and every muscle in me wanted to please him. He moved with the air, one stroke leading into the next, until he had a pile of drawings at his feet, like leaves dropping under a tree. These were the sketches that would lead to the finished work; Juan carried them away with great tenderness, as though Antonio had just delivered a newborn baby.

I posed this way for Antonio until midnight and then did the same for weeks afterward. Before long, I was his main model. We did *Vogue* Patterns, among many other projects, and it never really felt like work because I was so inspired and entertained by Antonio. As I watched him draw, I loved him more each day. He was one of the finest artists I've ever known. He could see deeply into the current moment but also mix past and future into his art. I felt sometimes that he was divinely guided, but he would always brush me off when I made comments like that. He never wanted to admit his spiritual side—he was always joking and playing down anything serious—but as far as I was concerned, he was working with a higher force.

So after my regular work and various go-sees and tests, I started going to Antonio's studio. Usually, he was just sketching me, but occasionally, he'd invite other models whom he wanted to photograph for his own portfolio. At one of those shoots, Antonio posed me nude, in an amorous embrace with a beautiful young (also nude) male model named Martin Snaric, whom I'd never met. It was a bit awkward to be entwined stark naked with a total stranger, but the two of us laughed it off and became fast friends. (That friendship deepened into something more about six years later, when Martin became my first husband.)

At the evening sessions with just Antonio, Juan, and me, we'd often break for dinner, which we'd always eat out because, while the studio was equipped with a kitchen, Juan couldn't stand the smell of food in the place. We'd usually go to a Cuban-Chinese joint on Ninth Avenue, where the food was cheap, plentiful, and delicious. Juan and Antonio were regulars, so they'd speak Spanish to the staff and other customers from the moment we walked in. At first everyone thought I was from Puerto Rico, too, because Antonio, that jokester, told them I was his sister (hmmm, this seemed to be a pattern of his). We'd order black beans and rice with thick greasy plantains and stuff ourselves until we couldn't eat another bite, then go back to work.

One night we were in the restaurant licking our fingers and sucking our mango sodas, when who should walk in but Maning Obregon. Unbeknownst to me, Antonio and Maning were rivals at *Vogue,* and Maning was incensed because while he was in Europe with Carrie Donovan, the powers-that-be had permanently replaced him with Antonio. Maning had received this unhappy surprise when he came in to work on the *Vogue* Seminars. Clueless as I was to these goings-on, I jumped up and ran over to Maning to say hello. I was delighted to see him; after all, he was one of my first and greatest mentors. Talk about a cold shoulder! Not toward me but toward Antonio. Maning grinned and joked but was clearly upset. "I see the enemy has taken over," he said.

Juan immediately asked for the check, and we ended up taking our boxed rice, beans, and gravy back to the studio. The three of us ate there, which tells you how unsettled the boys were, to let smelly food like that into their inner sanctum.

As for me, I was quite shaken up. I knew that Antonio and Maning respected each other and, deep down, even liked each other. If not for the politics of the business they were in, they'd have been fast friends, as they had been earlier in their careers. So often, it seemed, success came down to ego, ego, ego. It was a rude awakening for me, and as I gradually became more worldly-wise, I began cultivating a healthy ego of my own. It was the armor I needed to fend for myself in the often cutthroat environment of high fashion.

chapter 30

THE SONG IS ENDED

With Halston, who always watched
out for me. He gave me the roses.
Courtesy of Ron Galella.

$\mathcal{I}'d$ just finished a show with Halston for his new cruise-wear collection, and that night he threw a party at his studio for some of his favorite editors, designers, and models. I arrived with Marina and Elsa, feeling on top of the world. I noticed new wallpaper with a jungle design, with palm leaves that seemed to come together into an H. So I started to call Halston "H," which stuck as his new nickname.

The room was filled with society ladies (most of whom were dressed in Halston's clothes) and lots of other cool designers. Halston was in the corner of the room, leaning against the wall, smoking a cigarette and talking to Berry Berenson. Everyone was mingling and having fun—it was like my perfect dream of a marvelous party—and then I saw Matthew right across the room, standing in the dark by the door that led to the elevator lobby. He looked dirty, unkempt, and sweaty, like someone who'd been living on the streets, which in all likelihood he had been. With his Ramtree bass flute wrapped in its rough goatskin, he might have been a latter-day John the Baptist in the wilderness, coming to preach the word.

I noticed some of the guests sidestepping to avoid him, and an arrow pierced my heart. I ducked behind a curtain, hoping he wouldn't see me and would go away, but when I peeked through a crack, I saw he'd moved farther into the party and was standing near a table covered with orchids. *How did he find me here?* I wondered. My head started spinning. I couldn't tell if I was excited to see him or afraid of what his presence meant. My heart pounded over the sounds of the Jackson Five: "Never can say goodbye . . ."

One of the guards spotted Matthew and started elbowing him out of the party. That was when I knew I had to go to him and face the consequences. As I walked toward him, I saw Halston eyeing him curiously with a hard-to-read expression. When I reached Matthew, I said, "What are you doing here?" I heard my voice, and it sounded as ice-cold as the champagne I'd been sipping.

The guard stepped in. "Do you know this person?" he asked.

I do know him, I thought, *but from another time, another place. He doesn't belong in my life now.* These heavy feelings hit me with a force that left me panting as I stood there in front of him. I was caught at a fork in the road and knew I had to make a decision.

I couldn't speak. But my face must have signaled something to the bodyguard, because he stepped away. "I'm glad to see you," I said to Matthew. I wanted to kiss him on the cheek, but he reeked of traffic exhaust, cement dust, and a homeless smell that even a Rigaud candle couldn't disguise. How I missed the lemony-lime smell I'd fallen in love with all those years ago.

As if possessed, he whispered raggedly, "You could have invited me to this party." He fell silent, peering out into the distance.

"I didn't know where to call you," I said.

He didn't answer.

"You never give me your phone number."

Silence.

"What could I do?"

He whirled around to look at me. "You could leave this place," he hissed.

"Why?"

"These people are fake."

"What are you talking about?"

And then it was as if a dam broke and he started spewing all sorts of crazy gibberish about hell and sinners. I was used to his mystic proclamations, but this was a new, dark side he was tapping in to. For the first time, I had to confront the possibility that he was genuinely out of his mind.

"I'm going to play in the key of F, and then we can leave this place forever."

Maybe he's tripping, I thought. *No way is he going to play his flute here at Halston's. And why would I leave with him? What does he think he's offering me? A life in the gutters, suffering the slings and arrows of street poetry, just to prove our worth?*

Before I could even figure out how to answer him, he grabbed me, holding my arm so tightly that I felt I might break into pieces, and pulled me toward the door. I looked back into the room and met Halston's eyes. The look on my face must have done the screaming for me, because Halston rushed over. When he reached us, he instantly sussed out the situation. "Excuse me," he said. "I don't remember inviting you here. Please take your hands off her." Halston's fashion mask had dissolved, and he was somber. Matthew began pulling me again, but Halston blocked him. "You'd better let her go."

Then the situation exploded. Matthew pushed Halston across the room, and everyone in that area jumped to his rescue. Halston came right back at Matthew, with his assistant right behind him. "She doesn't want to go with you, she wants to stay here," Halston said, his face right up against Matthew's. "Can't you see that? Isn't that so, Miss Cleveland?" I was dumbstruck and stunned that Halston was defending me like this. "Let her go right now and leave. Or I'll call the police."

Matthew gave me a deranged look, then pulled my arm again. Halston took me by the other hand and waved his big bodyguard over. The bodyguard grabbed Matthew, and I fell into Halston's arms. My two worlds were colliding with me in the middle, and I felt crushed by the impact: *This is my poet boyfriend, a gentle soul whom I love deeply,* and *Here is my new friend.*

Everyone at the party was watching as the bodyguard, who was much larger than Matthew, pulled him toward the elevator and got him off the premises. Then they were gone, and the party continued as if nothing had happened. Halston went back to chatting with Berry, and the only memory of what had happened was carried in whispers.

Most of the guests kept a polite distance from me, but an older woman came over and said, "I wish I had a handsome, possessive boyfriend, honey. Nobody's ever fought over *me.*" I wasn't sure whether she was talking about Matthew or Halston.

Finally, Halston came over. "He's dangerous," he said.

"He's not usually like that," I said, fearful that the world I'd worked so hard to build around me was about to crumble.

"I can press charges against him for disturbing you," Halston said. "Shall I do that?"

"No, no. Please don't."

"If I were you, I'd stay away from him. He's crazy."

The bodyguard came back and told us that Matthew was in the lobby and refused to leave until I talked to him.

"Do you want to do that?" Halston asked. "You'd better watch out, Miss Cleveland."

He was right, but I had to talk to Matthew—*for his own good,* I told myself. So the bodyguard and I stepped into the bright light of the elevator, and my mind ran in circles: I saw Matthew and me watching Neil Armstrong walk on the moon; living in the commune; tripping out; playing flutes; going to jazz clubs and poetry readings; listening to Coltrane and Ravi Shankar; making love as moonlight streamed across the bed . . . The elevator stopped. The door opened. And there he was, in the lobby. The black-sheep son of Billy Eckstine, the love of my life, trying to get me to return to his world, where we'd wander with no money or place of our own.

He looked roughed up—had the scuffle upstairs actually *hurt* him?—and I felt guilt and sorrow wash over me. I walked over to him, the bodyguard at my side.

Matthew nodded at him. "You have to have a *bodyguard* to talk to me now?" he asked with an ugly sneer that I'd never seen before.

"You can't push people—" I began.

"These people don't care about you."

"Yes, they do."

His eyes were tired and red, and he looked completely worn out, as if the whole universe were warring against him. Standing there, he seemed to shrink in my eyes, like something from an imagined past or a Gothic romance novel I'd read as a girl. Well, I wasn't that girl anymore; I'd grown up. And I realized with absolute certainty that I couldn't be with Matthew. We were face-to-face but worlds apart. I gasped and said, "I'm not going with you."

"You'll be sorry," he said. He sounded like a wounded animal. The bodyguard was watching him closely, ready to pounce.

"You have to go," I said. "Please don't follow me like this. It's not good for either of us."

Matthew moved toward me one last time, but the bodyguard stepped between us. There was a struggle, and then the bodyguard literally shoved Matthew out the door. I couldn't stand to stay any longer, so I backed up into the elevator. As the doors closed, I saw Matthew's face through the glass windows. Then I was alone.

That night, after the party, Halston took me home. He'd never been so far uptown, and he was curious, looking out the limousine windows, about the neighborhood.

"Thank you," I said as his driver opened the car door for me.

Halston put out his cigarette and leaned toward me. "Never let that guy near you," he said. "You could be hurt, and I can't let anything bad happen to you."

I was surprised and gratified to hear him say that. Halston was an important person, and I was a nobody. That was my first inkling that this compassionate man, who would eventually become a dear friend and confidant, saw me as more than just a billboard for his clothes. I walked to the front door of my building, and when I looked back, he was still sitting in his limo. He waited until I was safely inside, and then he and his driver disappeared into the night.

chapter 31

LEAVING ON A JET PLANE

This photo was on the first
page of my portfolio, which
I took to Europe in 1971.
Courtesy of Charles Tracy.

$\mathcal{B}$y May 1971, all roads began pointing toward Europe. For starters, I never forgot what Wilhelmina had told me when she signed me—that I'd have to be a success abroad before I could make it big in America. In addition, I was getting fed up with the way my career was stalled in the States. I was working with major photographers like Bert Stern, Bill King (who shot me for *Harper's Bazaar*), and Irving Penn (whose exquisite photos of me appeared in *Vogue,* a major coup), but no matter how hard I tried, I couldn't quite break through to the top of the heap. I continued to get passed over for the best bookings. The photographers loved the portraits they shot of me, but the higher-ups at the various magazines kept saying no. Time after time, I was photographed for the cover of American *Vogue,* but time after time, the cover was given to a blonde or a foreign girl instead. It wasn't the fault of the editors, really, but of society as a whole. If people weren't ready to buy high-fashion magazines with black women on the cover, what could the magazines' staffs do about it? They needed to move copies on newsstands.

Even Hector, Stephen's assistant, was urging me toward Europe. One day when I was up at Stephen's World and Stephen was out of the room, Hector said, "You have to do photos with foreign photographers." He leafed through several magazines, then handed a few to me. "They have more magazines over there. The girls there look better; they have better style." His glasses kept slipping off his nose as he turned the pages of the French magazine *Elle.* "They really know how to put themselves together," he said, pointing at some fashion spreads. "You have to dress in other clothes, you know, not just Stephen's."

I giggled, but his comment bothered me. *Does Stephen know how Hector feels?* I wondered. Personally, I thought there was nothing better than dressing in Stephen's clothes. To wear his latest creation was what I lived for. I was Stephen's flagpole, his clothes my flag. I was part of his team. Now Hector was suggesting I leave the team?

No, not really. He was simply suggesting that I needed to branch out. And he had a point.

Antonio had left for France a couple of weeks earlier and was now living in Paris. He'd invited me to stay with him if I ever came over there. I'd managed to save three thousand dollars and wanted to visit—I was keeping up with the French lessons I had started—but I didn't expect that to happen any time soon. Still, it was tucked in the back of my mind as a possibility.

Then I got a call from Wilhelmina, who asked me to come in. She said she wanted to talk to me personally. She sounded so serious on the phone that I wondered if I'd done something wrong.

When I got to her office, she was in a good mood. A bunch of photographs of me were arrayed across her desk, and it looked as if she was rearranging the portfolio she kept of me at the office. "It looks like you're ready to go," she said. I had no idea what she was talking about. "Let's look at your portfolio."

I handed her the new portfolio I'd just purchased, with the recent test shots that I'd put in it the previous night. Immediately, she began rearranging the photos, carefully slipping the pictures out of the plastic sleeves and placing them on her desk, then putting aside the photos she didn't like. I sat quietly and watched her. "I have some good news for you," she said. "I contacted an agency in Milan. It's better for you to work in Europe at this time."

What did she just say? Did I hear her clearly?

"I like this photograph here," she said, patting my pictures as if they were precious treasures. I loved that about Willy; she was so gentle with me and my things. "So what do you think? Are you willing?"

"Yes, I'd love to go," I wanted to say immediately, but the words seemed to take forever to form, and it took a while before I actually responded.

Wilhelmina swirled around in her chair and pushed one of the numbered buttons on her phone. "Can you please get me the Milan agency on the phone?" she said to her assistant.

She spoke to the Italian agency and finalized all the details while I sat there nervously. I had to get my ticket and travel documents—passport, visa, and working papers—as soon as possible. I would need to visit the Italian consulate, since I'd be leaving in just five days. I could scarcely believe how quickly it was all happening!

☙

The following Tuesday, there I was with my mom and stepdad in their new Cadillac, on our way to JFK International Airport. Sonny was in the driver's seat, my mom sat in the front beside him, and I was in the back like a child. We drove across the Queensboro Fifty-Ninth Street Bridge, suspended high over the East River, and passed the island where I was born, Welfare Island (whose name would soon be changed to Roosevelt Island). I looked back at Manhattan, and the Empire State Building seemed to duck under the skyline and recede into nothingness. The traffic flowed through Queens, past Flushing Meadows–Corona Park, with the twelve-story Unisphere, the enduring monument of the 1964–1965 World's Fair.

At JFK, there was no way to miss the TWA terminal (though my mom was sure we would). With its sculpted abstract form, it looked like a futuristic spaceship in smooth white cement. We stopped at the entrance, and Mom got out with me while Sonny parked the car. We made our way to the long white check-in counters just under the soaring, intersecting concrete ceilings, which looked like seagulls in flight. My heavy pink suitcase was tagged and sent down the conveyer belt while I got my ticket and boarding pass. Sonny returned, and all three of us headed toward the gates where we would say goodbye. Mom was so excited for me, and I concentrated on what she was feeling instead of the fact that Sonny was standing beside her. She looked so helpless next to him. She didn't know, would never know, how much I hated him and that his toxicity—as much as my career—was one of the reasons I had to cross the ocean.

She hugged me, and he tried to, but I pulled away. I started down the long tunnel-like walkway toward the gates and turned back to look at her. As I smiled and waved, I could hear myself saying, "Oh, Mom, please come with me. Please don't stay with him. He'll hurt you." I could feel her heart breaking, just as mine was; the threads of our lives were that intertwined.

I quickly walked on, looking down at my feet. My Goody Two Shoes were holding on for dear life. As I picked up the pace, I was trying not to cry. The bright red color of the carpet bathed my senses, making me feel as though I were being born into my own future.

Aboard the brand-new Boeing 747, I settled into my first-class seat, eagerly accepting the champagne the flight attendants offered. I fell asleep, and when I woke up, we were flying over the snow-covered Alps. Incredible; it was already the next day. The pilot announced that we would be landing in Milan. I looked out the window at tiny terra-cotta rooftops in villages nestled in the foothills of mountains. As we made our descent, I prayed that we would land safely. When we did, the Italian passengers in the back of the plane applauded and shouted out *"Bravo!"* In my heart, I did the same.

chapter 32

I LOVE PARIS

Donna Jordan, me, and Corey Tippin
at the corner bar on Rue Bonaparte
in Paris, wearing our new Chloé coats
designed by Karl Lagerfeld, 1971.
Courtesy of Juan Ramos.

$\mathcal{I}$ always like to say that whenever I'm confronted with the dark, I turn away and move toward the light. Four days after landing in Milan, that was literally what I did, escaping a bad situation in Italy by taking off for . . . yes, the City of Light.

The Italian agency I was booked with was in fact one rather sketchy guy in a nearly empty office in what looked like a deserted area of Milan. The day after I arrived, this guy insisted on driving me far outside the city to meet his financial backers in a big secluded house in the woods that reminded me of a safe haven like you see in spy movies, where the CIA hides spooks who need to lie low for a while. Then my agent took off, leaving me there alone, still jet-lagged, in the middle of nowhere, with these strange men.

Somehow, I managed to talk one of them into taking me back to my hotel in Milan. On the way, I noticed in my side-view mirror that we were being tailed by a very cute guy on a Harley-Davidson who kept making indecipherable hand gestures to me whenever my driver was otherwise occupied (the car actually had a phone—in 1971!—and he yakked on it in Italian all the way into the city).

I know this story sounds crazy, but it's one of those stranger-than-fiction episodes that seemed to occur with regularity in my life back then, leaving me to make split-second decisions based on instinct alone. But there I was on the road when my driver stopped at a tobacco shop to buy cigarettes, and the motorcyclist rushed up and told me to hurry and get on his bike because I was in danger. "He's a bad guy!" he said. I had a second to make a decision, and as usual, I let my gut make it for me. *This Botticelli angel on a bike is someone you can trust,* my gut told me. I jumped out and hopped on, clinging to him for dear life. "I'm Marco," he said as we peeled off.

It turned out that Marco knew who I was and had heard I was in town from a friend of his who ran another modeling agency. Marco had been out riding his Harley when he saw me in the car with that man and knew he had to save me. "He and his friends are bad guys!" he kept shouting at the top of his voice as we sped down several small one-way streets. "Girls like you—he and his friends sell!"

"*Sell?*" I yelled. His Italian accent was adorable, but between it and the noise, I wasn't sure I'd heard him correctly.

"Into slavery! *Capito?* Understand?"

Slavery? I thought blankly, just before it dawned on me what Marco was saying: *sex slavery.* Good Lord. Thank you for saving me, Marco, my handsome Italian knight in shining armor. That was a close call.

☙

I phoned Antonio that very evening and took up his standing invitation to stay with them. The next morning I was on one of the first flights out of Milan. Juan met me at the airport.

We hurled my big pink suitcase into the back of the small convertible he was driving, top-down, and off we went. Our destination was 3 Rue Bonaparte, which was on the Rive Gauche, or Left Bank, of the Seine, Juan informed me. As we drove, he gave me a quick tour, which I was almost too excited to listen to. All the way into Paris, the red, white, and blue of the French flag seemed to wave a personal welcome to me.

I noticed a huge, ancient-looking church with a tall white tower poking into the perfect blue sky. "That's L'Église Saint-Germain-des-Prés," Juan said. "Parts of it date from the sixth century." *Wow, no wonder it looks old,* I thought, marveling at the way it sat there serenely, smack-dab in the middle of a busy intersection in Paris. Juan was quite knowledgeable about the neighborhood, which was also called Saint-Germain-des-Prés.

"We sometimes have breakfast there," he said, gesturing to an outdoor café opposite the church that seemed to wrap itself around the street corner and spill out all over the sidewalk. On this beautiful June day, Parisians sat languidly, faces forward, under the dark green awning imprinted with the words "Les Deux Magots," sipping wine and smoking cigarettes. It looked like a scene from a movie. "That café has been there since the nineteenth century," Juan said. "It used to be a favorite hangout for intellectuals in Paris, like Hemingway and Jean-Paul Sartre." I formed a pretty picture in my mind of Henriette Metcalf lunching there with her dear friend Isadora Duncan, the two of them looking impossibly chic and sophisticated as they clinked wineglasses. I remembered the *Madeline* book Henriette had given me, with the Eiffel Tower on the cover, and thought, *I'm finally here!*

We turned off Boulevard Saint-Germain onto Rue Bonaparte, and the movie set became even more charming and quintessentially Parisian. The street, paved with worn cobblestones, was barely wide enough for the car to get through. On either side were exquisite old buildings, none taller than about four stories, stone facades painted white like new gesso canvases, except with a few peeling surfaces that highlighted their beauty, like a gracefully aging face. Farther along, I noticed a courtyard flanked by two colossal stone carvings. Juan told me it was the home of the École des Beaux Arts, a famous school for painters and sculptors. Beaux Arts? That was the name of the costume balls in New York City that my mom and Auntie Helen used to attend. I felt a stab of sadness that Mom wasn't here with me to experience this enthralling city.

"We're here!" Juan belted out, bringing me back from my reverie. He seemed excited, which was unusual for him. But he knew how eager I was to see Antonio.

We stopped in front of a dark green lacquered door and piled out of the car, dragging my baggage with us. The bright light coming off the Seine, which I glimpsed just at the end of Rue Bonaparte, made everything around us glisten in tones of gray and violet that I would come to associate with the city. Juan pressed the buzzer, and we entered a dark hallway that led to a narrow stairway. We climbed up to the second floor, huffing and puffing from the suitcase and my assorted "dingle-dangle bags," as I called them. When Juan set my suitcase down, it took up most of the space in the room.

I sat on my suitcase, feeling a bit awkward. *What a tiny place,* I thought. *Where am I going to stay?*

I peeked into the other room, and whom did I see? None other than Donna Jordan! She was posing next to the wall on a daybed, sitting on a bolster-type pillow, straddled from behind by this handsome, boyish-looking blond guy. I stuck my head farther around the corner and saw Antonio. He was breathing the way he did when he was about to finish a sketch, his hand sliding across the page as though slicing it to shreds. It's a wonder the paper held up under the force of his creativity. Often at such moments, watching the way he would suck in air as he worked, as though taking energy from the entire universe, I'd imagine what he would be like while making love.

He stopped. The drawing was finished, and for a moment absolute silence prevailed. Then Juan said loudly, "*Fini!* The angels just passed by!" He used a playfully annoying voice, pronouncing the word "fini" with an exaggerated French accent to bring everyone down to earth.

Donna unwrapped herself from the erotic pose and beamed her bright green eyes right at me. "Hey, girl!" she screamed. That big smile of hers just lit up my heart.

"Hey, girl!" Antonio echoed, putting his work aside. As always, he seemed almost to be awakening from a dream. And as always, Juan was there to catch his drawing as though it were a precious treasure.

We all hugged and Antonio introduced me to the blond boy. "This is Joe Macdonald," he said. "The model." That was pure Antonio—adding an ironic little tag to someone's name.

He disappeared into the small room, then came out in a flash wearing three freshly pressed shirts, one layered over the next, pointy collars turned up. That, too, was pure Antonio.

"C'mon, guys," he said. "Let's get something to eat. I'm starving."

We walked exactly one hundred steps, including the stairs, to the Bar Bonaparte, which was situated in a small square facing the Seine. The bar was practically an extension of the boys' apartment, which had no kitchen. As I entered the bar, thrilled to be with my new Paris-based tribe of expats, I felt as if I had wandered into a Toulouse-Lautrec world. The walls were decorated with floor-to-ceiling mirrors and huge posters in bold red, yellow, and black. I was gawking at everything from the worn tiles at my feet to the ceiling fan turning slowly overhead. Antonio nudged me and said, "Keep moving." I couldn't take my eyes off the posters, especially one of a beautiful young woman dressed as a goddess, holding a drink up to the gods. It was signed Henri Privat. *I'm living in art,* I thought, again flashing to my mom.

We settled into a dark leather banquette, and Antonio, never much of a drinker, ordered a Coca-Cola. I noticed another beautiful poster with the word "Absinthe" printed across it, and I decided I simply *must* try the "drink of the green fairy."

Both Antonio and Juan discouraged me. "It can make you crazy, or cuckoo," Antonio said, twirling his finger beside his ear.

"*Muy loco,*" Juan added with a knowing nod. "It's like a psychedelic drug."

I didn't doubt that they had my best interests at heart, but I ordered it anyway, just to get a taste of the legendary liqueur.

"They say you get inspired if you drink absinthe," Antonio said. "That's why the poets in the 1890s drank it—to get inspired, to die!"

The bartender prepared the drink, putting one sugar cube in the glass, adding the emerald-green liquid, then pouring the bottled water over it until it magically turned a beautiful pale green. I took a little sip, then Juan removed it from my hand because I liked it—a lot. He took a sip and passed the glass to Antonio, then Antonio to Donna. We all had some, and after a few minutes, everything in the place seemed to brighten. All my senses were heightened, and I felt I could hear every word that everyone was saying, even if it came from the other side of the room.

Was it the absinthe? Probably. But it may have been Paris.

chapter 33

THAT'S WHAT FRIENDS ARE FOR

Getting cozy at the Rue Bonaparte flat with Karl
Lagerfeld (*center*), me (*top*), and Antonio Lopez, 1971.
Courtesy of Juan Ramos.

O*ver* the following days, I quickly adapted to the boys' routine, staying up until the wee hours, posing for Antonio to the strains of Erik Satie; sleeping late (Juan and Antonio in sleeping bags on the floor and Donna and I in the daybed, positioned head to foot); and then heading out at around three o'clock in the afternoon to the Café de Flore, another nearby restaurant with a long history of patronage by writers and artists. As in New York, Juan didn't want food in the apartment, which was provided by a mysterious man named Karl whom everyone was constantly talking about. I fell instantly in love with croque-monsieurs—so much more delicious than the humble American ham and cheese sandwich—and my new favorite comfort food, croissants. The first time I bit into one—all flaky and buttery, with sweet confiture inside—I thought I'd died and gone to heaven. I'd devour them for breakfast at any time of day, and wash down the jam-filled pastry with piping-hot café au lait. Goodbye, cornbread, biscuits, and fried eggs!

At the Flore, we were occasionally joined by another of Antonio's pals by way of Karl, Paloma Picasso, the daughter of the great Pablo (who, ironically, was one of the famous artists who'd frequented the Flore decades earlier) and the sister of Claude, whom I'd met in New York on the same day I'd first visited Wilhelmina's offices. I used to wonder how Paloma felt about having artists for parents. Had she ever drunk turpentine when she was little, like I did, or eaten clay? I never really found out, because Paloma was interested only in Antonio and never paid much attention to me. The fifth "regular" in our core gang was Corey Tippin, a makeup artist who was an old friend of Antonio's and Andy Warhol's. It was Corey, who shaved Donna's eyebrows and bleached her hair platinum white, creating her signature look.

After eating our fill, we'd order red wine by the glass. And after a few glasses, we'd get pretty boisterous. Antonio would always end up drawing on the paper tablecloths and even the cloth napkins—that's what artists do, after all—and then Juan and I would start drawing, too, covering one another's sketches as in a game of tic-tac-toe, laughing our heads off, until we'd filled the paper tablecloth all the way to the edges with our creations.

Corey's art was makeup, and he was always checking up on Donna and me. We'd apply lots of red lipstick, peering into our knives like narrow mirrors, with Corey directing us how to get the important upper (not lower) lip just right. Sometimes he'd get impatient and snatch the lipstick out of our hands and roughly pull our heads back, as if he'd just caught a squealing piglet, and apply the color himself.

Corey was mysterious, even a bit Gatsby-like, and Greek-god handsome, with golden hair and light eyes outlined in heavy black kohl. I asked him once how he got so good at doing makeup, and he told me he used to paint the faces of the corpses in a funeral home. "Honey, I'd pile that makeup on, and they wouldn't say a thing," he said.

As for Donna, the art she'd perfected was in not taking herself too seriously. It always tickled me that she could be so glamorous and high-fashiony one minute and in the next be so down-to-earth and hilarious. At the Flore, Donna would talk to the waiters in English, knowing full well they didn't understand a word she was saying. Like many French people, those waiters in those days had a snooty attitude toward Americans who spoke poor French. But Donna believed the world belonged to everyone. "We have a right to be here," she'd say. "We kicked ass for these guys during the war. There wouldn't *be* a Paris if it weren't for us Americans." She'd wink at us and shout in her loudest voice to the waiters, "Garçon! Knucklehead! Come here!" She'd gesture for a waiter to come closer, then turn to us and whisper, "He's so stupid, he doesn't even realize I called him knucklehead."

"Donna," I'd whisper back, "don't you think he might find out what you're saying?"

She'd just laugh and say, "Confidentially, honey, they're just a bunch of jerks. Try it with me."

I just couldn't. But waiters would be falling all over her even as she teased them—albeit with a coquettish manner. I have to admit it was funny to see people's reactions to Donna. She could really stir the soup, and Antonio loved it when she did. I was always afraid we'd be thrown out for being rude. I'd hear my mother's voice in the back of my head: *Trish, you must be a lady at all times.* Still, the fact that Donna got away with what she was doing was pretty entertaining; it was like watching a naughty three-year-old who's just learned to say no to everything. I guess she was saying no to the French attitude toward us gauche Americans. She toyed with them until she had them wrapped around her little finger.

Naughty or not, Donna was always the most glittering star in the room. She exuded this flamboyant tomboy confidence that contrasted dramatically with her bombshell movie-goddess appearance; she was a sort of modern-day combination of Mae West and Marilyn Monroe. After Warhol made her a superstar (she'd just finished his movie *L'Amour*, in which Corey also appeared), Antonio made her a fashion star. Next to her sun, I was the moon. Slowly, some of her bold radiance began to rub off on me, and we became best friends. We were like salt and pepper, like Jane Russell and Marilyn Monroe in *Gentlemen Prefer Blondes*. I was the brunette, and she was the blonde—"just two little girls from Little Rock, born on the wrong side of the tracks."

One of our great bonding experiences was posing together for the photographer Guy Bourdin. As usual, the booking came through Antonio, who was a friend of Bourdin's and wanted us to do test photos with him. Donna and I took a taxi one cold summer night—the shoot was scheduled for after midnight—to Bourdin's out-of-the-way studio, but the driver dropped us at the wrong address. After being caught in a torrential downpour, we finally found Bourdin's studio, which was a kind of modified garage, and we staggered in, drenched to the bone and dripping big puddles on the floor. No one greeted us, and the entryway was dark. Eventually, we saw a light coming out of what was possibly a dressing room. "Hello?" Donna shouted.

A girl came out and introduced herself as Christine, the makeup artist. She took us to a dressing room and gave us each a bathrobe to put on. It was such a relief to get out of those soggy clothes. Christine did our makeup and pulled our wet hair into tight, side-knotted chignons, using lots of hairpins and K-Y jelly (yes, the sexual lubricant—hairstylists often used it instead of hair gel back in those days) until our hair was rock-solid. It was really uncomfortable, but I didn't care, because I knew we were going to wear something wonderful and that Antonio would be proud if the photos came out beautifully.

"You are ready," Christine said.

"What do we wear?" I asked. "I don't see the clothes."

"You dress in just the shoes."

"Just shoes?" Donna didn't look pleased.

"Guy wants to do nudes tonight," she explained.

Hmmm. This is not fashion, I thought. I suppose it was Art with a capital A. But in my head, I heard Mom's voice again: *Never take off your clothes to do naked pictures.* True, I'd done it for Antonio, but he was like family, and the pictures weren't for public consumption.

"Are you ready?" Christine said in her sweet Swiss-French accent.

"I guess so," I mumbled, my mom's voice falling away.

Donna and I walked in our six-inch heels into the garage space, which was pitch-black except for the light on the set. The aluminum front door was partially open, and outside, the rain was still pounding down. Donna and I stood there shivering for what seemed like forever, waiting for Guy Bourdin to arrive. When he finally got there, we couldn't even see him.

"Hello," he said from behind the camera. "Thank you for coming." All I could see was his jacket and the outline of his shoulders behind a Nikon camera, which was sitting straight ahead of us on a tripod. He had us lit with a giant spotlight, rendering me all but blind, but I knew he was looking through the lens. Then, without saying a word, he walked away.

Christine came over. "I have to take your robes," she said. And there we were, nude as plucked chickens—or should I say geese, since Christine then put oil on our bodies and sprayed us with water so that both of us were soaked to the bone and covered from head to toe with goose pimples. We waited like that, in our birthday suits, wearing only high heels, until Bourdin finally returned to his position behind the camera. He directed us from out of the darkness, telling Donna and me to stand close and hold on to each other. We held the pose and he walked away again. He seemed to disappear into the darkness whenever he wanted to. I still hadn't seen his face. When he returned, I could tell he was smoking a cigarette by the orange glow. Then he put it out on the floor, and we went back to the posing.

"Bend back, holding each other," he said politely.

While we were executing this move, Donna and I conducted our own dialogue, as models often do when they're working. "Cover me up," she said anxiously. "You stay in the front."

"Like this?" I asked.

"Bend back more, more," Bourdin said out of the darkness.

"Okay," Donna answered as we struggled to pose in such a way to cover our girl parts, so that we were showing only our flank sides.

"Hide me. You have the bootie," Donna said.

"You have one, too."

"Yeah, but mine is flat."

"You have as much as I do."

"Lean back more, please," Bourdin said quietly. "*More.*"

"Show the shoes," Donna said. "Wait—where did he go?"

"He left again."

"*No!*"

"Yes. There he goes past the dressing room. I see his silhouette."

"Can't he close the door? I'm freezing."

"At least the light will keep us warm."

"My hair is so tight it hurts."

"Mine, too—and it's still wet under all the goop."

"It's probably seeping into our brains," Donna said.

"Did he even take a picture?" I asked. "I didn't hear a click, did you?"

Bourdin was in no hurry; that much we knew. Maybe this was how they worked in France, like sipping wine slowly.

"Don't move," he said,

"I have an itch," Donna said. At that point, we were standing so close together, I could almost feel her itch, too.

Pop! Flash went a strobe light. Bourdin finally took one shot. "It is good," he said in his monotone. By now it was two in the morning, and Donna and I were beyond caring what Bourdin was going to do with these photos.

Next, Bourdin's assistant created a little bench out of a plank, which he then covered with shiny black oilcloth. Bourdin returned to the scene, a voice in the dark. "Sit on the plank, very near each other, with your backs facing the camera, please."

Donna and I were like two hot cross buns stuck together, sitting naked on a baking sheet, ready to go into the oven, because now the spotlight was so hot that it burned our backs.

"It is good," Bourdin said again after taking the picture. I tried to look around at the camera. "Just your back," he said.

Now, *that* upset me. I wanted to show my face, wanted him to see *me*, but he seemed interested only in my backside.

"Thank you," Bourdin said.

"Thank *you*," Donna and I answered in unison.

"Where is he?" I asked Donna.

"He's gone, finished," Christine said.

At least the lights came on long enough for Donna and me to get dressed. Christine called a taxi and we returned home in a pelting rain. Ah, the glamorous world of modeling.

☙

I really appreciated Donna because, trust me, not all of the other models Antonio worked with were as fun-loving or just plain nice as she was.

Exhibit A was Carol LaBrie, another one of "Antonio's Girls" and the first black woman ever to grace the cover of Italian *Vogue*—or, for that matter, any edition of *Vogue* anywhere in the world.

The first things I noticed about Carol were her large doe eyes and her pixie haircut, slicked close to her head. She came to the apartment one day while I was posing for Antonio, so she went into the small room with Juan and Corey to wait for him. After Antonio finished a sketch, I joined them in the small room for a break and to stretch after leaning on one elbow for an hour. Carol looked at me, sizing me up, and said, "So what do you think you're doing with those?" She was standing right next to me, peering into my face. I had no idea what she was talking about. "Do you mind if I do something?" she asked.

"Do something?" I said, puzzled.

"Close your eyes," she said. And then, in under a second—*ouch!*— she ripped off both sets of my eyelashes at the same time. Not my real ones, thank heaven (though it felt like it) but my fake ones.

Juan and Corey began chortling. I actually thought they might be in on it. Then Corey said, "No, you didn't!" They all doubled over with laughter, including Antonio, who had walked in by then. "Did the mean puddy cat get to you?" he said to me as Carol smirked at him.

I was so hurt that I wanted to cry. "Here!" Carol said, handing me the lashes. "You won't be needing these anymore." She sashayed over to the door, opened it, and said, "Europe isn't America. You don't have to be fake over here." She looked over at the boys and said, "Doesn't she look *so* much better?" And with that, she made her grand exit.

As soon as the door shut, the boys collapsed in laughter all over again. I was so furious that I felt like smacking all three of them, but instead I started sobbing, my mascara running and streaking my cheeks. Having heard so much about Carol from Antonio, I'd hoped to be her friend, but in my book, you just don't do something like that to another girl the first time you meet her.

chapter 34

PLEASE PLEASE ME

A photo shoot for *Vogue Italia*, shot in
Karl Lagerfeld's Paris apartment, 1971.
Courtesy of Guy Bourdin.

Until I arrived in Paris, I don't believe I had even heard the name
Karl Lagerfeld. But in the days after I moved into the apartment on
Rue Bonaparte—where Antonio, Juan, Donna, and I were still living
like puppies in a box—it often seemed that I heard little else. It was
Karl this and Karl that, morning, noon, and night. Antonio explained
that he was a German-born designer who created the collections of the
French fashion house Chloé, and that he had hired Antonio to work
with him to illustrate the current collection. Donna knew Karl well
because they had appeared in *L'Amour* together, and she wore a lot of
his clothes.

One day Corey, another good friend of Karl's, came by the apartment
to say that Karl wanted us to come over that night. Donna was working,

so it was just me and the three boys. Off we went to Karl's apartment, arm in arm, skipping along the narrow streets. Finally, I was going to meet the mystery friend who'd been so generous to us all.

The boys had told me that Karl grew up in a castle. That sounded like a fairy tale; then again, just being in Paris and walking through its beautiful small streets on a summer evening was fairy tale enough for me. There is no greater feeling than being the only girl out with three gorgeous guys in the most romantic city on earth.

We nearly tripped when we walked into the garden courtyard of the building at 123 Rue de l'Université because we were laughing so hard at some wisecrack Antonio had made about Juan. When I got a good look at the garden, it took my breath away. In the center was a fountain with a marble statue of a dancer, and around the edges was white lattice covered with roses and jasmine, which reached up to an intricately carved iron balcony graced by tall French doors lit from within. I breathed deeply; the smell was divine.

"Which apartment is his?" I asked Juan.

"There's only one," Juan said. For the briefest instant, I experienced a flash of the intense class envy I had first felt at Madame Metcalf's house in Connecticut: *What I would give to be rich enough to live in a place like this,* I thought. Then I shrugged it off. *Be grateful you can even visit,* my inner voice told me.

From the garden, we ran up *l'escalier,* which wound up to what the French call the first floor. A pretty young maid showed us in, and as she walked in front of us, I noticed the seams up the back of her silk stockings. *I want those,* I thought as our heels clicked over onyx-colored marble floors. On the mirrored ceiling was a huge art deco chandelier that cast long shards of light on the dark mirrored walls. The entrance alone was three times bigger than the apartment we were staying in.

In awe, I stood there like a fish, mouth wide open, about to swallow a fisherman's hook. Antonio actually had to poke me in the ribs and tell me to close my mouth. I was lost in contemplation of a tall cut-glass vase of long-stemmed white calla lilies when someone said, "Boo!" I jumped.

"Karl!" Juan said in a screechy voice. "You scared us."

"Good," Karl said. "That was my intention, my dear." He chuckled in satisfaction.

"Come on, Karl, I know your tricks," Antonio said.

Corey was gazing in the mirror. "You should wear kohl on your eyes, Karl," he said, whipping out his kohl stick and ringing Karl's eyes with smudgy black circles. "There. That's better."

Karl glanced in the mirror. "Mysterious, like the old movie stars. Now we are all like Greta Garbo in *Mata Hari,* no?" Then he whispered in Juan's ear, and Juan laughed as if Karl had said something terribly naughty.

So this was the legendary Karl. I could see why they all loved him so much. He was very European-looking (though if Antonio hadn't told me, I wouldn't have been able to place his nationality), with thick, dark, wavy hair and a big smile. He spoke rapidly, in delightfully accented English. "How do you like Paris, my dear?"

The question was directed at me, but I couldn't speak. Antonio answered for me. "She likes it," he said. "Tell him you like it." I just nodded, feeling like an idiot.

"Is the apartment comfortable?" Karl asked.

"Yes," I managed, barely audible.

Karl held my hand in his and patted it kindly. "I must change," he said. "We are going out to dinner, and I can't go out in my smoking jacket, can I?"

While he was changing, Juan led us into a nearby room—also dark, mirrored, and spacious—that was filled with exercise machines. Antonio lay down on a push bench and rolled the heavy barbells over his chest and tried to pick them up. "Karl lifts these? I can't even budge them," he said, giving up. Juan tried but couldn't lift them, either.

"Wow, you two really need to work out," Corey said, but didn't touch a thing.

Karl came into the room. "Exercise is my new obsession," he said. "It's good for the body, don't you think?" He held out something to me. "Here, my dear. This is a little something I'd like you to wear tonight." It was a stunning black jacket, intricately beaded in rose flower patterns, with the tiniest deep red bugle beads. "It's a Schiaparelli," he said, draping it over my shoulders.

I'd learned about Elsa Schiaparelli's designs at school. Not only that, Berry Berenson had told me that Elsa was her and Marisa's grandmother (fashion certainly ran in that family!). This jacket was at least forty years old, and wearing it was like donning a piece of history. I was overwhelmed; I'd just met Karl, and already he had given me this incredible garment to wear.

The five of us went to a little restaurant that served Italian food just a few blocks away. The host guided us to a private room in the back, since we didn't want to sit at the tables on the street. I was feeling like a star in my beaded jacket. And then I saw Carol LaBrie. She was sitting at the table waiting for us, wearing a beaded jacket that at first glance was nearly identical to the one I had on. It sparkled, reflecting the candlelight, and as I got closer, my jacket did the same. We could have been twins. Carol was not amused. Come to think of it, neither was I.

❧

At the restaurant, Karl and Antonio arranged for me to accompany Antonio to Karl's atelier the following day. Bright and early the next morning, there we were in Karl's workshop, which was up a squeaky wooden stairway in a very old building. Inside was a wonderfully creative space. There were small sketches on corkboards, with attached squares of swatches, and along the walls were dozens of tubes of rolled-up silk, colorful bolts of wool, and smooth, shiny satin. The floors were covered with tapestries, which mingled, chameleonlike, with tiny pieces of unrolled bias tape, scraps of muslin, and shredded threads.

A short, sturdy French woman was kneeling on a green cushion, sewing a hem on a delicate long tulle dress draped on the croquis form in front of her. She looked over at us and went back to her work. Was she doing the double-hem stitch, or maybe the plain-hem stitch? I used to do those stitches, and I'd get knots in my threads from rushing—and I was *always* rushing. I watched her and thanked my lucky stars that it wasn't me having to hem that dress.

Antonio had begun to sketch when Karl came into the room, bristling with good cheer. "We must dress you," he said, putting his gentleman's purse on the sketching table.

Karl looked at what Antonio was drawing and got so engrossed that his face lit up. He sat down beside Antonio, picked up one of the markers, and quickly started a cartoonlike fashion drawing of his own. "Well, it's nothing like yours," he said, showing it to Antonio, "but you can get the idea, no?"

Karl looked at me and made a few marks on the paper. "We can turn you into anything," he said, showing me the paper. "This is you as Josephine, the woman who stole the heart of Napoleon." I was awestruck at how quickly his hands moved; he even wrote a short story beneath his drawings. "What do you think?" he said to Antonio. "She can be our empress."

Then Karl approached me, felt-tipped pen in hand. "You know, dear, you are missing just one thing." He extended the pen and drew a little round beauty mark on my cheekbone. Eerily, I heard my mom's voice in my head: *The beauty mark is like the period at the end of a sentence.* "There, now you look as though you are from the royal French courts," Karl said. He clapped his hands to get the seamstress's attention. "Madame! Bring the dress!"

La robe—"dress" in French—was thrown over my head. While I was worming my way into it, I could hear Karl discussing it in French with the seamstress. "Monsieur Lagerfeld . . . ," she said, and I could tell by the tone of her voice that she was protesting. I poked my head out, glad to get air. Really, dressing is sometimes like inching your way through a dark tunnel, especially if you've never seen the dress before. The good news is, it's a surprise when you manage to get it on, like being born again with a different skin.

In this case, I couldn't see my own image, which meant I was powerless to show the dress to its best advantage. Then I caught a glimpse of my reflection in a freestanding oval mirror set between two windows and saw Karl behind me with a white powdered eighteenth-century wig in his hands. He placed it carefully on my head and, with a big downy puff, applied white powder all over my face. "You are my Marie Antoinette," he said. "She said let them eat cake, but my dear, you look like the cake."

He stepped back and contemplated my appearance. "The fullness of the back, you see," Karl said as Antonio sketched away. "What do you think? I will make it more simple." With that, the seamstress got a terrified look on her face, as if she might have to take the entire dress apart. "Or pleated at the neckband, like a court lady . . ." The seamstress followed with her eyes as he pointed.

Off came the dress with a great deal of pulling and me dodging the straight pins. Being pinned is one of the hazards of being fitted; those tiny sabers scratch deeply, burn your skin, and leave scars.

Karl drew more ideas on paper, clearly naturally high on creating. His enthusiasm was contagious—Antonio was in a great mood, too—and it made me happy. Within the next hour, the two of them came up with many more sketches, and I had changed into a host of different characters in a host of different time periods. Karl had a great deal of intuition; he was creating me, as was Antonio.

That afternoon I added another name right next to Antonio's on the list of people I wanted to please: Karl Lagerfeld.

chapter 35

RHAPSODY IN BLUE

More posing at Karl Lagerfeld's
place for *Vogue Italia*, 1971.
Courtesy of Guy Bourdin.

$\mathcal{K}arl$ had invited us out to dinner, so Antonio, Juan, and I walked from our tiny flat over to Karl's art deco palace on Rue de l'Université. Donna and Corey would join us at the restaurant.

Karl greeted us in his evening smoking jacket and silk ascot. He looked like a perfect gentleman of the 1920s. "Excuse me, my dears," he said. "I must change my jacket."

He went into the other room, and when he came back, the maid was following him, carrying mounds of chiffon in the exact midnight blue of the candy boxes I'd been seeing in shops all over Paris. "My dear," Karl said, looking directly at me, "it is evening and you need something long, so I want you to wear this."

The maid accompanied me into Karl's exercise room off the foyer, where I stepped out of my own dress and she helped me put on the blue one, holding up yard after yard of pleated chiffon. It reminded me of a choir robe, but it was too transparent for church, that's for sure. As I slipped my arms into the sleeves, I remembered that I wasn't wearing underwear, because I hadn't wanted my panty line to show through the matte jersey dress I'd had on. There wasn't much I could do about that now.

The room had no mirror, so I couldn't see what I looked like. I quickly walked back to the boys, awkwardly covering the front of my body. With all those yards of chiffon flowing behind me, I felt ready to take flight. Karl and the boys' eyes seemed almost to pop.

"Brava, Miss Cleveland," Karl said, clapping. "I made this dress on Marlene Dietrich, but now I have decided it is yours. You are the only one who can wear this."

"*Me?*" I was nearly speechless.

"Do you like it, my dear?"

"Yes, very much." I was trying to digest what he had said. It was as if Karl had just given me a magic robe: That was how special it felt to be wearing a dress that had been made on Marlene Dietrich.

Antonio's eyes grew even wider, because he adored Dietrich, and he hated it when I was shy and didn't speak up for myself. "Say thank you to Karl," Antonio said. I had been just about to do that, but of course Antonio had to jump in and needle me, like a smart-alecky big brother.

"Thank you, Karl," I said quietly. I was too busy in my head to be mad at Antonio for embarrassing me.

I saw myself in the hall mirror, and I started walking up and down Karl's foyer, just expressing how I felt in that dress. I moved about until I was almost dizzy with excitement, then stood perfectly still and all the pleats landed straight. I lifted my arms and the yards of fabric looked like a cloud of blue mist surrounding me.

"You are our Blue Angel tonight," Karl said, grabbing his gentleman's purse, which he always had with him. (God only knows what he had in there, because he guarded it with his life.) Then we were out the door and into the car that was waiting in the courtyard, on our way to La Coupole, the largest restaurant in Paris and "the" place for people in the fashion world to see and be seen. As the driver maneuvered through the narrow streets on the way to Boulevard du Montparnasse, Juan, Karl, and Antonio discussed the rich artistic history of La Coupole, which had opened in 1927. "There are thirty-two paintings on the sixteen pillars that support the ceiling of the main dining room," the ever knowledge-able Juan said. "Léger did one of them," he added for Antonio's benefit, since Léger was one of his favorite artists.

We pulled up to 102 Boulevard du Montparnasse and the restau-rant—or, technically, brasserie—was bathed in a rosy glow emanating from the sign spelling out "La Coupole" in script above the long red aw-ning that stretched for nearly half a city block. There were lots of people sitting at the small tables outside, sipping wine and eating oysters. The driver opened our car door, and as we got out, the very act felt like the unveiling of a precious piece of art. Okay, that's a slight exaggeration, but that's how the fashion world feels sometimes when you're all dressed up and go out on the town.

I was swept along through the glass doors, which were open wide for summer, with the boys and Karl in front. As we entered the main dining room, I noticed the art deco motif on the tile floors. My elec-tric-blue chiffon hem was dragging on them a bit, so I lifted the fabric slightly. Above me, the chandeliers on the ceiling cast an amber light over the open dining area full of hundreds of Parisians. I could see the sixteen pillars, lit up with the painted frescoes that Juan had mentioned. Abruptly, the sound of silverware clinking against china plates brought me back to reality and the date: June 23, 1971. *Today is my birthday,* I realized. *I'm twenty-one years old, I've been in Paris for twelve days, and I'm wearing the Blue Angel. This is the dream I've had since I was five years old—and I'm living it.*

I whispered to Antonio, "Today's my birthday," and he promptly announced it to the group after planting a big kiss on my cheek. Just as the host was about to seat us, Donna and Corey showed up. "It's Pat's birthday," Antonio said.

"Wow, girl!" Donna was so happy that she kissed me in the French style, on both cheeks, and so did Corey. If nothing else, being in Paris had taught us the art of kissing.

I felt enveloped in love as the host took us to our table. I glided along in my high heels until, weirdly, I felt stuck. My hem had caught on one of the mosaic tiles and was pulling on the train of my dress, so that the length of it extended behind me like a wedding gown. *My God, the whole bloody thing is going to come off!* I thought in a panic. So I lifted my arms to pull it back on my shoulders, and the dress opened up in front. And there I was, moving forward in my birthday suit (it *was* my birthday, after all), the Blue Angel chiffon trailing behind me. Actually, the feeling wasn't dissimilar to that of walking the runway.

A great silence descended on the restaurant, as though the sound had been turned off. There was no talking, no tinkling of glasses, no waiters bustling around. It was if I'd dunked my head under the sea. And then, in a crash of sound, a wave of applause rolled over me. The Parisians were shouting, "Brava!" and forks were tapping on crystal glasses, and the waiters were all gathered together, cheering.

I heard Karl's voice in my ear. "They're applauding for you, my empress, my Josephine."

It was Karl's words that did it. Somehow they beckoned my regal alter ego, who arrived grandly on the scene and elbowed the shy New World bumpkin out of the way. I lifted my arms higher, gathered the train of chiffon, and wrapped it around my body like a veil as I walked to the table in what was unquestionably the longest thirty seconds of my life. When I finally sat down to dine, the entire restaurant lifted their glasses in my direction.

Karl raised his own glass. "Miss Cleveland, you are the toast of Paris," he said.

chapter 36

I COULD HAVE DANCED ALL NIGHT

Antonio and me dressed up to
go out to Club Sept, the hottest
nightclub in Paris, 1971.

One of the paradoxes of being a model is that you're constantly surrounded by sexiness—sexy people, sexy clothes, sexy talk—but when it
comes to actual sex, a lot of the time you're batting zero. Yes, it's true.
A model's life seems libertine, but the operative word is "seems." You
almost "wear" sexy people like sexy clothes, but at night, after you take
everything off, you're all alone, questioning whether you'll ever find true
intimacy with anyone.

At least that was my experience during those first weeks and months
in Europe. I was totally over Matthew; I knew I'd been lucky to escape
the destructiveness of that relationship, and having three thousand miles
between us made the breakup that much easier. A lot of my current

abstinence had to do with my preoccupation with Antonio. In those days, my emotional attention was focused pretty exclusively on him. Tragically, he was claimed by the AIDS epidemic in 1987, and even now it can be almost unbearably painful for me to think about him, especially the way he was in Paris in the early seventies—in his prime, his genius going at full throttle, and with me completely under his sway, almost giddy at being allowed into his inner circle. Believe me, I wasn't the only one he had this effect on.

We loved each other but weren't lovers. The energy between us, however, was undeniably sexual. Instead of openly acknowledging that fact, we danced around it—verbally, of course, with our relentless provocative sparring, but also literally. Our dance partnership, which became something of a local legend (if briefly), was born at a hot new club at Sept [7] Rue Saint-Anne, called simply Club Sept. Our dance of choice was the Apache tango (Apache is a highly aggressive, almost violent dance style that supposedly originated among Parisian street gangs and is said to simulate a fight between a prostitute and her pimp). The first time we did it resembled something out of a movie. Think the rumble scene in *West Side Story*.

We got there at around ten in the evening. Taxis were dropping off well-dressed groups of people in front of a small door with a square peephole and a single light over it. (Like Le Club from my high school days and so many other exclusive nightspots, Club Sept had no sign outside announcing its existence; only those already in the know could go there and expect to be let in.) Inside, a huge, ornate gold-framed mirror blocked off the dining area from the bar. When our little gang— Antonio, Juan, Karl, Donna, and me—came in that night, Fabrice, the manager, greeted us with a glass of champagne at the bar. But as soon as I heard the sounds of Marvin Gaye's "Mercy Mercy Me" sweeping up the stairs from the basement down below, I knew I had to go to where the music was. I had all this excess energy to burn; besides, I loved to dance.

The disc jockey at Club Sept was a Cuban fellow named Guy Cuevas who had a way of spinning the vinyl, blending and mixing sounds from all styles and periods of music, that was way ahead of its time. When he saw Antonio enter the room, Guy put on the most exciting music he could find—in this case, the theme music from *Shaft,* the new blaxploitation movie directed by the famed photographer/filmmaker Gordon Parks (the same Gordon Parks who'd booked me for that first issue of *Essence*), which had just opened in New York. Antonio disappeared to dance with the flock of beautiful French boys who instantly surrounded him. I stood for a moment with Karl, watching the bodies writhe on the minuscule dance floor. "You should dance, too," Karl said. I nodded and threw myself into the middle of the action.

Before I knew it, I was doing a heavy-duty bump-and-grind with some not so shabby French boys. When Antonio saw me dancing with them, he stopped dead in his tracks. And then good old Guy, with his impeccable sense of musical timing, put on a gypsy tango record. Antonio looked at me from across the room and—this is the straight-out-of-*West Side Story* piece of it—the crowd on the dance floor *parted* to make room for us. In a split second, Antonio grabbed me and pulled me so close to his body that I almost fainted. I wrapped my leg completely around him, and he threw me down on the floor. Oddly enough, he had worn a black-and-white striped T-shirt under his shirt that night (those striped shirts are associated with Apache dance), and he ripped off his outer shirt, grabbed me by the arm, dragged me across the floor, and once again pulled me close to his body.

Now I got what he was doing: He wanted to show off. *Okay, if that's the game you want to play, Mr. Lopez, you have met your match*, I thought. *Nobody throws me across the room and gets away with it.* So I grabbed him back and held his body tight to mine—so tight I felt like I was nearly squeezing the life out of it—and I whispered in his ear, "So you want to dance?"

"To the death," he whispered back. Everyone else on the dance floor had stopped and gathered around to watch our choreographed battle. Antonio would drop me on the floor, then pick me up and embrace me passionately. I even slapped him in the face and he came back for more. By the time we finally stopped (out of sheer exhaustion), we were both dripping wet, and my dress was ripped up the side and nearly torn to rags. I didn't mind. A little ditty kept running through my head: *In the heat of passion / Who cares about fashion?*

❧

Call it symbolic sex, because that's clearly what it was. And that was all fine and dandy, but sometimes . . . well, *ain't nothing like the real thing, baby.*

A week after that night at Club Sept, I moved out of Rue Bonaparte and into a nearby hotel. It was time; I'd imposed long enough on Juan and Antonio's hospitality. Besides, they were moving, too—to a bigger place nearer to Karl's. Now, loaded down with the large piece of luggage I'd brought with me to Europe (the hotel refused to hold it for me until I got back), I was in a taxi on my way to Gare du Nord to board the night train to Berlin. I'd accepted one of those last-minute bookings a model gets when another model doesn't call the agent back. It meant that I would miss the first few days of our holiday with Karl in the South of France, which was disappointing, but I needed the work because my savings were running low.

Luckily, the jobs were starting to trickle in. Antonio had been calling some magazines for me—*L'Officiel, Lui, Ambre*—and Donna had introduced me to Christa, her agent in Paris. As soon as Christa learned that I was represented in New York by Wilhelmina, I was in because the two agencies worked hand in hand. That was a huge thrill; half the time, I still couldn't believe people paid me for doing what I did. And the deutsche marks I'd make on this booking would be enough in French francs for me to live on for two months.

My reservation was for the 8:46 train, second class. I was running late because it was raining hard outside, and as the driver maneuvered the cab through the traffic like a pinball, I fretted about getting to the station on time. We got there at 8:42 and I raced to the platform, ran into the first car I saw, and collapsed into a seat. It was my first time on a European train. My destination was a town a few stops before Berlin called Potsdam. I repeated the name to myself several times so I wouldn't forget it.

"*Mademoiselle, le billet s'il vous plaît,*" the conductor said. I handed it to him and he shook his head. "Sorry, you are in the wrong coach," he said, switching to heavily accented English. "You must move."

What did I know? I was just glad to be on the train. Hoisting my heavy pink suitcase, I followed the conductor into a section with wee subsections called couchettes running the length of the car. I could feel my old back injury give a *ping*; suitcases didn't have wheels on them in those days, so you needed strong arms and back muscles to carry them.

I had just settled into my new seat when in wandered two bouncy little boys of about three and four. They were followed by their pregnant mother, who was holding a small girl who looked very sleepy, and their father, who was loaded down with bundles that looked like they would double as a tablecloth. They both spoke to the children politely in a language I'd never heard but eventually discovered was Turkish. I helped them settle the children, and they made themselves a little picnic, which they sweetly offered to share with me. But I decided to go to the dining car, whose delicious smells I could detect from six cars away. I shared my table with a Swiss businessman who spoke several languages. We ate goulash and talked about art, and he paid for my meal, which was lucky for me, because I'd overtipped the cabdriver and didn't have enough cash to cover the whole cost.

When I returned to my car, the children and the father were asleep, and the mother was singing a beautiful Turkish lullaby to her daughter. I had just gotten comfortable and was happily snoozing when the lights came on full blast and the train stopped. Two East German policemen stepped into our coach and asked to see our passports. I got mine out quickly and handed it over. They looked impatiently at me and then at the family. They probably thought we were all together until the father handed his papers to the police and spoke to them in German. They gave me back my passport and we were at peace again. The train was soon humming along the tracks on its way to Berlin. The children had slept through it all, and I, too, fell into a deep sleep with my temporary family.

It must have been about two-thirty in the morning when I was abruptly awakened by a stopping of the train followed by a backing up. I figured we were changing tracks, the way trains did in America. But when I looked out the window, I saw that we were stopped in the middle of nowhere. *They must know what they're doing,* I thought, and nearly dozed off again. Then I realized something was wrong. We had been motionless for at least half an hour, and the train's motor was turned off. Even the lights in our cabin and hall were off. It was pitch black, and the only source of light was the waxing moon. We'd made other stops along the way, but they were quick. This was weird.

In the corridor of the coach, other passengers were leaving the train with their suitcases. *In the middle of nowhere, with no station in sight?* I thought. *How strange.* Then a new conductor appeared and knocked loudly on our cabin door. "Last stop," he said in English.

What? Is he serious? I asked him where we were, but he didn't answer. He just said that we had to take our luggage and leave the train. Immediately. The mother and father started whispering, looking frantic. I didn't know what was happening as I watched the exodus of passengers. The father said to me in English, "I believe we are in a train strike."

"Strike?" I said. I remembered being at a party in New York before I left for Europe, where a guy had told me, "You'll know you're in Europe because there will be some kind of strike every other day." I guessed this was what he'd been talking about.

"Yes, the train will not go," the father said, gesturing with his hands to amplify the point. I looked around and realized that we were the last people on the train.

Then we were out on the tracks, with the children and all our baggage, looking (and feeling) like refugees in the second book of the Bible. I held one child's hand, and in my other hand I clutched my heavy suitcase. The gaps between the train rails and timber slabs were vast chasms, deep and rocky. Thank heaven for the cork soles on my high-heeled Goody Two Shoes; they provided a little cushioning.

I was freezing cold in my light summer dress, but what could I do, open my suitcase and rummage around for a sweater? I wanted off those tracks, but there was no place else to walk. Plus, I was now carrying one of the little boys, who'd fallen asleep, on my hip. "Mind over matter," I kept repeating as the muscles in my arms started to shake and my back felt nearly ready to give out. "Mind over matter." I'd lift the suitcase and step over the sharp stones onto the slabs of timber again and again, praying I wouldn't sprain an ankle in the process. *Pretend it's a game of hopscotch,* I thought cheerlessly.

We walked probably a mile to the station platform, a mass of other luggage-carrying passengers paving the way. One nice man came to help me with my bag, bless his soul, so now I had only the little boy to carry. I thanked God for that man, the stars in the sky, and the fact that it wasn't raining. When we finally reached the station, the sign was

Donna Jordan and me, near Café de Flore, Paris, 1971.

Me wearing Chloé for a photo shoot at Karl Lagerfeld's Paris apartment for *Vogue Italia*. Grace Coddington did the styling.
Courtesy of Guy Bourdin

Helmut Newton's wife, June (also known as Alice Springs), took this photo of me at the Newtons' Paris apartment, 1971.
Courtesy of Alice Springs

The boys who crowded into my room at Karl Lagerfeld's St. Tropez vacation home, 1972: Jacques de Bascher (*top*); Sylvain, Peter Lester, Billie Hall (*middle row*); Pelito Galvez, Joe MacDonald, and Kenzo's favorite model in the 1970s, Jaime Santiago Closa.

Cover shot for *Harpers & Queen*, London, 1972.
Courtesy of Barry McKinley

Me in Peter Lindbergh's second shoot for *Vogue Italia*, Rome, 1972. The image was later part of an exhibition of Lindbergh's photography that COMME des GARÇONS sponsored at Paris's Centre Georges Pompidou in 1986.
Courtesy of Peter Lindbergh

Me, being chased by the photographers Helmut Newton (*holding camera*) and Jean-Paul Goude (*wearing the white suit, at far left*) on the way to Yves Saint Laurent show, Paris, 1972.

Shoot in Mexico for *Stern*, 1972.
Courtesy of Helmut Newton

Interview cover by Richard Bernstein.
Photograph by Berry Berenson at her
apartment in New York City, 1972.
Courtesy of BMP Holdings, LLC

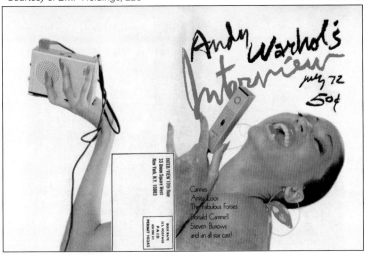

Platonic love with Richard
Bernstein on Fire Island, 1972.

(A) With Yves Saint Laurent backstage after his show, 1972. Afterward, we went to the top of the Eiffel Tower.
Courtesy of Roxanne Lowit

(B) My first time at the top of the Eiffel Tower, 1972. I went up with Roxanne Lowit, Yves Saint Laurent, and Antonio Lopez.
Courtesy of Roxanne Lowit

Relaxing with a young Massai man in a tree in Kenya, 1972. I was there for a shoot for *Harpers & Queen*.
Courtesy of Barry McKinley

Posing with the model Ted Dawson in Capri, Italy, for the cover of *GQ*, 1973.
Courtesy of Barry McKinley

With Hubert de Givenchy, walking
down the Hall of Mirrors in the
Palace of Versailles after the
fashion show, November 1973.
Courtesy of Bill Cunningham

Winter in Ethiopia, 1970.
Courtesy of Oliviero Toscani

With one of my idols, Josephine Baker,
autumn 1973, alongside Juan Fernandez
and fellow model Donyale Luna.

Me, backstage after the finale of the
Karl Lagerfeld show, Paris, 1978.
Courtesy of Roxanne Lowit

Runway finale with Thierry Mugler,
Paris, 1976.

Carrying groceries on the runway in a
Franco Moschino show, Milan, 1975.

Finally, a cover of *Vogue*: in Valentino,
photographed by François Lamy for
Vogue Italia, 1978.
Courtesy of 1978/2 September, issue 330

One of my many finales with
Valentino, Paris, 1978.

The Studio 54 gang (*from left*): Sherry Gordon, me, Steve Rubell, Grace Jones, and Potassa de la Fayette. New York City, 1977.

With another one of my idols, Diana Ross, filming *The Wiz* at the World Trade Center, New York City, 1977.

The night I sang at Régine's as Josephine Baker with my friend, Andy Warhol.

Fun shoot in my room at the Ritz in Paris, 1978. I ordered the bananas from room service.
Courtesy of Alan Kaplan

A dream come true: wearing Valentino, being
photographed by Horst for *Vogue Italia*, 1979.
Courtesy of Horst Estate

On tour in Japan, 1980, with Kenzo and
Xavier de Castella.

With my friend André Leon Talley after
the Yves Saint Laurent show, Paris, 1981.
Courtesy of Roxanne Lowit

lit: Potsdam. It was my stop! At least I wouldn't have to get on another train.

We had to climb up on the platform, which was about six feet above the tracks. The men helped the mother and her children first, then the baggage, then me, then one another. We were all exhausted, but a local train had arrived on the other track, and the passengers were directed toward it. It would take them to Berlin. Everything seemed to happen in a flash. Suddenly, the family was gone and it was just me and my pink suitcase, all alone at the station. Not a single other person remained.

I thought I'd sit in the waiting room until dawn, but no such luck: The station was locked. I made my way around the side toward the street, where one light at the end illuminated a taxi stand. I dragged my suitcase toward it and wondered where the cabs were. There was no sign of activity whatsoever. I was trying to figure out what to do next when my body made the decision for me: I fell asleep on my suitcase. I awoke to the sound of a man's voice, speaking in English with a German accent. "You are waiting for a taxi, but you will not find one at this hour in Potsdam," he said. He looked like a decent kind of guy, so I took his word for it. "I will take a room at the hotel over there." He pointed across the street. "You are welcome to stay in my room."

Although I would have given practically my right arm for a decent bed just then, the red alert went off in my head: *Danger! Danger! Strange man plus hotel room equals dead girl.* So I politely told the man a little fib, saying that one of the other passengers had gone to the parking lot for his car and was giving me a lift to my hotel. I must have been a great actress, because he fell for it, and walked across the street to his hotel with no hard feelings. That was when I realized I should have simply said, "No, thank you," because I could have gone to the hotel and sat in the lobby. But having told the lie, I was afraid he might catch me in it. That's what lying gets you: *nothing.*

So there I sat on my pink suitcase, alone by the taxi stand. There was a telephone booth, but I had no German coins to use in it. There was no music in my head, no joy, just dead, cold fear surrounding me in those dark hours before dawn. I missed home. What I would have given to be cuddled up on the couch with Mom at that moment, watching an old movie on television.

I have never been so happy to see the sun rise; its fiery presence was like a long-lost friend with a heart brimming with love. It took a long time before even one taxi showed up. When a Mercedes finally pulled over, I simply thrust Christa's telegram at the driver, with the address of the studio printed on it. I was so zonked at that point, I could barely read and didn't trust myself to pronounce the words right.

The studio was in a small factory outside town. I arrived in time for breakfast and was greeted by a woman dressed in a dark green vest, a flowered peasant skirt hitting midcalf, and white stockings (yes, long white opaque tights in summer). I'd already noticed from the cab window that this was how most of the women on the streets of Potsdam dressed. The woman paid for my taxi, then gave me a tour, first through rooms where women were knitting by hand or on knitting machines, and then into the studio, where I was welcomed in both English and German and immediately offered cheeses and meats from a lavish buffet. I ate and ate all day long, even between shots.

The photo shoot, which was for the factory's catalog, went well into the evening, with me struggling not to show my exhaustion. I drank coffee but no beer, which everyone else, even the stylists, guzzled as if it were soda pop. (Beer for the Germans is a lot like wine for the French.) Everything was extremely efficient, and at the end of the workday, I was handed an envelope full of deutsche marks. I felt deeply gratified. As the taxi drove me to the train station to catch the train to Berlin, followed by the night train to Paris, all I could think about was the little bed of my own that I'd have in the sleeping car. My desire for that bed was so intense, it was almost like a sexual fantasy.

That night on the train, a gorgeous, delectable-looking young man delivered a dinner menu to my cabin. I ordered my meal, trying not to stare. I mean, this guy was handsomeness personified, a tall, slim drink of deliciousness. He returned minutes later with my dinner. When I was done eating, I was disappointed to see that someone else came to take my dishes away. But then *he* came back into the cabin to prepare the berth and turn down the covers. He kept his eyes on me as he fixed the bed, and I must have given him some signal, because in the middle of the night, he came back.

I woke up right away. I grabbed him, and he grabbed me, the wheels of the train gliding smoothly on the rails beneath us. I let go of the bag of pistachios that I'd fallen asleep gripping, and within seconds we were both naked. From that point on, my hormones were in charge. Every so often, as we lusted away, a small part of my brain would step back and ask, *Is this acceptable behavior?* But I was too distracted to pay attention.

After my German-Italian lover (I did find out that much about him, along with his name, Roy G. Biv) left my cabin to return to duty, I looked in the mirror and thought, *You are someone who just had sex with a total stranger.* Later, as I lounged in my seat, cracking pistachios all the way to Paris, I actually laughed out loud, savoring my secret and my new recreational sport—men!

chapter 37

ENGLAND SWINGS

Me with the fabulous designer
Zandra Rhodes in the *Vogue*
studios, London, 1971.
Courtesy of Clive Arrowsmith.

As Wilhelmina had predicted, Europe was more accepting of me than America was; relocating there was a good career move for me. Somehow the Europeans seemed less hung up on race and on labels, and they appeared to have moved away from the lily-white, blond, blue-eyed ideal of beauty that retained a tight grip on the imaginations of magazine editors and art directors in the States. In Europe, my color just wasn't an issue. Or if it was, I didn't notice because I was too busy: The year 1971 was shaping up to be my most successful yet as a model, as I appeared in top magazines in both Europe and America and walked the runway for all the collections on both continents (as well as in Japan for Kenzo). For the first time I felt my career was on solid ground, and as my experience widened, I gained confidence that I'm sure made me more appealing to clients. It was kind of like playing an instrument: The more you practice, the better you get, and the more people want to hear your music.

But if I was thriving professionally, I sometimes felt a bit out of control personally. A typical week might find me in Milan on Monday, back in Paris on Tuesday, and off to London on Thursday for five days. My body—and mind—felt the strain. My old back injury flared up, and my feet ached incessantly. If there was an airborne virus, I'd catch it. (It turns out that sixteen-hour days and a diet of croissants and croques monsieurs tossed back with champagne aren't the best ways to build up resistance.) I'd vacillate between feeling adventurous and up for anything and exhausted, sick, and ready to collapse. And more than a little homesick. On balance, though, the ups certainly outweighed the downs, and I knew how lucky I was.

My first trip from France requiring air travel was to London, where I was introduced, in roughly this order, to: (1) a whole new batch of delightful accents (including Cockney, in a monologue from my Heathrow taxi driver that had me in stitches); (2) left-side-of-the-road driving (which had me clutching the car handle with white knuckles); (3) British *Vogue*'s legendary Grace Coddington (a flame-haired, Pre-Raphaelite beauty who was a consummate professional); (4) the great photographer Norman Parkinson (who'd just finished photographing Princess Anne and scared me when he said, "You are very odd-looking, not at all the kind of model I am used to photographing," since the phrasing was so similar to that of the snobby Patrick Lichfield, whose elevator was the scene of my near rape—but unlike Lichfield, Norman was joking); (5) the brilliant hairdresser Didier Malige of Jean Louis David in Paris ("Not to be confused with Jacques-Louis David, the history painter," he said endearingly before offering to do my hair); (6) my lovely, maternal English agent, Eileen Green (who is hands-down one of the nicest people I've ever met); and (7) compliments of Eileen, a proper cup of English tea and scones with clotted cream and jam (which—need I even say it?—I fell in love with on first bite). And that was just in my first four hours in the country!

I learned so much from that *Vogue* shoot with Grace Coddington and Norman Parkinson, and I had so much fun doing it (Parkinson could have been Bartholomew Cubbins from the Kingdom of Didd because he put on a different crazy hat for every shot), that I developed a permanent soft spot for London and the United Kingdom as a whole. I met some of my favorite people and had some of my most unforgettable adventures on British soil.

On my second trip, I stayed at Eileen's house in London. I had gotten back very late at night after finishing a shoot in a remote London pub with David Bailey, the hottest photographer in England, if not the world. The next day Eileen woke me with a tray laden with toast, marmalade, a hard-boiled egg, and a pretty flower in a vase—and some exciting news. "Guess what, my dear?" she said. "You have a job for a very important show, and the designer is Mr. Yves Saint Laurent. But you must get over there as soon as you have breakfast. It's close to eleven. I let you sleep in."

Meeting Yves Saint Laurent was a dream come true, and my heart began to race at the very possibility. He was a hero of mine, not only because I loved his designs but also because he was one of the first French couturiers to use black models on the runway. I cursed myself for leaving my Saint Laurent dress—the one I'd bought on Madison Avenue the day Halston hired me—back in Paris. My Stephen Burrows wrap dress was a good second choice. I threw it on, and in no time, I was bumping along on the wrong side of the street in a big English taxi, headed to the London Planetarium for a charity fashion show.

I felt as though I'd entered the bottom of a fish bowl when I looked up at the building's dome, with the entire universe displayed on it via a twenty-foot-tall projector that stood in the center of the room. Wrapped around the projector was a narrow catwalk. I had never seen such a peculiar space for a show: proof to me of how eccentric (if charmingly so) the English could be.

During the rehearsal, I could hardly concentrate on walking that perilous platform, which was seven feet above the floor, because I was so distracted by the intricate dance of stars, planets, and constellations on the ceiling. There was a choreographer backstage, and lots of English models, hairdressers, and dressers. It was nothing like a Seventh Avenue show or, for that matter, anything I'd ever done. With thirty different outfits to change into, which wasn't unusual back then, I felt like a celestial body moving in an elliptical orbit around a star, the star being

Yves Saint Laurent, who was sitting somewhere in the audience, hidden among the hundreds of other stars held together by their adoration of fashion. I had seen him once in Paris, on the day his collection was being shown. He had driven himself right up to the door of the building in a black Volkswagen Beetle, jumped out without locking the doors, and quickly gone inside. Imagine—no Rolls, no entourage (boy, those were the days)! He had looked like a sexy bookworm, quite handsome, with a luscious mane of hair that turned golden in the sunlight, oddly geeky and shy-seeming, with those oversize black glasses.

As I returned backstage to change, the dressers were buzzing about the fact that Princess Margaret, Queen Elizabeth's younger sister, was supposedly in the audience. I'd had a special interest in Princess Margaret ever since I'd seen her royal wedding to Antony Armstrong-Jones (a commoner, my mother had explained) on television when I was a child. Now there were two people in the audience I desperately wanted to impress. I resolved to do my best show ever.

In the end, Saint Laurent didn't even come onstage, though I did get to see him from a distance when a spotlight lit him in the audience. Backstage, all the models had somewhere to rush off to. Disappointed at not meeting Monsieur Saint Laurent, I changed back into my beautiful Stephen dress and left by myself. Eileen had said she'd have a cab waiting for me at the end of the show, so I made my way to the Planetarium's entrance, where the crowd was filing into the lobby and a small reception was taking place.

There were so many people that I just went with the flow—it was shoulder to shoulder—and found myself in an exhibition of carnival mirrors. I stopped in my tracks and looked into the mirrors and started to have fun with them, bending this way and that, just playing while I waited for the crowd to thin out. It was full of the crème de la crème of London society, and I got a kick out of seeing the whole scene distorted behind me in the mirrors, like a kaleidoscope of reality. The stream of people was so thick that I had to stand closer to the mirrors, and at one point, I almost lost my balance. I felt my high heel step back on to something soft, like clothing. I looked down at the floor and saw that I was standing on the hem of a woman's dress.

"Oh, dear," a voice said, and the entire crowd stopped moving. When

I turned my head, I realized the person whose dress I'd stepped on was none other than Her Royal Highness Princess Margaret. She even had on her tiara. She smiled and toasted me with the drink in her hand. I was almost too stunned too respond, but then, as if on cue, we both turned to the carnival mirrors and started to laugh. I was so much taller than she was, but the mirrors' distortions were an equalizer: They rendered us both with short legs, wide bodies, and little arms. Like children, we bent and weaved for a couple of moments, looking over our shoulders at our backsides, giggling.

Then she extended her free hand, bedecked with jeweled rings, and took mine, and we stepped and shifted to the next mirror and repeated the routine. As we laughed out loud at ourselves for looking so silly, we were no longer a royal and a commoner, a princess and a pauper—just two innocent kids being free and having fun. Then someone in her royal retinue pulled her away, and she walked back onto the carpet and into her official role as British royalty.

That encounter with Princess Margaret taught me that when it comes to joy, there are no class barriers.

ℰℐ

My next trip to England was to be photographed a second time by the enigmatic Guy Bourdin. Believe it or not, I was even colder on this shoot than I was on that first one with Donna. *Way* colder. The client was Max Factor, so I was really excited. *I'm going to represent the makeup of the Hollywood stars!* I told myself. Guy's brilliant idea was to paint me blue and photograph me nude on a platform in the middle of the North Sea. Oh, and did I mention that this was in January? Not only was the paint itself itchy and uncomfortable, but I couldn't cover myself between takes, because the paint would peel off. I was blue with cold underneath the blue paint; my goose pimples had goose pimples. Christine, the sweet assistant whom I'd worked with on other shoots, kept saying, "You poor darling, you poor darling."

The assistants were all standing knee-deep in the water, waiting for the master to show up. When he did finally, he stood on scaffolding as I was carried out into the sea—which was gusting with high waves—and placed on a tiny plank of wood on my belly, facedown. As I looked into the water just below me, I could hear Guy shouting out, "Stay straight," so I stretched my arms and legs out as far as I could and balanced my weight on my abdominal muscles and held that position. I actually muttered to myself, "You are a seagull, and flying over this water is natural to you." Without this pep talk, I'm not sure I would have made it through the whole ordeal.

The waves kept moving, the metal pole holding the plank kept swaying from side to side, and I kept peeking to see whether Guy was shooting or if I had been left there to die. Every muscle in my body was screaming for help when I saw the assistants and crew bundle up onshore in their coats and blankets. *Please, God, let him get the shot, please hurry up, please, please, please,* I begged as the cold entered my lungs—a heavy, damp feeling. I was there, naked, in the dead of winter, for a good half hour before I was released and back on dry land.

Two days later, I was in bed with pneumonia at the Portobello Hotel, as sick as I can ever remember being.

chapter 38

I'M A BELIEVER

For one of my first modeling jobs in
England, I got to hang out with Teddy
Boys at the Swan Club in London, 1971.
Courtesy of David Bailey.

Despite enduring that epic bout of pneumonia, I have fond memories
of the Portobello, a boutique hotel in Notting Hill that was a favorite
of the music and fashion crowd back in the seventies. I had memorable
encounters there with more cool people than I can recount, but two in
particular stand out.

The first was Mick Jagger, whom I met when I was at my sickest. I got
a call from a London friend who told me there had been a Mick sighting
at the Portobello and that if I didn't go down to the dining room immediately to meet him, he would come over and drag me down there himself.

"I can't," I said. "I'm in bed. I think I'm going to die."

"You can die later. You have to meet Mick. Do it for me. Promise."

I staggered out of bed and looked in the bathroom mirror. The face staring back resembled the survivor of a shipwreck. I gulped down two of the antibiotics the doctor had prescribed (he'd made a house call to my hotel room) and felt so dizzy that I dropped my glass of water. The phone rang again.

"Are you dressed?" asked my friend.

"Not yet, I—"

"Go. Now. Before he leaves. Or else I won't speak to you again." And he hung up.

I went to the closet, pulled on a colorful dress, and left my room for the first time in two days. The front-desk clerks looked startled to see me, since the meal trays they'd been leaving at my door had gone untouched. I smiled at them wanly and walked down the short stairway to the dining room. And then I saw him sitting alone at a table by the bar.

The room was spinning, and I had just decided to turn around when Mick looked up at me with big bright eyes and smiled. He was the cutest thing on two legs, with so much hair that he looked like a fourteen-year-old. He gave me a nod and I nodded back. What did that mean? Then he did it again, which said to me, *Why don't you come over?* So I did.

"Hello!" he said in the unplaceable British accent that his critics like to call "mockney."

"Good morning," I replied in American.

"I'm waiting for breakfast," he said. "They're slow."

I couldn't concentrate, and the room seemed to be spinning, so I sat down next to him on the bench to regroup. It was a tiny space, so we were sitting very close. We looked at each other.

"I'm Pat," I said.

"I'm Mick," he said. "Nice to meet you."

Just then an exotic-looking, dark-haired girl walked over to us, gave me a dirty look, and sat down across from Mick. She looked like she wanted to take a bite out of me. Mick looked awkwardly at me, then at her, then at me. "This is Pat," he said finally.

"Really?" the dark-haired girl said, watchful, like a lion protecting her cub.

"Excuse me," I said. "Nice to meet you both. Don't let me disturb you."

I slid out over the leather bench and went back to my room, where I promptly fainted. When I woke up, the concierge was beside my bed with a doctor. I was in that hotel room for a week, with the doctor visiting daily, until my fever broke.

It wasn't until 1975, some three years later, that Mick and I finally had some fun together. He was between relationships: His first marriage, to the dark-haired girl I'd met that morning, Bianca Pérez-Mora Macias, had ended (though they weren't officially divorced), and he had not yet met his second wife, my good friend Jerry Hall (I'd gotten to know her in Paris through Antonio, who was crazy about her and thought—correctly—that she and I would hit it off).

Mick and I reconnected in New York through the photographer Ara Gallant, a friend of both of ours. Mick was in town and wanted to go out with a nice girl and asked Ara if he knew anyone. Ara suggested me, and I thought, *Why not?* So it was arranged that I would meet Mick at the Sherry-Netherland Hotel at midnight.

I was really nervous walking into that grand Manhattan hotel, especially since I knew Mick was somewhere in the tower, hiding under the fake name. I'd written it down in case I forgot it, because the people staffing the front desk would show me the door if I asked for Mick Jagger. "Mr. Lawrence" was the password I must whisper to the gatekeepers of this hidden treasure.

When I got to the suite, the door was ajar, so in I walked. Voices were coming from down the hall, and I followed them until I saw Mick standing there talking to the rest of the Rolling Stones: Keith Richards, Charlie Watts, and Ronnie Wood. They were all sitting on the sofa, smoking. On a low coffee table by their feet sat a pizza box, overflowing ashtrays, beer cans, and empty champagne bottles. Keith Richards saw me and pointed. Mick turned around. "Hi! You made it. I'm Mr. Lawrence. No, I'm Mick."

"No, you're not Mick." Keith laughed, plucking on his guitar in slow motion.

Mick and I shook hands, but then Ronnie shouted, "Kiss her!" so Mick kissed me on the cheek. "There, satisfied?" he said to his band-

mates. "I'm going out. You'd better be ready to work when I get back."
He turned to me and said, "These guys are so lazy . . ."

There was an awkward pause while Mick hatched a plan. "I have a
car downstairs. You hungry?"

"Sure," I said.

Mick and I got in the elevator. When the doorman opened the front
door, Mick poked his head out and said, "Got to see if the coast is clear."
We ran for the car and dove into the backseat.

"Where to, sir?" said the driver.

"To that little Italian place on Eighth Avenue."

"The same one as last night?"

"Yeah," said Mick. "I go there after the studio," he explained to me.
"It's not too far."

Gosh, this is a real date, I thought.

"I can only go out late at night," he said. "Fewer people around, more
space just to be."

I recognized the restaurant as a place Ara liked. We sat down at a
table in the back and ate American-style spaghetti and meatballs and
drank red wine. When we got back to the hotel, we went straight to his
suite, which was fancy and candlelit, and he set the scene by throwing
rose petals over a fur throw. I thought this was romantic and stylish, and
soon we were making love.

Afterward we lay in bed next to each other and talked and talked
about our shared love of music, art, and fashion. I knew he was the
biggest rock-and-roll star on the planet, but to me he came across as a
vulnerable boy, especially when he mentioned his earliest years in England during World War II. At one point, Mick jumped up, put on his
Chinese silk robe, and did the strangest thing. He just stood there at
the foot of the bed looking at me, as though taking a picture with his
eyes. And then the moment passed and we fooled around some more,
like two kittens.

I fell asleep, and when I woke up it was morning and time to go to
my booking. That evening Mick called and we met again for dinner. He
took me home in his limo—I was living at the Upper East Side townhouse of my beloved agent, Zoli Rendessy (with whom I signed after
Wilhelmina accused me of "tarnishing" her agency's reputation by ap-

pearing in a spaghetti western, something I never did, by the way)—but instead of saying goodbye, Mick came in with me and sneaked up to the room where I was staying, which had a piano in it. We kissed a bit, and then he saw the piano. "Nice," he said. "You play?"

"Just for fun," I said. I'd been practicing a little, because I had my heart set on launching a singing career at some point. The two of us sat down at the keyboard. He played a few chords pianissimo, and we rhymed words together, laughing so hard that the maid in the house knocked on the door and told us to pipe down. She padded away, never realizing she'd just shushed the front man of the greatest rock-and-roll band in the world.

Mick and I tried to be as quiet as mice. We whispered the words, and he told me that the vowels are the most important part to sing, and that the higher I sang, the better. I was thrilled to get this advice (the *vowels?* who knew?), and I thanked him profusely as I walked him to the front door. With one last kiss, we said goodbye.

"Tomorrow?" he said.

"Tomorrow," I said.

But Mick got caught up in his work, and I in mine, and it was nearly a week before I heard from him. He invited me over to his studio. He talked to the tech guys for a while, we grabbed dinner, and then he had to return to the studio to record. By then, it was two in the morning, and I had an early-morning booking, so I bade him good night. How could I have known it would be years before I'd see Mick again, and by that time he'd be with Jerry and I'd be cast in the role of her old pal from the Paris days?

∾

The other Portobello-related incident that stays with me was the hand-written note left there for me by another English rock star. I met Ringo Starr in 1972 because I'd heard through a hairdresser friend in London that the film studio of Apple Corps, the production company formed by the Beatles when they were still together, needed an actress for the opening scene of a film they were shooting. I wanted to break into acting almost as much as I wanted to be a singer (even at that relatively early stage in my career, I sensed that modeling wouldn't be enough to satisfy my artistic yearnings), so the next morning my friend took me to the studio and said to the director, "This is the perfect girl." I was sitting in a chair in the waiting room, not knowing whether I'd end up doing anything or not, when someone popped her head out and asked, "Are you ready?"

I was incredibly nervous, but I jumped up and said, "Yes, yes, of course."

She said, "Did you bring anything to wear?"

I said, "Yes, I have this." I produced my Blue Angel dress and gold spray-painted Goody Two Shoes high heels, which I adored even though they pinched my toes something awful.

"Well, put it on," she said, and I retreated to the bathroom in the hallway to change. When I got onto the set, I realized how different shooting movies was from shooting still photos. The lighting was much more dependent on natural light, and best of all, I didn't have to stand motionless and wait for the shot. I could move! There was a blower on the set that hit my dress just so; its pleats billowed up and flowed behind me, my hair blew back, and with my posture as erect as I've ever had it, I probably looked like the emblem on the front of a Rolls-Royce.

When the director announced a break (I can't recall the name of the film, and I'm not sure it was ever released), I walked out on the terrace and sat down on a bench to give my feet a rest. Someone said, "Hello there," and I looked up and it was Ringo. The first things I noticed were his hands. On every finger, he wore a big chunky silver band—the accessory that had earned him his moniker—and he was dressed in a silk indigo-blue suit with a purple satin shirt. He asked, "What are you into?" and we chatted about colors. I told him that I saw colors every day, and he told me he did, too. "When I was in New York," he said, "I saw everything yellow—yellow cabs, yellow traffic lights." It was a playful conversation, and he ended it by asking me to join him and some friends for dinner that night.

The dinner was in the private dining room of a private townhouse restaurant. There were three couples—Ringo was with Maureen, his first wife—and me, seated around a big round table. I sat next to Ringo, and at one point he asked me, "How do you like London?"

"I love it," I replied. "I can't believe I'm here!"

He smiled and said, "Well, luv, you got to believe in believing." *Believe in believing*. It was a throwaway line, but I found it oddly profound, and it has stuck with me all these years. The next morning, the desk clerk at the Portobello handed me an envelope. Inside was a handwritten note on stationery, "Apple Corps Ltd." embossed at the top along with the company logo, the image of a green apple. It read:

Dear Pat,
   Thank you for being straight.
                           Love, Ringo

chapter 39

OF THEE I SING, BABY

On stage at the Versailles fashion show, 1973,
for the curtain call just after the finale with
Liza Minnelli (*left*). I'm at the far right.

$\mathcal{A}$*fterward,* a lot of people said, "It was just like the war. Versailles
was crumbling. And who swooped in to put it back together? The big,
brash Americans."

That's a simplification, of course, and it's not quite the way I remember the so-called Battle of Versailles, a now legendary fashion show
at France's Palace of Versailles in November 1973. The event, in which
French designers competed against American ones, was a fund-raiser to
repair the palace's rapidly deteriorating roof. The American "victory"
came against all odds; we were definitely the underdog. Still, I'll admit
that it felt great for this sometime expat to be on the American side that
night, especially since we not only showed critics on both sides of the
Atlantic that American fashion could hold its own against the very best
in the world, but we also made history with the record number of black
models who participated.

Out of the thirty-six models used by the five American designers included in the show, ten of us were African-American: Billie Blair, Beth-ann Hardison, Amina Warsuma, Charlene Dash, Ramona Saunders, Norma Jean Darden, Barbara Jackson, Alva Chinn, Jennifer Brice, and me. En masse, the three dozen girls who walked the show ranged from the lightest-complected blondes and redheads to the darkest-skinned brunettes. We were the original United Colors of Benetton, a living, breathing emblem of America in all its glorious diversity. In 1973 that was a breakthrough of epic proportions (and a sweet vindication for me, since I'd had to move to Europe to find more acceptance), and like everything else that happened that night, it was proof positive that times were changing.

The show, the brainchild of Eleanor Lambert, pitted five French couturiers who were considered *the* preeminent fashion virtuosos in the world—Yves Saint Laurent, Hubert de Givenchy, Pierre Cardin, Eman-uel Ungaro, and Marc Bohan of Christian Dior—against five on-fire American designers: Anne Klein (who was accompanied by her pregnant number two, Donna Karan), Oscar de la Renta, Bill Blass, Halston, and Stephen Burrows. It was very much Old World versus New.

It was just after Thanksgiving, which I'd spent in New Jersey with my mom and stepfather, who'd bought a house there soon after I'd left for Europe. They seemed to be doing okay—moving out of the city had been good for them—but I still loathed Sonny and constantly had to hide my revulsion from Mom. Besides, extreme cold had already come to the New York area, so a free trip to France was just the thing to brighten my mood.

On the flight over, the Versailles-bound crew felt like we were having a private party, with free-flowing champagne, singing, and dancing in the aisles. The clothes were all in the belly of the plane; as far as I and my fellow models were concerned, we had everything we needed to put on a terrific show. The pay was low (as in really, *really* low), but our pride was high because we knew we were the best walking girls in the business, and we were being asked to help rescue Versailles from ruin. Our attitude was like Mighty Mouse's: "Here we come to save the day!"

In Paris, a bus took us from Orly Airport to the Hotel Saint Jacques in the Latin Quarter. The digs were perfectly fine but hardly at the level of the Plaza Athénée, which was where Oscar de la Renta was staying.

We girls bunked together, two or three to a room, and slept until another bus came at the crack of dawn to take us to the palace for rehearsal.

At Versailles, the snowflakes fell like lace on the fragile rooftop, and the cobblestones in the courtyard glistened as everybody got off the bus. Like schoolgirls, we tried to catch snowflakes on our tongues; we didn't mind the cold, because we figured we'd be warm inside. *Wrong.* The space was tiny, damp, and drafty. This was the first trip to Europe for some of the girls, and what a rude awakening it must have been: no central heating, no food, and worst of all, ancient toilets that lacked even the simplest amenities—like *toilet paper!* By the time the designers joined us, it was nearly dark, and we girls were like sheep huddling together just to keep warm. When they saw what was going on, Stephen Burrows and Anne Klein spoke up and managed to get us some cheese sandwiches.

Meanwhile, out front, Halston, Bill Blass, and Oscar de la Renta were trying to get our segment of the show set up, but it was no-go because the stage crew union had called it quits for the day. Then Bill, Halston, and Oscar's wife, Françoise (an editor at French *Vogue*), got into a tiff over the order in which the designers should go. Stephen was his easygoing self, and Oscar really didn't care; he was busy rounding up his models to go back to his suite at the Plaza Athénée for a stealth rehearsal.

For now, though, we were supposed to rehearse at Versailles, and everything seemed to be going wrong. Halston's good friend Liza Minnelli was to open the American show, and in addition to being a model for the designers, I was one of Liza's backup dancers. Kay Thompson, Liza's godmother, was set to choreograph and direct. Kay was an idol of mine because she'd written one of my favorite children's books, *Eloise*, and had coached Audrey Hepburn in one of my favorite movies, *Funny Face.* I was overjoyed just to meet her, let alone work with her.

Kay was standing downstage with Halston when Liza's backup dancers, including me, went onstage to rehearse the opening number. (Liza was arriving the next day.) From where I stood, Kay and Halston appeared to be quarreling. She was waving her long arms and making hand motions at the stage as Halston pointed here and there with his extended cigarette holder. His face was contorted in anger, and so was hers.

Meanwhile, Joe Eula, the celebrated fashion illustrator who'd been recruited to design a stage set, looked traumatized, and the reason was evident. He had painted a very large Eiffel Tower on an even larger swath of seamless paper, but on that humongous stage, with its forty-five-foot-high ceiling, the painting looked like a hand towel flapping on a clothesline.

There was no lighting, no stage assistants, no stage crew. It was midnight when we were told the obvious: The rehearsal would have to wait until morning. So it was back in the bus and off to Oscar's semisecret rehearsal at the Athénée, where we ate caviar and drank champagne as Oscar directed our show number, featuring Billie Blair as a genie who charmed the rest of us into dancing in a circle around her and set to the music of Barry White's Love Unlimited Orchestra. By the time we got back to our hotel, it was nearly time to get up. Billie and I flopped down on our queen-size bed and slept in our clothes until the bus came at six-thirty to take us back to the palace.

The first thing we learned was that Kay Thompson had walked off the job. She couldn't handle the infighting among the designers, so she quit. At least the Opéra Royale stage was buzzing with activity—even if it was all for the French designers. There were three hundred people working up there, including the famous French hairdresser Alexandre de Paris. I couldn't believe how much scenery was being moved on and off the stage. There were enough sets, by Jean-François Daigre, for five operettas and two orchestras. Meanwhile, the Americans had Joe Eula's hand towel and a master cassette tape.

Baroness Marie-Hélène de Rothschild, one of the show's French organizers, was trying to assist us Americans, but she kept complaining to the French designers that we hadn't spent enough money for props. and that we had no orchestra. Finally, she just left, and we waited as the French conducted their leisurely rehearsal. They had corralled some big-name performers: Rudolf Nureyev, Zizi Jeanmaire, Capucine, the nude dancers from Paris's Crazy Horse, and the legendary Josephine Baker (who, it's worth pointing out, could as easily be claimed by the Americans, since she was born in Saint Louis—a city she left because *my* great-aunt Leanna had urged her to do so!).

On my way to the bathroom, I sneaked out of our dressing space to watch the French rehearsals. I was running so fast in my high heels through the dark backstage area that I accidentally stepped on Nureyev's toe as he prepared to leap onto the stage. He shot me an irritated look but didn't miss a beat. I stood behind the curtain and watched him dance flawlessly to *Swan Lake*. When I rushed back to our dressing area to tell the others what was going on out front, Billie decided to come with me to "use the loo."

This time a group of dancers was encircling a tall woman with a feathered headdress. In the middle stood Josephine Baker, decked out as a showgirl. This was a larger-than-life, near-mythic figure whom I'd been hearing about since childhood; she was an inextricable part of my personal folklore. I couldn't just stand there and gape. "Come on, Billie," I said. "Let's say hello."

"No, no, I can't," Billie said, pushing me forward. "You go, Patty."

"Okay, I will," I said, but I hooked my arm in hers and brought her along with me. We were both shaking in our high heels, and then I noticed Billie duck behind Josephine and begin to pluck feathers out of Josephine's boas. I don't think anyone noticed, but I looked so guilty as I was saying hello to Josephine that she must have thought I was strange. Sixty-seven at the time, Josephine was dressed in a nude catsuit, her long legs covered in fishnet stockings with pearls dripping off them. Her headdress of ostrich plumes was so enormous and high that I figured whatever balance she had came from having to hold up that thing. She had on eyelashes so heavy that all I could see of her eyes were two tiny twinkling slits. She gave me the briefest of smiles, like a silent film star, as I said hello. I would have loved to say, "My great-aunt Leanna—the music teacher who told you to get out of St. Louis—is the reason you're here today," but the guards caught Billie and me watching her from the wings and ordered us to return to our dressing area.

Billie was so proud of her stolen plucked feathers that she handed me a piece of her plunder. "Here, Patty, these feathers will make us stars, too," she said, hugging me. I still have that scraggly black feather—and I *still* think it's magic. If nothing else, it reminds me that I managed to meet the great Josephine Baker before she died, which happened less than two years later.

The French rehearsal took most of the day, and by the time we got use of the stage, the stage union had quit again. This time Halston literally put his foot down—he stamped it hard on the floor and threatened to walk out. His little temper tantrum worked; mysteriously, they were back on the job. But the lighting assistants were not helping, and we had the biggest star in the world—Liza Minnelli, who had just come off a Best Actress Oscar win for *Cabaret*—opening the show. We were forced to rehearse with a simple spotlight, and that was when the eureka moment came: no sets, just spotlights! Genius. Necessity *is* the mother of invention.

Joe Eula helped each designer with his lighting—lots of pale blue, rose, and magenta—and since the music was already in order on the cassettes, all we had to do was be in our place on time. Each of the designers directed his own section in rehearsal: Bill Blass went first for seven minutes, followed by Stephen, then Anne Klein, then Halston, then Oscar. Somehow we just pulled together as a team. We finished rehearsals at around half past nine, and there was a party to attend at Maxim's, given in Liza's honor. Finally, a fun night out in Paris. I table-hopped all night long, hobnobbing with the likes of the Duchess of Windsor and Andy Warhol, and once again got to sleep in the early-morning hours.

The sight of Le Château de Versailles as we approached on the bus the evening of the show was one of the most magical scenes I have ever witnessed: It felt like being inside a snow globe as snowflakes drifted down on the lit-up palace. We entered through the front gates, and everything seemed golden and full of life.

None of us could see any of the French portion of the show beyond what went on backstage, though I did hear that Princess Grace of Monaco was in the audience. A giant pumpkin, like a Cinderella coach, was rolled onto the stage, and we were told that a ballerina would bounce out of it during the Dior show and dance to the music of Prokofiev. We couldn't hear the music from where we were standing. It seemed so silent, it was hard to believe a show was going on out there.

I knew that Josephine Baker was the finale of the French portion of the show, and missing that one killed me. I would have given anything to sit out front and watch her. But as one of the girls in our gang said, too bad, too sad. We realized the first half of the show was over only when someone came backstage and said there would be a champagne interval, the way there is at the theater. *Well, why not?* I thought. *This* is *theater.*

Then it was showtime. The backup dancers took their place onstage, with the heavy curtains still closed. We could hear the audience milling around, getting back to seats. We lined up like racehorses behind Liza. My place was in the second row after the lead dancers; I kept a good eye on a dancer in front of me so I wouldn't miss a step.

"Bonjour, Paris!" Liza shouted as the curtain rose. Then she began to sing: "I want to step out on the Champs-Élysées . . ." and I could feel goose bumps all over my body as those of us onstage started to step in sync to the music. We were moving as fast as our feet could go; the energy level was sky-high. It seemed like only an instant before the opening number was over and the audience was applauding wildly. I quickly shuffled offstage to change into my first outfit for Anne Klein. Everything was going fast-fast-fast. The next thing I knew, I was running to change into Stephen's finale dress—a hot pastel multicolored creation with a dragon-tail train—and the trumpets and funky R&B guitar of Al Green's "Love and Happiness" enveloped the whole theater. The lyrics were all about loving, and I thought, *That's what we're here to do—to spread the love and happiness.*

The show was moving like a locomotive, and my heart was beating to match. I moved to center stage, where I would come into the spotlight to walk the stage alone. But Bethann was to walk out first, and she got an unexpected case of stage fright. She turned to me and said, "I can't go out there." I decided to make a joke of it: "If you don't go out there, I will kick you out. Just do it!" I gave her a reassuring look, and she seemed to take a gulp of air as she strode out like a warrior, feather and bone in her hair and a defiant look on her face. By now the crowd was really warmed up; they'd seen all these beautiful black girls onstage, and Bethann was the crowning glory. Then it was my turn. The drums beat out *Love and happiness / Love is . . .* In order to keep the beat, I had to hold my long train in my hand. As I walked, I picked up speed, waving the train about as though it weighed nothing, until I got to the front of the stage. And then—bam!—I dropped it hard with attitude and made a sharp turn. I could feel the weight of the train dragging behind me almost the length of the entire stage. As swiftly as I could, I returned to the top of the stage to meet the other girls, and when I turned again, the funky drumbeat picked up. This was the kind of runway move—more like a dance—that

I had become known for and loved through and through. (Years later, *Vogue* would describe my style as "Broadway meets flamenco," and I think that gets it about right.) I was the point of the arrow for the girls to follow in a V formation behind me, spreading out downstage in the blue light as Stephen had told us, an arrow shot from Cupid's bow straight into our audience's heart. With Al Green's voice lifting us up, we could do no wrong. The audience simply *had* to fall in love with us.

Posing there at the front of the stage in our V, we looked out into the audience. This was the true origin of voguing, where it really began, with us walking girls. We were just happy moving with the rhythm of the music, like waves to the shore, coming at the audience, who went crazy wild, standing up, cheering, almost dancing along with us. Talk about the power of love. They felt it, all right.

Stephen's presentation stole the show, and I was over the moon for him. But there was no time to bask in the applause; I had another solo number for Halston. I rushed to change into his evening dress, constructed of layers of beige chiffon. The music from Visconti's *The Damned,* with its classical guitar, played as we Halston girls—Elsa Peretti, Marisa Berenson, China Machado, and a few others who usually did H's shows—posed in sharp beams of pin lighting. The choreography was by Martha Graham, with whom Halston and Joe Eula had consulted when Kay Thompson quit so abruptly.

Onstage, Elsa carried a silver compact that she'd designed, China fluttered a black raven-feathered fan with a silver handle over her bare breasts, and Marisa wore transparent sequins. Then it was my turn in the spotlight.

Alone onstage, in complete silence, I could see nothing. Everything was blacked out except one dramatic beam of light that waited for me. I started spinning into it in my mind even before I left backstage, and within seconds the spotlight was following me. All I could hear was Halston's voice in my head shouting, *Spin, spin!* And I did. All I could feel were the layers and layers of chiffon, a vortex all around me in which I was spinning. I was on the very edge of the stage until I was virtually in the audience; such was my momentum. But somehow I managed to grip the soles of my high-heeled sandals with the balls of my feet and prayed that I would stop before I tumbled into the crowd. My prayers were answered: I made a dead stop, and then the vortex of chiffon reversed itself and I started to twirl and spin at high velocity in the other direction. What had come over me? I'm not sure, but something held me in balance. I heard the roar of applause and whistles, and my heart felt as though it would pop from joy.

The rest of the show was a blur. I joined the other girls in Oscar's number as Billie's genie hypnotized us to the swirling violins of Barry White's Love Unlimited Orchestra. I didn't take part in Bill Blass's section of the show, which was Gatsbyesque, with music by Cole Porter, because I had no time to change.

Then the curtain dropped and all the models were back onstage, dressed in black and seated at tables for a restaurant scene. Liza came out to center stage and threw us all a big kiss. The curtain rose, the spotlight was aimed, and Liza stepped into it, surrounded by rainbows. In her appearance and her movements, she looked so much like her mother, Judy Garland, that if you'd squinted, you would have sworn it was Judy herself up there.

As Liza sang and danced like the world-class entertainer she was, everyone in that palace—onstage, backstage, in the wings, and in the audience (where people were throwing their programs in the air like confetti)—knew without a doubt that American royalty was in residence at Versailles.

chapter 40

COME SAIL AWAY

Mombasa, Kenya, 1973.
Courtesy of Barry McKinley.

I looked up from my game of shuffleboard and took in the craggy face of one of the world's natural wonders: the Rock of Gibraltar. A shiver ran down my spine. *This,* I thought, *is the reason I became a model and not a designer—to see sights like this instead of being stuck in an office.*

I was aboard the S.S. *Michelangelo,* and we were maneuvering through the Strait of Gibraltar en route to Genoa, Italy, the ship's home port. The photographer Barry McKinley had chosen me to be part of a big fashion feature for *GQ* magazine that we'd been shooting as we sailed across the Atlantic on this magnificent ocean liner. I was the only woman; the other three models in our group—Peter Keating, Tony Spinelli, and Ted Dawson—were male (and totally gorgeous). After Genoa, we were going to Capri, and from there, Barry, Peter, and I would take another boat to Mombasa, Kenya, and then fly from there to the interior for another photo shoot for *Harpers & Queen.*

I'd been warned that Barry, a red-haired, somewhat quirky Australian, was a "perfectionist" (which, in my experience, is code for "difficult," which is code for "jerk"), but he and I had been getting along just fine. The theme of the *GQ* story was "elegance," Barry explained, and the aesthetic that he was going for was Duchess of Windsor chic. The clothes I wore were varied and exquisite, and I examined them from top to bottom. I had become more interested than ever in the finer points of clothing design when, a few weeks earlier, Antonio had taken me to the Chelsea Hotel in New York to meet one of his heroes, the eccentric and utterly brilliant couturier Charles James, who lived in a single room at the Chelsea amid his draping mannequins and cutting tables. Charles, who'd been Halston's teacher and Marlene Dietrich's favorite designer, had awed me with his knowledge and impeccable design instincts. He was the first designer to cut fabric on the bias and thereby introduce one-seam construction, and he showed me how the lines of a well-made dress echo the wishbone shape of a woman's body. As a former seamstress (emphasis on "former;" I was *not* sorry that I had dumped my sewing machine once and for all), I had always paid attention to the way clothes were sewn, but Charles made me more attuned to the way they were *made.* This trip with Barry, whose own fashion sense was peerless, advanced my design education by leaps and bounds.

Our little gang aroused a lot of curiosity from the other passengers on the ship: the three handsome male models and me, all dressed up in designer duds; the tall redheaded guy with the camera; and the crazy stylist/hairdresser/makeup artist Richard Adams, who'd drape me in pearls to wear with a swimsuit. "*Very* Duchess of Windsor," he'd always say. He and Barry both had a thing for the Duchess of Windsor, who was widely considered the best-dressed woman in the world at the time.

We'd work hard during the day, grinding out the looks that sold the dream of elegance. And at night we'd party hard. We ate dinner with the ship's captain, but not before testing out every cocktail lounge on every level of the ship. We'd drink and drink and get so wasted that we could barely walk up and down the stairs. We'd just fall down and laugh at how hilarious it all was. It sounds kind of ghastly when I describe it now, but I was having a ball. During the day when we weren't working, I'd lounge by the pool and have lunch on the deck. If this is what's called a working vacation, I'll take it.

When we reached Genoa, we immediately caught a boat to Naples and from there we marched along with our Vuitton trunks to catch the hydrofoil to Capri, where we continued our shooting. I wore sun hats and holiday clothes and posed with the boys, who at this point had become like my brothers. Just before our final photo, we went to lunch and downed such large quantities of white wine—a fixture at Capri lunch tables—that we could barely keep it together for the photo. I had to stand by myself at the top of a tall rock—Ted Dawson sat at my feet on the side of the rock—and it's a minor miracle that I didn't fall down and crack my skull. But as usual, Barry pulled a rabbit out of the hat and got a great shot. No one looking at that beautifully composed photograph would ever guess our state of inebriation.

⌘

Capri was the end of the road for Ted, Tony, and Richard; Barry, Peter, and I headed on to Africa, the land of my mother's ancestors, or at least some of them. And that was where Barry's notorious "difficult" side surfaced, perhaps because we were no longer enjoying all the perks and first-class accommodations that the developed world had to offer. He and Peter, who were romantically involved, started fighting *constantly*, and a day rarely passed that Barry didn't throw a temper tantrum—or two.

The small plane that picked us up in Mombasa to take us into the interior was almost too tiny for the enormous amount of luggage we were towing. As we flew to Lake Nakuru National Park, the herds of water buffalo, giraffes, and zebras on the ground all merged, looking from the air like one long undulating body snaking across the brown earth. Our little plane dived down to let us get a closer look; the sheer abundance of animal life was breathtaking.

Barry and Peter got into a huge row as soon as we got off the plane, and in the middle of it, Barry said he was calling off the shoot. I wasn't about to let that happen. "You do not come all the way to Africa to not take the photos," I told him. "You are going to take them. And you're going to stop fighting."

We spent the day crossing an arid plain to a Maasai village. Once the sun set, the sky was almost pure black. For dinner we ate snake cooked over an open fire, along with a drink made of cow's milk and cow's blood, just as the Maasai do. On the way back to our huts with our guide (he was a Kenyan-born Brit who led safaris), we had to walk along a river. Suddenly, our guide told us to stay very still. There was a black leopard in a tree eating the carcass of an antelope. We could hear but not see him feasting; only his huge greenish-yellow eyes glinted through the darkness. I was petrified. What if that leopard preferred American fast food—like me? (Our guide told me later that the villagers put sheep carcasses in the branches of the surrounding trees at night to keep the leopards satisfied so they wouldn't go after the people.)

That night I lay in my hut alone, trying to get to sleep on my little straw mat, but I was upset because Peter and Barry were quarreling in the hut they were sharing and scared because of all the hungry animals nearby. The fruit I'd been given on arrival had been half-eaten by monkeys that got into my hut when I wasn't there, and at that very moment I could feel an elephant eating off the top of the hut. He snorted and brushed up against it, which terrified me. Our guide was in the next hut, and I told myself that he'd protect me if the elephant decided to stampede. With that in mind, I finally dropped off to sleep out of sheer exhaustion.

I woke up earlier than the boys and decided to go relax by the river with a book and a banana. Sitting on the sand cross-legged, I closed my eyes to meditate, and when I opened them, I was completely encircled by large hungry-looking yellow monkeys with long teeth. I remained silent; my first thought was that they wanted my banana. Then a gunshot rang out, the monkeys scattered, and I felt myself being pulled roughly across the sand by my shirt collar. It was the guide, and he was furious with me. He said I was in grave danger and that I should never, *ever* go off by myself like that again. These animals were dangerous and could eat me alive. I realized that I'd been very lucky that morning.

We were going to shoot some photos during the day that involved taking a Jeep out over the plains. Peter and Barry were still mad when we set off. I was trying to apply eyeliner and a bit of rouge and eye shadow as the Jeep bounced along over the bumpiest, dustiest roads I'd ever been on in my life (the Jeep had no roof). Our ride soon turned into an impromptu safari, as we were treated to the sight of giraffes, elephants, rhinos, and even lions grazing right out in the open. I was marveling at these majestic beasts, so close we could almost touch them, when Barry announced that he had to relieve himself. The driver stopped the Jeep, and Barry jumped out and ducked behind a bush.

As it turns out, a lion's mane is indistinguishable from a dry beige bush. All of a sudden, Barry was running like a bullet for the Jeep, shouting "*Lion!*" Our driver started up the motor and started to pull out. Barry yelled at him to stop, but the driver just kept going. When Peter told the driver, "Keep driving!" I couldn't believe my ears! Was Peter really so angry at Barry that he'd leave him here to be killed by the lion?

"Are you insane?" I screamed, grabbing Peter's shoulders and shaking him as hard as I could. "Stop this car!" I was shouting at the top of my lungs. Barry, his face redder than his hair, was running alongside the Jeep, which had slowed but was still moving. I reached out and pulled him, hard, into the back of the Jeep, where we both tumbled onto the floor. *These people are out of their minds,* I thought as we sped away, leaving a spray of rocks behind us.

That night, as usual, I could hear Barry and Peter arguing, but I couldn't make out the words. If I had to guess, I'd say Barry was bawling out Peter for nearly leaving him there to die with the lion. Those two weren't exactly ambassadors for coupledom; witnessing the viciousness with which they went at each other, I began to wonder if the whole concept of a romantic partnership was inherently flawed and doomed to failure. Maybe we should all forget about finding Mr. or Ms. Right and resign ourselves to being alone. That was how I felt in the tent that night—a million miles from everything that was safe and familiar and more lonely than I can ever remember being. But I also remember thinking that loneliness had to be better than fighting nonstop with a so-called lover who's so furious he's willing to let you get torn apart by a lion on the side of a road in Kenya.

The next morning we went back to our village, where I made friends with one of the Maasai young men who appeared with me in some of the photographs. I loved posing in the tree with this slim beautiful Maasai warrior. It was a bit odd to realize that though we were around the same age, our worlds could not have been more different. He was expected to kill the lion; I was expected to pose prettily for the readers of *Harpers & Queen*.

A group of Maasai girls came along to our next location. They sang all the way in voices that reached pitches several octaves higher than any I had ever heard. Their songs had no words, or at least none that I could discern; they were just sounds, pure and joyous. This transcendent music must have soothed Barry's and Peter's spirits, too, because they actually stopped squabbling for a whole day.

Three days later, with many more photos under our belts, we were back near Mombasa, in a village on the Indian Ocean. Barry and Peter had a huge row—*again*—so Peter and I decided to go to the beach to give Barry some time to calm down and come to his senses. We went into the water and floated peacefully. The villagers had warned us not to go any farther than the reefs, because beyond them were sharks. After a while, Peter got out of the water as I drifted out some more, doing the backstroke. I went pretty far, but well short of the reefs. I looked up dreamily at the big blue sky, and then at Peter, who looked like he was getting smaller, like a dot on the shore. Then I heard a dog barking before I spotted it running at the edge of the water. The dog was barking at me, telling me to come back. Slowly, I backstroked toward the shore, following the sound of the bark. When I got out of the water and petted the dog, whose tail was wagging wildly, I swear I felt an almost electric current flowing between us—and with it, the certainty that the dog had saved me from the sharks.

Barry finally arrived at the beach, evidently recovered from yet another temper tantrum. He and Peter were talking calmly as I danced on the beach by myself in the soft, fading daylight, relieved to see them walking together in silence. We'd worked long and hard for this fragile moment of peace.

We stood on the shore, looking at the horizon. We could see the reefs, far out in the water, and just beyond Barry spied a small fishing boat coming in. When they got closer, I could see three tall, skinny Kenyans.

One of the men jumped into the water, pulled the boat closer to the shore, put a basket on the sand, and went back to the boat. They were about to shove off again when Barry waded into the water and spoke with the young men. They nodded at whatever Barry said, and he got into the boat before gesturing to Peter and me to join him. When I got near, he said, "Jump in—they offered to take us out." The African men smiled at us.

The boat looked like a long dark wooden salad bowl. I couldn't imagine how it ever stayed afloat. "They made it out of a single tree trunk," Barry said.

Great, I thought.

"Really authentic," he said. "Hand-carved." Barry loved stuff like that—ordinary objects to the locals that to us are extraordinary. It was like something you'd see in *National Geographic.*

The moment I put my foot on the boat, though, the Africans' attitude changed. "No women! No women!" they said to Barry, who was able to understand a little of their language. There was a horrified look in their eyes. But I smiled in a really friendly way, and they relented and let me on. Then Peter climbed aboard. The tallest man said something to Barry, and Barry translated. "The fishermen have a superstition about women on boats. They think it's bad luck."

I didn't exactly feel welcome, but once we arranged ourselves, the three African fishermen at the back and the three of us at the front, the fishermen started to relax about my being on the boat, and began to sing or, more accurately, chant rhythmically as they paddled.

The boat was sitting low in the water, and I didn't feel safe at all as we went up to and over the waves, one after another. The water out there—we were well past the reefs—seemed to want to push us back to shore, and it was rough. Then we got to a section where the water was still but much darker—almost black. It was close to sunset, about nine in the evening. I began to feel okay as we moved along in the water, though how far or how deep we were going, I did not know.

Barry said they were going to get more fish. *Ugh,* I thought, *the boat smells fishy enough already.* But I loved the sound of the chanting, especially the call and response from one man to the next. The rhythm was almost hypnotically soothing. I glanced behind me at one of the men, thinking that perhaps if I looked at his mouth, I might understand how to pronounce the words. All three of the Africans smiled at me as they sang, and in that moment one of the men got out of step with the others' rowing. The second man's oars hit his, and then the oar of the man behind him. There was a strong jolt, then a moment of confusion. I looked around and saw one of the men let go of his oar. As he bent into the water to retrieve it, the boat tipped slightly. One African started talking fast to another one, and that was when I realized the boat was filling with water. One of the African men jumped into the water, causing the boat to dip and the water to rush in.

"Oh my God," Barry said, sounding slightly hysterical. "It's true—women are bad luck."

Peter didn't say a word but shot me a sympathetic look. The boat was sinking, and I didn't know what to do. Barry jumped into the water. Peter let go of the side he was clinging to. I stayed on that tip end of the boat; I just could not bring myself to jump into that deep, dark nothingness.

The last one left on board, I stood as tall as I could on the front tip of the boat. I was running out of options, but I knew panicking was the worst option of all. I started to pray and chant "*Om*" with as much vigor as I could muster. Then I saw a star in the sky and attached my soul to it. As I was doing so, I heard one of the Africans yell in English, "*Shark!*"

There was big game in the water, and it was coming directly toward us. The shark started to circle. There was a look of terror on Barry's face, and Peter began gripping the boat's edge again. Meanwhile, the water was so high that my feet were getting wet. I must have looked like a flagpole on the tip of that boat as everyone else was dodging the shark's fin, which had punctured the surface of the water. Not knowing what else to do, I stood perfectly still and chanted and put out a call to God.

Against all odds, my call was answered. I saw a sailboat in the distance and flagged it down. It arrived in the nick of time and scooped all five guys out of the water. They flopped on board like wet fish. One of the sailors on the big boat threw out a rope; I caught it and he and another sailor pulled me in and hoisted me up into their boat. Just in time. All but the very tip of our little boat was now underwater.

Peter was relatively calm, but when I looked at Barry, he was shaking all over, a total basket case. The shark had come closest to him. The Africans were basket cases as well, talking loudly and pointing at me in an accusing way. I may have saved their lives, but the sinking of their ship was all my fault. Nothing I could say or do would convince them otherwise. So that was what I said and did: nothing.

chapter 41

A HOT TIME IN THE OLD TOWN

Salvador Dalí (*left*), Juan Fernandez, and
me at Dalí's apartment, Paris, 1974.

After three years of jetting (and boating!) all over the world for
bookings and basically living in hotels—including months over a fish
market at Paris's fabled La Louisiane, in a room so tiny that my trusty
pink suitcase doubled as my dining table—I was starting to feel a bit *too*
nomadic. I wanted a place to call home, somewhere to put down roots
(or my version thereof). The Americans' little coup d'état at Versailles
had aroused in me more warmth than ever toward France (paradoxically,
perhaps, but there you have it), so I settled on Paris, renting my very
first apartment ever on Rue Saint-Martin in the Châtelet neighborhood.
Today, with the nearby Pompidou Center and several big shopping
areas, that area is a beehive of activity, but back in those pregentrified
days, it was dangerous and not really residential.

At night, when I'd walk home by myself, tired to the bone, I'd see
the local "ladies of the evening" with their stockings, garters, and corsets

(like something straight out of Toulouse-Lautrec), looking even more tired than I felt. They were my protectors, accompanying me to my front door; if someone followed me, they'd get aggressive and chase off the would-be assailant. Sometimes they'd even wait outside for me while I stopped at a little Moroccan restaurant for my take-out dinner. They were always interested in my clothes and often asked for fashion and beauty advice. I'd sometimes buy inexpensive scarves or cosmetics for them and then show them how to wear them. They were my very own welcoming committee, and in their unorthodox way, they made me feel safe and comfortable in my new community.

My apartment, on the top floor of a six-story building, consisted of a tiny living room that overlooked a lovely Catholic church (in the entire time I lived there, I never saw the inside, because the door was always bolted shut to keep thieves out), a kitchenette, and a skylit sleeping loft, reachable by a stairway with a rope banister. I loved my little home, but I was often lonely—I longed for a romantic companion, of course, but nothing was happening in that department—so I was happy when my old high school friend Juan Fernandez (the fellow raccoon-coat wearer) became my roommate.

Juan had been in Paris for several months when we reconnected. Until he moved in with me, he'd been living in one room filled with portraits of himself painted by Salvador Dalí. I'm not sure how they came to know each other (though Juan's father was a diplomat from the Dominican Republic and at one point had been based in Spain, Dalí's homeland), but Juan was one of the great artist's many muses and often accompanied him to Spain. When Dalí was in Paris, he stayed at a venerable old hotel near the Place Vendôme, where he had a special apartment with a wraparound terrace.

One fine early-autumn day, Dalí invited Juan to high tea on the terrace, and Juan asked me to come along. When we arrived at the apartment—which was very grand in the French style, with red velvet curtains with gold tassels and ornate gilded furniture—I expected to see a horde of hangers-on, but it was just Juan and me. From another room, we could hear a couple bickering in Spanish mixed with French. Juan whispered that the voices were those of Dalí and his wife, Gala.

There was a silence, the bedroom door opened, and out came Dalí, who didn't even realize we were there until Juan said something to him in Spanish. The artist immediately opened his arms to Juan, and the two embraced and began talking in very animated Spanish. I felt like a hothouse flower left in a vase with no water, until Dalí noticed me out of the corner of his eye and came over and embraced me, too. He was about my height, dressed in a velvet smoking jacket, and smelled deliciously of Spanish oranges and sandalwood.

It turned out that we were an hour early for high tea, so Dalí asked his maid to get us biscuits and tea. Gala never emerged from the bedroom. As we sat down to have the biscuits, Dalí asked if I would come into another room with him. I followed him into a makeshift studio with a large table full of all sorts of canvases, brushes, paints, and other art supplies. The smell was heavenly and instantly evoked some of the happiest moments of my childhood, when I'd sit and watch my mother paint. Then Dalí surprised and delighted me by asking quietly, "Would you pose for me?" *Would I? The great Salvador Dalí?* I simply nodded, dumbstruck. He pulled out a very large sheet of copper and a tool for etching into the metal. He asked me to stand on the table and gently helped me up. Then he asked, "Do you mind to be nude?"

I hesitated for no more than a second. "No," I said, and quickly removed my dress.

He walked around the table, twirling his trademark handlebar mustache, looking at me from every angle. "I have to get the perfect pose," he said. "Can you get down on all fours?" I dropped into the doggie position, on my hands and knees. "Now can you arch your back?" I did, and he walked around me again. "Now can you stick out your tongue like this?" he said, demonstrating. I was beginning to feel embarrassed and rather silly but did as he requested. "Yes, perfect," he said. "Hold it right there."

He got busy etching, first from the front, then from the side, digging with his tool into the copper. Then he went around to the back of me, where I could no longer see him. I had no idea what he was doing back there for so long, and I began to wonder, *Is he just a dirty old man, taking a good long look?* Then he said, "Yes, I've got it! Perfect!"

He didn't show me the picture. I slipped my dress on. Back in the living room, it was as if nothing had happened, and I began to feel as if

I'd been had. But then I reminded myself that one of the greatest living artists in the world had just done my portrait (though later, when I told Juan what had happened, he laughed and said, "Yup, that's Dalí—dirty old man"). I was sipping my tea when Dalí left the room. He came back a minute later and pulled me onto his lap. "Here's a present for you," he said. "I gave this opera purse to Gala, but she has so many that I want you to have it."

I was quite honored to receive a gift from the master (though I did hope that he'd gotten the okay from Gala to give away her purse). Juan snapped a Polaroid of Dalí with me on his lap, holding the purse. That was when I saw Gala for the first time. She was tiny, very compact, and old-seeming. She walked straight toward us out of the bedroom and, without saying a word, grabbed the purse out of my hand. Dalí jumped up, nearly knocking me off his knee, as Gala stomped back into the bedroom and slammed the door. He went after her, came back thirty seconds later with the purse, sat me back on his knee, and handed me the purse again. "Don't mind her," he said. "She's just jealous."

I didn't know what to think. I hadn't even met this woman properly and already she hated me. Then Dalí said, "To me, the most creative thing a woman can do is have a baby; that is the greatest creation, and one that men are incapable of." I knew he had no children, and his words touched me. On the way back to our apartment that day, Juan said Dalí had told him that he wanted to have a baby with me. I shook my head in disbelief. In any case, I never saw Dalí again, though I did hear that he put the copper sketch of me on display in his home in Spain. And I still have the purse he gave me.

❧

Juan had almost no money during that long winter we spent together in Paris, when the cold and damp were nearly unbearable. In the wee hours of morning, as we walked home from a night of dancing at Club Sept, we'd pass the closed bakeries and food shops where bags of supplies would be delivered and left outside the doors. Juan, who had an oversize raincoat with lots of pockets, would say, "Let's go shopping," and he'd load up his coat pockets with baguettes, milk, and any other food he could scrounge, and we'd walk away as quickly as we could in the direction of the apartment. I always felt guilty (though not so guilty I couldn't eat), but Juan said it was a gift from the gods.

At home, we'd spread a blanket on the floor, picnic-style, and dine on café au lait and our stolen bread with jam. God forgive us, but honestly, even though I was working regularly, there were times when I could barely afford the rent, which was surprisingly high, given the iffy neighborhood. Just before dawn, we'd tuck ourselves into the loft right below the skylight and count the stars until we fell asleep. Or we'd read to each other from *The Hobbit* and *The Lord of the Rings,* partly because Juan wanted to hear English, since we had no television or radio. Our friendship was completely platonic, but we told neighbors that we were married because if the landlord found out that a non–family member was living in the apartment, he would jack up the rent.

One day Juan, who loved playing host, decided it was time to entertain our friends. So we threw a big glamorous party, the likes of which the Rue Saint-Martin had never seen. For atmosphere, we decided to illuminate the space with lit candles—two hundred in all, lining the floor of our apartment, the ledge of our window, and each of the narrow steps leading directly to our front door. That staircase led only to our apartment, so we didn't see the harm.

We had talked the owners of Club Sept into giving us free champagne and a cook for the evening, and we flung open our doors. In all we had about a hundred people coming and going. The music ranged from Latin, R&B, and jazz to Edith Piaf and Josephine Baker. Jerry Hall arrived with Antonio, followed by some photographers I knew, including Helmut Newton, whose studio was nearby, and my great friend Hans Feurer. How we all fit in that tiny space, I'll never know.

It was about midnight when Valentino, with whom I'd just done a photo shoot on the Spanish Steps in Rome for *Vogue Italia,* dropped by with his longtime partner, Giancarlo, and I experienced that over-the-moon feeling a host gets when she knows her party is a success. Not a minute later, I had a crisis on my hands: The rope banister to the loft bedroom, which was being used for posing and playacting (a Thai transsexual was doing a striptease to end all stripteases), broke just as Jerry and Valentino were descending the narrow steps. They came crashing down on the guests below. Jerry landed flat on top of Valentino—they looked beautiful lying there together—and Giancarlo went running over to help, saying, "I wish it was me that Jerry fell on." They all laughed, but I was scared to death they'd been hurt. They were all so drunk, though, that nobody felt a thing.

Suddenly, there were flashing lights and the sound of fire sirens. Before we knew what was happening, several firemen were crawling through the window with hatchets. Apparently, someone had reported a fire in the building, probably because of all the candles. And with that, the party came to an abrupt end, even though we invited the firemen to join us. I actually think they were tempted, but there were just too many people on the premises. Everyone had to leave. A fire hazard is a fire hazard, and the law is the law.

chapter 42

WALK ON THE WILD SIDE

Mom and me on her visit to Paris, 1974.
She'd waited a quarter of a century
to make this trip, and the city was
everything she'd dreamed and more.

$\mathcal{M}om$ came to visit me at my apartment in Châtelet. It was her first trip to Europe—she'd been about to go on the *Queen Mary* when she got pregnant with me, so Aunt Helen had gone instead—and I don't remember her ever being so excited. She brought loads of fancy clothes for partying, and I did not disappoint her. She had waited twenty-four years to get there, and I was going to make sure she had the time of her life.

First I took her to the South of France (I had a job there), where the highlight of the trip was a visit to the Musée Picasso in Antibes. Mom spent a full day there, just soaking up the genius of one of her favorite artists. When we got back to Paris, we saw all the sights that she'd heard about for years from Aunt Helen and from my godmother, Henriette Metcalf. We walked past the houses where Gertrude Stein had held her famous salons and where Isadora Duncan's brother Raymond used to live (once, when I was in that neighborhood, I'd gotten up the nerve to knock on the door of Raymond Duncan's house, and it was answered by Jessica Lange, then just another American in Paris who was studying mime and subletting the place); we visited the cafés and restaurants that Henriette and her circle had frequented; and we ascended to the top of the Eiffel Tower and gazed at all of Paris laid out before us. Most gratifying (for me, anyway) was when Mom purchased a sketchbook and some pencils and began drawing the city's muted gray beauty one chilly afternoon as we floated down the Seine on the Bateaux-Mouches. It had been years since I'd seen her making art, and my heart was flooded with joy. *Thank God for fashion,* I thought, not for the first time. Because of all that fashion had done for me, I was able to spirit my mom away from my awful stepfather and bring her to the city of her dreams, even if it was only for a week and a half.

For the pièce de résistance, we had a night out on the town. Thanks to Antonio and both Juans, I knew plenty of boys, and we had about nine of them as our escorts. Mom, decked out in a long evening dress with a feathered boa, fit right in. We went straight to Club Sept, where we had dinner next to Liberace. When the dancing started, I strutted over and set a candelabra in front of him. He threw back his head, roared with laughter, and gave Mom, who was directly to his right, a big kiss. She was tickled pink. Afterward, we all walked down toward the river holding our champagne glasses, with the boys singing under the moonlight, serenading Mom. Everyone adored my mother, and I never saw her have so much fun.

A couple of days later, my friend Roz came to visit from the United States, and I prepared a beautiful lunch for the three of us. Can you believe we all got food poisoning? My mom and Roz had a minor case; I got so ill I almost died. All I remember is Mom and Roz crying over me in the ambulance as I was rushed to the hospital to have my stomach pumped, and me thinking, *After almost drowning in shark-infested water in Kenya,* this *is how I'm going to die—from eating bad fish in Paris?* Fortunately, I survived, but the doctors kept me in the hospital for an extra twenty-four hours for observation. Mom had to go back to America the next day, but at least she knew I was alive. As she was leaving for the airport, she told me, "I always wanted to live in Paris, but I never got here until now. Thank you for making my dream come true."

"I know, Ma," I said, still groggy from my ordeal but aware that this was an important moment. Mom wasn't big on verbalizing her emotions, so I had to make sure she understood that I understood. Hugging her as hard as I could manage, I whispered, "I know, I know. I'm living your dream for both of us. You're with me every step of the way."

Not long after that, Juan left for London, and then I began to feel *very* lonely. Hans Feurer, one of my favorite photographers (not to mention one of the nicest people on earth), came over sometimes to keep me company. Funny, a great listener, and a fantastic cook—he taught me how to prepare a Swiss fruit dessert according to a recipe that had been handed down in his family—Hans filled a void, and we had some great times together. But what I really hungered for was love.

౭౩

In that year of living dangerously—I mean, *two* near-death experiences (three, if you count the threat of fire in my apartment)—there was one more dicey episode that brought me closer than I cared to be to criminal behavior, though only by association.

I had become pals with a Venezuelan artist with the improbable name of Victor Hugo (perhaps this connected up karmically with the stolen bread and Juan, the latter-day Jean Valjean). Victor had started out as a hustler and a call boy, but Halston had become obsessed with him and, designating Victor his "in-house artist," gave Victor the entire top floor of his townhouse to live in. Victor was every inch the wild and edgy Latin artiste, and he was a ton of fun to boot. He loved to do naughty things and never apologized for them. And he *was* talented in a provocative way. He created daring window displays at Halston's boutique on Madison Avenue and later worked as an assistant to Andy Warhol at the Factory, where one of his special duties was peeing on Andy's series of "oxidation" paintings (canvases that Andy coated with copper-laced paint that reacted chemically with Victor's urine to produce beautifully iridescent, strangely colored imagery). Andy and his minions found this uproarious because Victor was so exceedingly well endowed.

There's no question that Victor used Halston, who was a naturally trusting man, but Victor did genuinely love him. Every other word out of his mouth concerned Halston: *Will Halston like this? Will Halston be there? This is for Halston.* I loved Halston, too; Victor and I had that in common. One day I ran into Victor on the Left Bank just as he was getting out of a taxi in front of a cheap hotel in the Latin Quarter. He was in Paris for a week, he said, and despite the Louis Vuitton luggage he was carrying (it belonged to Halston), he had very little money and couldn't afford a decent hotel.

I had no bookings the following day, so Victor and I made a date to see the sights. Clad in our matching black Yves Saint Laurent capes, which were all the rage, we set off the next morning from the lobby of his hotel. Our first stop was the Louvre. We'd been enjoying the art for about an hour when we came to an area underneath the museum where there was a storage room. (Electronic surveillance was in its infancy back then, and it was relatively easy to wander all over in a place like the Louvre without alarms sounding.) Victor told me to wait outside while he had a look around, so I did. Five minutes later, he came out, holding his cape tightly closed in the front. "C'mon," he said, "let's get out of here."

"Why?"

"Don't ask, just hurry up."

I had no idea what was going on, but he was walking so fast that I just ran along behind him in my high heels, following him out of the museum and back to the hotel. He sprinted up three flights of stairs with me tagging behind, quickly opened the door to his room, yanked me inside, slammed the door, then reached into his cape and pulled out a rolled-up canvas. "I just stole this painting," he said.

Whaaaaaaaat? I thought. *Who steals a painting from the Louvre?* He unrolled the painting, a small landscape with figures whose creator's name he never divulged (perhaps he didn't know it), and spread it lovingly across the bed. "I'm the only person in the world who should have this painting," he announced, stepping back to survey his plunder.

Flushed with excitement at his caper, Victor grabbed me and began kissing me and tearing off my clothes in a kind of frenzy. What can I say? He was a really attractive guy, and that kind of sexual ferocity is contagious. We paused just long enough for him to roll up the canvas and place it on the desk before we toppled onto the sheets together. Afterward, he said, "I'm going to give this painting to Halston as a present when I get back." *Wait,* I thought. *Didn't you just tell me* you *were the only person in the world who should have the painting?* Consistency wasn't Victor's strong suit.

I didn't see Victor again during his visit, and he left Paris a few days later. As for the painting, that was the first and last time I ever laid eyes on it. Maybe he returned it. Otherwise—since neither he nor Halston is around to ask—its whereabouts are anybody's guess.

chapter 43

LOVE HURTS

Being so scantily dressed was a risk
in a place where women cover up
to their eyes. Luxor, Egypt, 1975.
Courtesy of Pelito Galvez.

One of the lasting legacies of my long involvement with Matthew was my continuing quest for spiritual enlightenment. Matthew had turned me on to some of the writings and practices of Hinduism, Buddhism, and Christianity, and my curiosity about these traditions stayed with me long after our relationship ended. Unfortunately, the world of fashion was not always compatible with this side of my personality: Many of the people I met during my modeling career cared about very little beyond clothes or their own image. But when I got together with Pelito Galvez, a raven-haired, green-eyed Argentine photographer who was also a devoted yogi, I thought I'd finally found a kindred spirit, someone who shared my own commitment to mindfulness and meditation.

I'd met Pelito in 1972 when I visited Karl Lagerfeld in Saint-Tropez—that was the trip when I introduced Karl to his life partner, Jacques de Bascher, and first encountered the divine André Leon Talley (then a new college graduate who nervously approached me in the train station to say how much he admired me)—but Pelito and I didn't become a couple until late 1974. By then I was an acolyte of the esteemed guru Swami Satchidananda and an ardent practitioner of hatha yoga, which the swami helped popularize in the United States. (Remember, back in the seventies, yoga was still quite rare; the only person I knew who did it was my friend Roz.)

Meeting the swami was one of those life-changing events that happen seemingly out of the blue but in retrospect feel predestined. I was in New York on a business trip from Paris in late 1971 and was coming back after a long day's work to the Greenwich Village apartment where I was staying with a friend. I was strolling along West Thirteenth Street when a peaceful feeling came over me. Something was drawing me toward a building across the street, so I crossed over and found myself standing in front of a storefront that looked like some sort of hangout for hippies. An Indian-print bedspread covered the window, and the scent of incense wafted over me. In the corner of the window, I noticed a small sign that read "Integral Yoga." The door opened, and a young man with a welcoming smile ushered me inside. I felt buoyant as I followed him up the stairs to the second floor. There, in a big room, were about a dozen people dressed in white, sitting cross-legged on the floor with perfect posture. The young man asked if I wanted to join them for a class of hatha. I had nothing else to do, so I said yes. I sat in the room with the others, closed my eyes, and tried to relax every muscle in my body. When I opened my eyes, there before me was the founder of Integral Yoga, Swami Satchidananda. His name was an amalgam of three Sanskrit words meaning essence, consciousness, and bliss.

Swami became my teacher, and for the next few weeks, while I was in New York, I was a regular student, practicing all the postures and breathing techniques he taught me and learning to chant the *Om Namah Shivaya* (I Bow to Shiva) mantra. Before I left New York, I was considered one of the most dedicated students of hatha yoga at Integral

Yoga, so I, along with a few other aspiring hatha yoga teachers, was invited to a private dinner for Swami Satchidananda.

The day of the dinner, I was stuck until quite late at one of those hectic, frenzied shoots, and there was no time to go home and change. So I went straight from the set to the dinner, which was at an ashram on the Upper West Side, wearing black leather pants, boots, and vest, and carrying my heavy model bag. My face was covered in a thick layer of white powder, my lips were bright red, and my eyes were coated with sparkly eye shadow and three pairs of false eyelashes. I came into the ashram panting because I was late and rushing; the ten other invited guests were already seated at a long table.

The room seemed lit with a peaceful yellow light as Swami, looking beatific in his white robes, long white hair and beard, and contented smile, entered. Everyone stood and listened to Swami as he welcomed us and urged us to ask him any question, which he would then try to answer. My hand shot up, and Swami bowed his head in my direction. "Namaste, Swami," I said, bowing with my hands in prayer position. "I have only one desire."

"What might that be?" Swami smiled patiently.

I took a deep breath and screwed up all my courage. "I would like to be a yoga teacher."

Swami looked at me and started to chuckle. I thought he was pleased with my question until I realized that I'd forgotten what I was wearing. In all that black leather and makeup, I looked like the devil himself. The other yogis looked on in horror as Swami smiled at me without speaking. I wanted to melt into the floor. Then Swami said, "Are you a good yogi? You can become a siddha if you practice sincerely."

"I am," I said to Swami.

"Then, my dear, I say to you with all my heart that you could become a model guru."

I felt I had failed. What did he mean by "model guru"? That didn't sound like a teacher. Was he making fun of my profession? Plenty of people knocked modeling as superficial and frivolous. Was that what he believed, too?

"I see you are a good yogi," Swami continued, "and you will be a very good teacher."

When he uttered those words, my heart felt as if it would burst with joy. *He sees the real me,* I thought. *He sees past all the paint and the clothes all the way to my heart.*

He gave me his blessings, and I bowed and thanked him. And I have carried the jewel of his blessing and his teachings (which draw on many faiths, not simply Hinduism) ever since.

∽

Given how profoundly affected I was by my interactions with Swami Satchidananda, and how interested I was in yoga, I was understandably drawn to Pelito when I met him for the second time in Paris in 1974. Pelito was studying the *I Ching* and the tarot and was deeply into yoga and meditation. He was the most exciting man I'd met in ages, and we seemed like a perfect fit in every way, not least because he was a photographer and I was a model. We made several trips to Amsterdam and London, doing pictures for the UK-based *19* and *Honey* magazines, and everything we did turned out beautifully. All the editors and art directors to whom we showed the photos fell completely in love with them.

Our life together was somewhat less smooth, most likely (I say this with the benefit of hindsight) because I loved him more than he loved me. Indeed, the word "love" doesn't even capture how I felt about him, though I was convinced that in him I had found the great and lasting love I'd long been seeking. "Obsessed" is more like it. Whether Pelito realized it or not, I saw him as my spiritual superior—my guru, really—and I worried constantly about pleasing him. Indeed, looking back, I'm staggered at the amount of energy I spent simply trying to keep Pelito happy, to stay on his good side. In the end, nothing I did was sufficient.

Our big plan, after shooting in various European cities for paying clients, was to go to Egypt together and explore and take pictures on our own, selling them afterward. We were confident we could do so. In London, at the *Vogue* offices, Grace Coddington and Norman Parkinson were so taken with the work Pelito and I had done for *19* that they gave us bags of Capezio clothes to take to Egypt and photograph me wearing them "any way you want," and told us they'd find a way to use the pictures. (They ended up liking Pelito's photos so much that Norman Parkinson replicated them almost exactly with a different model, and

Vogue published *his* photos!) It says everything about our relationship and its balance of power that Pelito unilaterally called off the trip several times before we took off. We had terrible fights, and he would tell me he was leaving. I had to beg and beg, in English and in Spanish, for him to stay and go to Egypt with me as we'd planned. I'm not sure if it was love or pity that caused him to capitulate.

We started out in Spain, where we took beautiful photos in Ibiza. We had packed all our personal belongings into one small rucksack each, which we had bought at an army shop in a London flea market. (For once, I left my pink Samsonite behind, knowing it would stick out like a neon sign in Egypt.) Each bag held a toothbrush, black pencils, two changes of underwear, one book (the *I Ching*, which we faithfully studied), a pack of tarot cards, which we'd learned to read from a teacher in a sketchy part of Paris, and—oh yes—a considerable amount of money in traveler's checks, supplied by me.

One thing we did consistently on our trip (indeed, throughout our entire relationship) was meditate; this was a lesson we'd learned in Amsterdam, where I received my first mantra, "I am." I wasn't really sure what it meant, but I repeated it every morning.

Pelito, whose father was a famous racecar driver in Argentina, spoke Spanish, French, and Italian in addition to flawless English. His gift for languages—including, I discovered in Egypt, a smattering of Arabic— was one of the qualities about him that captivated me; his voice and his way with words were like music. He was smarter than I was about so much; he knew where to go and how to get around with ease almost anywhere in the world.

We arrived in Cairo without a hotel but found one on a side street and went out in search of a drink of strawberry or watermelon juice. It was unbearably hot, but we decided to visit the Pyramids. That was why we were here, after all—to see the sights. We entered the first one crawling on our hands and knees. The space was large enough to accommodate one very bulky person at a time; after that, the tunnel grew smaller and narrower. A German couple behind me turned back when the passage got narrow. I soldiered on. All at once there was no light. Pelito said I was crawling too slowly, so he sped ahead of me, leaving me alone. The guide, an Egyptian man dressed in white linen pants, white robe, and turban, had been in front of Pelito, so I was truly on my own.

The dust, the darkness, and the tiny space started to get to me. Then the space got even tighter and I was no longer on all fours—I was on my stomach, unable even to arch my back. I inched along, hoping to see light, and you can be sure that I spoke to God, especially when I got to the bend in the tunnel. I called out to Pelito in the blackness, and he didn't answer. So I kept sliding forward, my entire body trembling, my spine throbbing, for the next ten minutes. I could feel that the tunnel was descending deeper into the tomb, and there was no way to turn around. I was thinking about the vipers and the snakes and wondering what would happen if I encountered one. Instead of a viper, it was a rat that I ended up nose to nose with. Thankfully, the rat scurried away, leaving me with only the roaring drumbeat of my heart and the old pain in my spine, which started to radiate throughout my body. I crawled on, hoping, quite literally, to find the light at the end of the tunnel. Suddenly, I found myself all alone in a large square space with natural light coming from above; I believe it was the king's chamber, or maybe it was the queen's.

Praying to God to help me be brave and singing an old Stephen Foster song to quell my fears, I crawled back into another tunnel that I thought would be the one to lead me out. It wasn't the right one, but luckily, I met up with another guide, who helped me. Pelito was nowhere to be seen, but when I got out into the blinding light of day—my God, what a relief!—there was Pelito, sitting casually on a rock. And then *he* got angry at *me* for singing, "Oh Susanna, don't you cry for me" like a loud, boorish American. I understand that it may have been annoying, but I'd begun singing it because he'd left me alone underground and it helped me feel less afraid. With Pelito, I realized, my heart sinking, I was on my own. I had to learn to be strong. That was one of the lessons of our relationship. And to be fair, it was a useful one. I had never depended on a man before, and I don't know what had possessed me to think I should start now, and with Pelito, of all people.

We stayed only one night in Cairo—we didn't have money for two— and the next day we made our way through insane Cairo traffic to the train station. The drivers in Cairo were unlike any I'd seen anywhere;

it was as if they were *trying* to hit one another and any pedestrians they could. There were no rules or traffic lights, the roads were unpaved, and left turns were made from far-right lanes (insofar as there *were* lanes).

At the station, pure chaos reigned, with live chickens pecking around underfoot, people with baskets instead of luggage, and the pervasive smells of body odor and rotting produce in the air. The few women we saw were dressed in burkas; Pelito had already decided that I should pretend to be a boy to avoid notice. It was easy to pass because I was so skinny and dressed in pants and a T-shirt, with my short hair tucked under a cap. As we headed for the train—I was limping from straining my back in the Pyramids, and my only concern was finding shade and a seat—I blended right in because of my skin tone. So did Pelito, except for his bright green eyes. We looked so much alike that we could have been brothers.

The train was made of wood and resembled something out of the 1800s. We found a place on the wooden benches between the veiled women and the bearded men with faces so deeply wrinkled from the sun that they looked like road maps. The eyes of our fellow passengers were dark and smiling as the train started, and the heat and dust coming in through the open windows got even more intense. Pelito and his smaller, younger brother were on their way to Luxor.

৩

The rest of our time in Egypt was exhausting but rewarding. Whatever else there is to say about Pelito, he was an extraordinary photographer and he took great pictures of me, both as a woman (for *19* and other magazines) and as a boy, which was pretty much the way I dressed the whole time I was in Egypt. There is one of me in the Nile with a hippopotamus lurking nearby that I still marvel at. How did he ever get that shot?

Things fell apart after we left Egypt and went to Greece for a few days of R&R. We were on the island of Mykonos when Pelito pulled his disappearing act again, this time for three days. Sick with worry, I had no idea where he was or if he was okay. Finally, someone in the town told me that she had seen him on Paradise Beach, one of the resort areas in another part of the island. I took a boat over to that region and went hunting for him, and lo and behold—there he was, lying on the beach naked, in a clinch with a new lover! That did it. I was so angry, I pulled him by the hair, then took a big rock and aimed it right at his head. (He was lucky I had poor aim and missed.) I left him there, got my stuff together in my rucksack, and took off.

But there was a wee problem: I didn't know where to go. I had signed over my apartment in Paris to another model because I'd been delusional enough to believe that Pelito and I were headed for happily ever after. I couldn't face the thought of living in another hotel out of a suitcase. And then the thought came to me: *Maybe I should go back to America.* When I'd moved to Europe to find better professional opportunities, I'd vowed not to return to the States (to live, that is) until a black woman appeared on the cover of American *Vogue.* Well, that had just happened: The August 1974 issue had made history by featuring the face of Beverly Johnson, a stunningly beautiful African-American, on its cover. If I wanted to go back, there was nothing stopping me; I had nothing more to prove in terms of modeling. And if, as I hoped (but rarely articulated because it sounded so arrogant), to launch a performing career, then New York or Los Angeles was the place to be. I knew my agent, Zoli Rendessy, would put me up in his townhouse on the Upper East Side. Why not give it a try?

Pondering my next step, I lugged my rucksack down the main street of Mykonos's main town. A nice older Greek man, a poet named Anastasi, said hello and asked me to have a lemonade with him. I ended up staying with Anastasi at his gorgeous home in the country, in a totally chaste relationship (though he would have liked it to be otherwise), for several days of perfect serenity, until I was able to gather my wits about me and book a flight to New York. Anastasi kept asking me to stay a little longer, but at that point the prospect of living in a place that lacked indoor plumbing held zero appeal for me, even if it did have a wide-open, unobstructed view of the Aegean. I was ready for the asphalt jungle of New York City.

chapter 44

THE MAN THAT GOT AWAY

The New York Post ran a picture
of me with Richard Avedon at the
opening of his photography exhibition
in 1975. That was the night I met
Warren Beatty (*bottom center*).

The model who's in a relationship with a rock star is almost a cliché. While I had nothing against rock musicians (hello, Mick!), my own preferences ran more toward Hollywood types. My modeling life often put me in close proximity to these men and—why be coy?—I took full advantage of opportunities that knocked.

In those heady days of the mid-to-late seventies, when I was single, newly returned from Europe, and living at Zoli's townhouse on East Sixty-Second Street, I had what I called flings, which lasted anywhere from a few nights to a few months, with several of Tinseltown's biggest stars. These included Ryan O'Neal, Michael Douglas, Helmut Berger, and Jack Nicholson (who was everything you can imagine and more).

Here's a gossipy tidbit: I was at a huge A-list party at an East Side townhouse, and Bob Rafelson—the director of *Five Easy Pieces* and *The King of Marvin Gardens,* both starring Jack—was in attendance, sitting sullenly in a corner. I went over to the piano and plunked out a few notes to Carly Simon's hit "You're So Vain" and began to sing. The next thing I knew, Carly Simon herself (who, unbeknownst to me, was at the party) scooted onto the piano bench next to me and said, "Can I play, too? I wrote this song." Carly and I were singing together, having a ball, when she whispered, "The song's about him." She pointed to Rafelson. (Later, in her own memoir, published in 2015, Carly claimed the second verse was about Warren Beatty—an eminently songworthy fellow, as I would soon discover—but declined to say who inspired the other two verses. The guessing could go on forever, but I will say that whenever I hear the opening phrase, "You walked into the party . . . ," the face of Bob Rafelson springs into my mind.) In any case, Carly aroused my curiosity, and I sidled up next to Rafelson to see what she'd found so enthralling. I wound up leaving with him that night.

But there are movie stars and then there is Warren Beatty. In my universe, he was a constellation unto himself. Good grief, I'd had a crush on the man since I was eleven years old. (To this day, I'm incapable of *not* watching *Splendor in the Grass* in its entirety if I catch of glimpse of it when I'm channel-surfing.)

In September 1975, my dear friend Richard Bernstein, a brilliant artist whose portraits of me appeared several times in Andy Warhol's *Interview* magazine, and I had both been invited to an opening of Avedon portraits at the Marlborough Gallery, so we decided to go together. I dressed up in my favorite summer non-color, white, and when Richard picked me up, he tucked a big white gardenia into the side of my chignon. He thought it gave me an exotic Dorothy Lamour/Billie Holiday kind of allure. I was partial to gardenias because they gave off such an intoxicating scent, especially at night.

The exhibition, which featured Avedon's non-fashion work, was a very big deal because its presence at a Fifty-Seventh Street gallery signified the "arrival" of photography in general, and Avedon in particular, into the realm of fine art. It was one of those New York events that drew glitterati from every celebrity sphere: Gloria Vanderbilt and Lauren Hut-ton were there, and so were literary heavy hitters such as Susan Sontag and Norman Mailer.

I noticed Warren Beatty as soon as he stepped off the elevator. And I suppose he noticed me, because Andy Warhol and both Richards (Avedon and Bernstein) were gathered around me, sniffing my gardenia. Although I wouldn't have thought it possible, Warren was even more handsome in the flesh than on celluloid. The photographers and cameras had been trained on Andy, the Richards, and me until Warren walked in. That was when the flashbulbs really exploded. We were left in the dust as the paparazzi did an about-face and rushed en masse to swallow Warren up in their bright lights. But for a split second, he caught my eye, and an ineffable *something* passed between us.

My insides were churning like mad, though I thought I was doing a pretty good job of keeping my cool. Evidently not. Richard Bernstein and Andy Warhol noticed my agitation and guessed instantly what was up. "You *must* have him," Andy stage-whispered when Avedon was pulled away to be photographed with some other boldface name who'd just arrived. "Get over there," he hissed, nudging me in Warren's general direction.

I was tempted—I could feel my soul reaching through the crowd to be near the person I'd worshipped from afar nearly my whole life—but my nerve failed me. I couldn't move. So I let it go. Richard and Andy seemed to know what was going through my mind, and I saw Andy take Richard's arm and whisper something in his ear.

The party went on in the background, but before we'd even had a chance to mingle, Richard took my arm and started to pull me toward the exit. "What are you doing?" I asked. "We just got here."

"We have to leave before he gets away."

"Who?"

"You know who. Warren. He gave you the eye."

"What?" I said, faux-innocent. "*Eye?*"

"Come on," Richard said, hustling us toward the elevator. "He just left. This is your chance, if you hurry."

"Richard, I can't run after a guy."

"You can because I'm going with you," he said. "This is no time to be shy."

It took forever for the elevator to come and descend to the ground floor, so Richard was practically sprinting when we got to the street. I felt like a little sister tagging along behind her big brother as we rushed down the block toward Tiffany. When we got to the corner, there was a red light, and standing all alone in his white suit was none other than Warren Beatty.

"Good evening," he said. "Nice night. I saw you two at the opening. I wanted to say hello, but it was so crowded."

The traffic light turned green, but we just stood there, watching the empty street. Fifth Avenue and not a car in sight: What were the odds?

"I was walking my friend Pat home, but I have to get back to the party," Richard began. Evidently, he communicated with Warren in some kind of unspoken bro code, because the three of us crossed the street together, Richard said so long, and presto! There were two of us standing on the corner. As in Warren Beatty and . . . *me*. It was actual magic. Richard Bernstein was a magician.

"I can walk you home," Warren said, all smiles.

I couldn't look him directly in the eye, but I managed to say to his vest, "Sure, walk with me."

It was one of those dreamy late-summer nights when New York is a perfect version of itself. The air was warm, the moon full, and the pink-colored streetlights suffused the whole scene with a rosy glow as the two of us strolled along in the breeze, both dressed head to toe in white, as if we'd planned it.

With each step, things between us began to feel more and more natural, though I still couldn't believe that my lifelong crush was escorting me home. At least I'd regained my capacity to speak. When we arrived at Oasis Zoli (my nickname for Zoli's townhouse, because that's what it was for me), it was lit up inside, radiating warmth and New York sophistication. I felt like the female lead in the most romantic movie ever made.

Warren took my hand and kissed my fingertips, then looked with his starry eyes directly into my face. I could have fainted on the spot, but I held my composure. "I'd like to see you again, if you don't mind," he said.

Mind? Would I mind a chariot descending from the sky and lifting me up to heaven?

"When may I call you?"

I started to give him my number, but neither of us had anything to write it on. He said it didn't matter, that he would memorize it. So I recited it to him, and he repeated it back three times with his eyes closed. It was the sweetest thing to watch.

"I know where you live now," he said, giving me a naughty wink. "If I can't remember, I'll just show up here, looking for you."

Looking for me? Oh, Warren, I thought, *you have no idea how long it's been the other way around.* I unlocked the front door, and when I turned to say goodbye, he gave me a quick kiss on the lips. I closed the door and leaned against it, not wanting the moment to end. *Did that just happen?* I kept asking myself.

The next morning when I went down to the agency, everyone in the booking office was buzzing. "Pat! Someone very important left a message for you and sent these flowers!"

A dozen red roses sat on the counter. The attached note said, "Please call me. Warren."

And so our romance began. We'd get together every time he came to New York City, and I would cherish every moment. He was funny, considerate, and astonishingly sensual. He'd always send a car to pick me up and another to drop me off. But whenever he asked me to fly out to California, I'd decline. I was well aware of his reputation as a womanizer, and I didn't want to chase him. There were so many women, and that was intimidating to me. I didn't feel comfortable casting my lot with that whole Hollywood scene. Ultimately, what could I, Pat Cleveland, give Warren Beatty? He was such a gentle soul and had so much faith in me, but on some level, I felt I wasn't rich enough or smart enough for him. I didn't speak foreign languages; I had no talents that made me truly special. I was just young, and obviously, youth doesn't last forever.

To process it emotionally, I compartmentalized, putting my affair with Warren in a lovely little box, grabbing the moments that I could— and they were marvelous—but not expecting a whole lot. It was like handling the yellow diamond at Tiffany. It's behind glass, but you can touch it, try it on, be the proud owner for an enchanted moment or two. And then you have to put it back behind the glass so someone else can get a chance. We drifted along this way for years, fitting each other in between our work and our other relationships, romantic and otherwise.

That said, Warren always wanted more from me (or at least he claimed to), perhaps because the strict boundaries I erected around our affair presented a challenge to him. In early 1978, just after I'd married my first husband, Martin (more on that later), I stopped answering Warren's phone messages. I was a wife now, and I took my vows seriously. Then I decided that I at least owed Warren an explanation. With the noblest of intentions, I went over to his place the next time he came to town. I steeled myself for the moment of truth, but I had forgotten one vital fact: Warren could charm me from here to eternity. And that was exactly what he did. He was irresistible, as usual, and I succumbed. We had sex—*great* sex—with him still blissfully ignorant of my altered marital status. Warren just seemed to melt that day and was more ardent than I'd ever seen him. The guilt was killing me, so I finally blurted out the truth. "I got married," I said.

"What?" he said. "Why did you do that? You were supposed to marry *me*."

He crossed the room, dropped into a chair, and assumed the posture of Rodin's famous *Thinker* statue. It was almost comical, but I could see that he was upset and trying to figure out what to say next. He looked up and said bluntly, "Don't stay with him. Divorce him and marry me!"

"I can't," I said. "I can't do a thing like that." Was it true? I wondered. Here was a man I'd idolized since I was eleven years old, saying words I'd always dreamed of hearing. And I was *refusing*? Had I lost my marbles? Maybe. But I also knew in my heart that Warren would end up hurting me. There would be other girls like me—many, many other girls—and I wouldn't know how to cope. I couldn't leave Martin for him (though I sensed even then that Martin and I were not destined for the long haul).

Walking away from Warren that day was one of the toughest things I've ever had to do. Still, we weren't quite finished with each other. We continued to speak on the phone now and then, and I got together with him a few times when I was "between marriages," as the euphemism goes. The final time we saw each other was in late 1981. He called me when I was sick in bed with hepatitis A, which is the least serious variety in that it's contracted through eating or drinking something contaminated with the virus (in my case, I'm convinced, it was airplane food) and the patient usually makes a full recovery, which I did. At the time, however, I felt like I was about to die. My skin had a weird yellow hue, and I was feverish and weak as a kitten.

The last thing I wanted, of course, was for Warren to see me in this state. Our relationship had always been conducted on his turf (in all those years, he'd never come to my apartment) and only when I was done up in full makeup and runway-ready outfits. But I literally couldn't get out of bed to visit him, and he begged me to let him come over. Bored and desperate for some company, I relented. *What the hell,* I thought. *What harm can it do?* Within an hour, he was ringing the buzzer of my apartment at 100 Central Park South.

I could see the profound shock on his face the moment he walked in. Smiling tentatively, he slowly advanced toward my bed, where I sat propped up by pillows, yellow and frail, my hair a greasy mess. He stopped short of the bed and didn't kiss me; he kept his hands clasped behind his back. We made awkward chitchat for a few minutes, and then his eyes fell on the bookshelf next to my bed, where I had placed a framed picture of Jesus Christ. Warren cleared his throat, then gestured toward the picture. "Well, maybe He can help you," he said. "I don't think I can." He quietly retraced his steps and let himself out my front door.

And that, dear reader, was the last time, outside of a movie or television screen, that I ever saw Warren Beatty.

chapter 45

THERE'S NO BUSINESS
LIKE SHOW BUSINESS

With Sterling St. Jacques, my
dance partner and lover, 1976.

The model who wants to be an actress or a singer is as much, if not more, of a cliché than the model who hooks up with a rock star. Well, then, mea culpa: I *am* that cliché. Born with the performing gene—witness my delight in dancing as a five-year-old for Mom and Aunt Helen's friends—I'd nursed a desire to sing and dance professionally since high school, when Bobby Seligman had me whisper-croon Burt Bacharach tunes from the upstairs lounge at Le Club. And while I like to think that I brought an element of performance to runway work (I practically *bounced* down that catwalk!), I was getting frustrated with the limitations of modeling and yearned for a larger stage and a more fulfilling method of self-expression. I was always practicing, pretty much anytime, anywhere. On at least one occasion, I got the seal of approval from an authoritative source.

My friend Billie Blair and I got a kick out of singing together whenever we could. One night in Paris, after midnight, she and I were waiting at the taxi stand on Boulevard Saint-Germain in front of Le Drugstore and across the street from Café de Flore, belting out our version of "Chapel of Love," when a private car pulled up. A black woman who looked to be about fifty rolled down the window and growled from within the depths of the backseat, "Hey, you girls are *good*! You should come to the studio sometime and sing with me." Billie peered into the car, did a double take, and asked, "Wait a minute! Are you . . ."

"Nina Simone?" came the answer. "I most certainly am. And I'm hungry." She drew out the first syllable and pronounced the word as if it were spelled with a short O: "hong-gree." "Why don't you gals get in and take me someplace where I can get a bite to eat?"

After we calmed down (*Is she who she says she is, and did she just say what I think she said?*), Billie and I conferred. Paris, alas, has never been the late-night town that New York is, and we couldn't think of any place that would be open at that hour. Then, with a what-the-heck shrug, we piled into the car next to Miss Simone, who was sprawled across the backseat in a white fur coat (it was the middle of summer), seemingly a bit tipsy. We told the driver to take us to La Coupole on Boulevard du Montparnasse. We figured the sidewalk café might still be open, even though the actual restaurant would no longer be serving.

When we got there, we sat down at one of the outdoor tables, and Miss Simone told us she'd been living in Switzerland, and that it was a no-man's-land and we should never, ever live there. She said she was out of money, dead broke. As if we didn't believe her, she announced again that she was hungry—and proved it: As a waiter walked by with a tray bearing a big lobster on a plate, Miss Simone grabbed it, broke off the tail, and began gnawing on its underside. Billie and I looked at each other and burst out laughing. As with so many other moments in my life, the central thought running through my mind was: *Wait till I tell Mom about this!*

That episode notwithstanding, Miss Simone was one of my heroes, and her raw, soulful voice never failed to give me chills. When we parted that night—Billie and I paid the bill, and I hooked Miss Simone up with some friends of mine who helped her find a cheap place to live—she told both of us to keep singing and reminded us that she wanted to record with us sometime. I took that last part with a grain of salt, obviously, but her encouragement did strengthen my determination to make a go of it.

The trouble was, I wasn't sure that singing was my true calling. Maybe it was acting. Or dancing, which never failed to make me feel truly alive. Or some combination of the three. All I really knew was that I wanted to express myself creatively in a way that went beyond modeling. I'd begun lessons at HB Studio in New York when I was living at Zoli's house, and while I loved them, I had to keep a low profile about that part of my life because in the fashion world at that time, mixing modeling with the stage or screen was very much frowned upon.

In addition, my limited experiences with show business had been somewhat frustrating. I'd been cast in the opening scene of the 1975 Diana Ross movie *Mahogany,* for instance, and had jetted off to Rome to film on location with Berry Gordy, the director, as well as Tony Perkins, the costar and by then the husband of my old *Vogue* buddy Berry Berenson, who was there with him. I was looking forward to a fabulous time (the story, after all—about a poor girl from Chicago who becomes a fashion designer and then a top international model—was partly based on my life) but instead ended up feeling dejected and disillusioned. The day my scene was filmed, I was last to arrive on the set because I'd been the last among a large group of actresses to get my makeup and wardrobe done that morning. Diana Ross went ballistic and accused me of deliberately holding things up. "Just who do you think you are, Little Miss Star?" she screamed. She threatened to cut me out of the picture, but in the end my "blink and you'll miss it" appearance stayed in. (I was less fortunate a few years later, when I had a part in another Ross film, *The Wiz,* and my entire scene ended up on the cutting-room floor.)

Given my batting average in both love and show business, I thought my luck had changed when I got together with Sterling St. Jacques, who seemed to embody everything I was looking for in a man, personally and professionally. I met him one night in July 1976, when I was dancing under the disco ball at Hurrah, a hot new nightclub on West Sixty-Second Street, just off Broadway. It was a who's-who club that was difficult to get into unless you were a fashion person, a music star, or some sort of jet setter.

I had recently moved to my own apartment at 100 Central Park South, which was nearby, and I went to Hurrah often, both alone and with friends, because it was close and I loved to dance. I was turning under the disco ball by myself one night, feeling rather lonely, when I felt a hand on my back. Before I knew what was happening, I was lifted off my feet and twirled around by a very tall, breathtakingly handsome young black man with a radiant smile. It felt like the coolest carnival ride of my life. "Hello," he said, still holding me in his arms, "my name is Sterling. Would you like to dance?"

We started to swirl around the room, and I felt as if we were flying. I was wearing one of my chiffon Stephen Burrows dresses, and the layers of fabric seemed to become part of him while we moved as one; my Charles Jourdan heels barely seemed to touch the floor. Our steps were perfectly synchronized, and then Sterling picked me up in his arms. I pretty much stayed there, through better and worse, for the next year.

Sterling was a well-known man about town, very dapper—he wore cashmere suits, expensive shoes, and diamond jewelry—and debonair. Women were always swarming around him, but until me, he had slept only with men, including a long affair with the great designer Hubert de Givenchy (whose fragrances I can never smell without thinking of Sterling). Sterling and I became a famous dancing couple, a kind of latter-day Fred Astaire and Ginger Rogers, going to all the top nightclubs together—Hurrah, Regine's, and once it came on the scene, Studio 54—and being constantly photographed for newspapers and magazines. He was "Twirling Sterling" and I was Pat, the "top model turned dancer." We performed together on the television show *Soul Train,* and at Lincoln Center for a benefit, where we were introduced by Bob Hope, the master of ceremonies, as the "best dancing couple in America." *People* magazine went even further, dubbing us the "hottest couple in America." I was in heaven, and it wasn't long before we were engaged and Sterling moved into my apartment.

One of the collaborations that I was most excited about was a Broadway play called *Let My People Come.* Billed as "a sexual musical," this risqué show celebrated sex in all its wild and wacky varieties. It had been a huge hit off-Broadway and was set to open in autumn 1976 at the Morosco Theatre on West Forty-Fifth Street (one of those small but legendary Broadway houses that later got torn down to make room for the oversize Marriott Marquis Hotel). Phil Oesterman, the director/producer, wanted to see us as a couple, so we went down to audition. That day was like a classic moment out of a forties movie (or maybe that other Broadway musical playing nearby at the Shubert Theatre, *A Chorus Line*), with all the dancers lined up, showing their legs, and dancing their hearts out, hoping against hope to get the part. When our names were called, we didn't walk out onto the stage; we danced out and did our patented twirling, swirling routine.

We were cast as players in the larger company. I had about seven small parts to play, from a child in a school scene to a new dancer in a scene in which Sterling also appeared. As I mentioned, the show was all about sex, so the actors were nude in many of the scenes. I, however, refused to appear without a G-string, which Phil Oesterman agreed to. (Sterling gave me a powder-blue leather G-string with rhinestones on it—very trendy—at one of the rehearsals.)

The girls in the cast had their dressing room on one side of the theater and the boys on the other. I had my own teeny-tiny dressing room—there was barely room enough to reach into the open closet to get my costume, and every time I did, I'd be hit by wire hangers—on the top floor of the spiral staircase. I didn't care; I loved my little stall, and I decorated it with pictures and pink cushions.

There were two months of rehearsals before the show was set to go into previews in front of live audiences, and not a soul in the fashion world knew what I was doing after work. Every evening Sterling and I would ride our bikes down Broadway from my apartment and sneak into the theater for rehearsal. I was terrified that if anyone in fashion found out about my role in this musical, I'd stop getting work as a model. The divide between the two worlds was massive back then. It was kind of like being a photo model and also walking the shows; it simply "wasn't done." But I'd always done it all. That's how I liked it, and I wasn't about to change now.

At rehearsal, I had a blast standing around the baby grand piano with the whole cast, all quite young but terrific singers and dancers.

They coached me in how to hit the high notes and how to harmonize. Nothing beats the "learn while you earn" method—not that I was earning much. The pay was only about three hundred dollars a week, but I wanted to do this musical so badly that I would have worked twice as hard for half as much.

Finally, the first day of previews arrived. I was standing just behind the heavy red velvet curtains right before the first scene. I can remember looking at the hems on the curtains, almost as tall as I was, and at the way the curtains draped on the floor. The guy standing at the ropes of the curtains smiled, his face sparkling with joy. The cast was dead silent; there was no talking backstage. All of us were totally professional—no jokes, no looking around, just do your part, hit your marks, and the play will proceed like a well-oiled machine.

The orchestra was in the pit, and the music started up. The sound of the curtain slowly rising gave me my first glimpse of working live on a Broadway stage—and that was of footlights so bright I was nearly blinded. I knew the audience was there, but I couldn't see them at all. I had no idea where Sterling was, and I felt like I would jump out of my own skin from the excitement. Then we all started to move into our positions as the first dance number began.

My tap dancing had improved somewhat, but I was still insecure. *Shuffle-ball kick, one-two-three, circle round, then left stage, downstage, upstage, jump, and circle again.* It was dizzying and dazzling and perfectly timed: I knew that if I missed a single step, I would screw it up for the other dancers. We danced the first number, ran into the wings for our next costume change, scrambled up the spiral stairs to the dressing room for another change and makeup, and hurried back down the stairs and onto the stage again. This up-and-down-the-stairs thing was so difficult that I finally convinced Phil Oesterman to please let me change just behind the stage.

At night after each performance, Sterling and I would have dinner at Sardi's, where our show had reserved a table across from the one reserved by the show Rita Moreno was starring in. It was fantastic. I would wave at her and she would wave back. It was just like high school, with all the various groups at "their" lunch tables in the cafeteria, but instead these were Broadway stars. I would look around Sardi's at all of the framed caricatures of Broadway celebrities done by Alex Gard and feel as though I were in a dream made real. John and Ethel Barrymore, Alfred Lunt and Lynn Fontanne, Richard Rodgers and Oscar Hammerstein. And now I was here, too—not on the wall (though a girl could dream, couldn't she?) but in the flesh, often until the wee hours of the morning because Phil would have notes for the whole cast. He'd go over that night's show, pointing out flaws in the performances or places that could be tightened.

By the time those sessions were over—around two in the morning—I would be ravenously hungry. I was on what turned out to be an ill-advised diet of steak and grapefruit. Given the multitude of dance numbers in the show, I sometimes felt close to starving. I was all muscle, no body fat whatsoever, and when I did eat, I'd devour a huge steak for strength and drink grapefruit juice backstage between scenes.

It ended in disaster. In around the third month of previews, I was in the back row of the chorus during the second act. Standing in the back gave me a chance to rest up for my next dance number. Suddenly, I started to sweat so profusely that my eyelashes popped loose on the edges. Then I felt a sharp pain in my back just under my shoulder blades, as if a Mack truck had plowed into me, and I fell backward. Luckily, the actor standing next to me caught me and helped me stay standing until the song was finished. That was when I blacked out. When I woke up, I was on a stretcher, on my way into an ambulance. One of the dressers came with me to the hospital. Sterling stayed behind. The show must go on, after all.

Both my kidneys had blown out because I had kidney stones, probably the result of all the acid in the grapefruit juice I'd been drinking night and day. I was bedridden for three months, stir-crazy and unable to do any kind of work. I simply sat in bed and healed; in the meantime, Sterling stayed in the show until it closed after 108 performances, all of them previews. It never officially opened.

At the time I was devastated, but it didn't take long for me to see that I was lucky to get out. All that work for a paltry three hundred bucks a week? What was I thinking? True, modeling wasn't the most creative work in the world, but I needed to make a living and couldn't jeopardize that. Fortunately, I got better in time for the fall fashion season in New

York, so I was able to walk the collections and recoup the money I'd lost while convalescing.

In the meantime, Sterling and I had a beautiful affair—until we didn't. We held on for nearly a year and a half, but ultimately, I had to accept the deeply painful fact that, despite our deep devotion to each other, his sexual preference was clearly for other men. I craved intimacy in every sense of the word, and part of him lay forever out of reach, even on the occasions when we did have sex. One night we had a huge fight, ostensibly over the whereabouts of two diamonds he had given me—one in a ring for my finger and another in a pendant to hang around my neck—and he disappeared. I saw him around after that from time to time, and then he *truly* disappeared, moving to Europe and dying in 1984 from AIDS, though his death was never officially confirmed. That was pure Sterling: Even in death, he retained a certain mystery.

I made a few other forays into show business after my kidney-stone fiasco. I sang occasionally at New York's Mudd Club (the "underground" venue where punk groups like the Ramones first found fame) in the early eighties, appeared in a 1981 episode of the television show *The Love Boat* in a cameo with Halston (an experience that brought us closer than ever), delivered a killer rendition of "Makin' Whoopie" at an event with the great jazz vibraphonist Lionel Hampton in 1983, and went to Rio de Janeiro to make a sexy Portuguese-language crime drama called *Rio Babilônia* (released in 1983, it has since become a kind of cult movie). All of these gigs were fun—some more than others, of course—but nothing I tried ever stirred the unparalleled zest for performing that I had during my brief romp on the Great White Way.

chapter 46

ALONE AGAIN (NATURALLY)

Posing for John Taylor, Adel Rootstein's master sculptor, 1977. What a privilege to be made into a mannequin.

$\mathcal{I}$ guess you could call it an experiment, and like many experiments, it failed. I had spent my early twenties getting my career in order, and relationships were secondary in my mind, at best. I wanted love and passion as much as the next girl, but my adolescent obsession with Matthew had introduced a note of caution into my heart: Grand passions were awfully draining, so watch out. Still, as I moved into my late twenties, I began to think more and more about how wonderful it would be to have a life mate with whom I could have a family. (My mother's warning was always ringing in my brain: "Do *not* miss your chance to have children," she would tell me, and I'd wonder if she was sorry she hadn't had more than just me.) Like most women of my generation, I was weaned on happily-ever-after movies and books and truly believed that if and when I ever got married, it would be the most romantic moment of my life, a sign that I had finally found "the one." To say that it didn't work out that way is an understatement.

Martin Snaric was my best friend. That's a phrase people often use to emphasize the undying love between two spouses, but for Martin and me, it meant we were close pals and probably should have remained so. Martin was an American actor and model (born of first-generation immigrants—Yugoslavian on his dad's side and Italian on his mother's) whom I had known since the early seventies, when Antonio Lopez had introduced us, then shot us naked for his photography portfolio. By the late seventies, Martin, like me, was sick of what I'll call (for lack of a better term) the dating game. Essentially, we decided to get married as a way to get other people out of our hair, to tell them, "Keep off!" We would try marriage, he and I agreed, give it five years, and if it didn't work out, we'd get divorced—no harm, no foul.

What were we smoking? As if any relationship, let alone marriage, could ever be that simple, especially for a diehard romantic like me.

Martin and I ran in the same circle, and we were both extremely social and extroverted. One November evening in 1977, we happened to be in Paris at the same time and were riding in a taxi with Maning Obregon, the illustrator I'd worked with at *Vogue,* who was Martin's friend as well as mine. All three of us were laughing our heads off about something or other when Martin suddenly kissed me and said, "Will you marry me?"

"Sure!" My response was instant and nonchalant.

That was when Maning got the brilliant idea that we should all go to London that night, via the ferry from Paris to Dover, and show up at the office of Adel Rootstein, the world's preeminent maker of mannequins, first thing in the morning to see about having my mannequin made. Martin had already had his perfectly proportioned physique reproduced by Adel, and replicas of it were in store windows all over the world. Adel, who had emigrated to England from South Africa, had started out making mannequins in her kitchen and became famous for them because she created them in the images—including the bodies and the faces—of stars like Twiggy and Joan Collins. No one else had ever done that (though she also made mannequins, like the one based on Martin, that were excellent at their primary job: looking good in clothes).

Adel's method was painstaking and artistic: First her in-house artist, John Taylor, would sculpt a clay version of the model, who sat for days (or in my case, stood with my arms crossed) like any artist's model as John threw clay on a metal amulet and shaped it into the model's form. Once finished, that clay statue would be cast in fiberglass and, from there, replicated and mass-produced for sale to stores all over the world. Adel's great innovation, in addition to modeling her mannequins on real people, was to have them assume natural, realistic poses rather than look stiff and unnatural like . . . well, *mannequins.*

I think it was that moonlit ferry ride across the English Channel from Paris to Dover that sealed the deal for Martin and me. The three of us stood on the deck, huddled in Scottish blankets, and acted out our idea of a glamorous little movie. Martin gazed at me adoringly and sang, "Blue Moon, you saw me standing alone / Without a dream in my heart / Without a love of my own . . ." Yeah, sparks definitely flew between us that night.

We got to London around dawn and killed time in a coffee shop on King's Road until it was time for Adel to arrive at Shawfield House, where the Rootstein offices were located. Kevin Arpino, the company's creative director, whom I knew from the Paris shows, met us there, and he and Maning talked me up to Adel, trying to convince her that I would make a great mannequin. I got lucky. "I'm going to do new batch of mannequins next month," she told me. "And I'd like you to come back in December to take part." I could scarcely believe my ears. I floated out of her office.

Martin and I flew back to New York, where I met his parents, devout working-class Catholics who lived in an unassuming house in Brooklyn, and his twin sister, Pat. We definitely felt engaged but decided not to tell anyone. Then we jetted back to London, where I had one of the most wonderful months of my life. I spent my days sipping tea and posing for John Taylor as he sculpted my mannequin out of clay in his lovely little English house with a garden. At night Adel and Kevin wined and dined us all over London. I remember one evening we went to the Royal Ballet; after a superb performance of *Swan Lake*, Kevin took us backstage to meet the principal dancer, who was a friend of his. After we'd all shaken hands, the dancer said to Kevin, "I have so many runs in my stockings, I almost couldn't dance."

I was wearing a gold woven-metal dress by Stephen Burrows, and I couldn't resist chiming in. "You think *you've* got runs?" I said, lifting my skirt and revealing the dozens of zigzaggy tears the metal had cut into my tights. "Now, *these* are runs!" We all had a good chuckle over that.

A week or so into our stay, Martin and I went to the registry in Chelsea and got married. I had always loved the television show *December Bride* when I was a kid, and somehow I wanted to be one, too—fresh and white and crisp. I wore the wedding dress that was made for my mannequin. It was lovely but heavy and terribly uncomfortable because it wasn't meant to be worn by a real woman. Fleetingly, I wondered whether my mom—or Martin's parents—would have wanted to be there, but I put the thought out of my mind. This was a spur-of-the-moment thing; it was a nice ceremony, but not the kind of wedding you fly across the Atlantic to attend.

Somehow we had achieved celebrity status in London—Adel and her mannequins really did confer a certain kind of fame—and the local newspapers got wind of our marriage and put it on the front page. I don't remember the exact headlines, but they were something along the lines of "Two Dummies Tie the Knot." We laughed at that, too. We found everything hilarious during that brief, wondrous time. Adel put us up in a sweet little apartment at the Nell Gwynn House near her offices, and Martin would wake me in the morning with small gifts or by singing show tunes in my ear. We both adored Rodgers and Hammerstein, and I would sing back to him, "I'm in love with a wonderful guy." And I was.

If only we could have sustained that feeling once we returned to our real lives. Instead, we got mired in the classic two-career trap, and my career was by far the more successful. That first year of our marriage, I realized one of my greatest career goals: I appeared on the cover of *Vogue*. No, it wasn't American *Vogue* (that goal has proved elusive) but the September 1978 issue of *Vogue Italia*, which, as with its American counterpart, was the biggest, fattest fashion issue of the year. Not too shabby. I wanted Martin to be happy for me, and he was, but I could tell he was conflicted because my career was eclipsing his. His effort to move from modeling into acting had stalled. He'd been cast as Valentino in *The Last Remake of Beau Geste* with Marty Feldman and Michael York, which was released in 1977, but subsequent movie parts just weren't materializing, and he was understandably frustrated. Martin was (and is) one of the most talented people I've ever known, but he was discovering a basic truism of life: It's not easy to reinvent yourself.

We lived in my two-and-a-half-room apartment on Central Park South, though the demands of my job meant that I spent very little time there. Neither did Martin, evidently, because whenever I called him from wherever I was, he never answered the phone. I was constantly traveling for work, and my absence did not make our hearts grow fonder. Au contraire. Martin pulled away and grew closer than ever to his oldest friend, Alban, a chef who wanted Martin to start a pie-baking business with him. I felt like the odd person out. Even when I was in New York, Martin would be with Alban and I'd be in the apartment by myself, trying not to cry.

On the occasions when Martin traveled with me, as he did when both of us modeled for Kenzo on a working trip to Japan early in our marriage, we often quarreled. I remember vividly a side visit that we made to Bali during that job in Asia. We accidentally ate some sort of psychedelic mushrooms—dopey us, we thought we were simply enjoying mushroom soup and omelets—and we had terrible hallucinations for nearly three days. Martin and I got into a horrendous fight and I remember thinking, *Here we are in paradise and we can't get along. What hope is there for this marriage?* Right then and there, I tied a ribbon to a tree, said a prayer to a murti of Lakshmi, the Hindu goddess of prosperity and good fortune, that I'd purchased—it was a small carved wooden statue—and vowed that if I were ever lucky enough to come back to Bali, it would be with my true love.

The word "divorce" surfaced early, though at first I didn't take it that seriously. But I couldn't help noticing that the subjects of our future together and the possibility of children were particular sore spots. Any time I broached them, Martin would get angry and accuse me of rushing him. "I wasn't ready to get married," he'd say. "You never gave me a chance to get on my feet." When he wasn't making me feel like I was pressuring him, he took to teasing me in a way that was supposedly affectionate but subtly stuck in the knife and twisted it. "Oh, look at you with your fuzzy hair," he'd say. Or "Oh, you poor thing, you're so skinny."

I think I saw the curtain start to come down on our marriage during the historic world tour both of us made in September 1980 with Halston and his usual retinue of "Halstonettes"—ten of his favorite models—and around a dozen or so other advisers and assistants. The highlight of the trip, which included fashion shows, publicity, and round after breathless round of lunches, dinners, and sightseeing excursions in Los Angeles, Japan, China, and Paris, was unquestionably China, where Halston (thanks to some string-pulling by his brother, a high-ranking diplomat in the State Department) managed to get permission to tour the country's silk factories with an eye to possible trade. Like all good designers, Halston understood that fashion is ultimately about fabric, and he wanted to show his clothes to the Chinese manufacturers so they could see firsthand some of the ways their silk—the best in the world—could be turned into beautiful garments.

The United States had established diplomatic relations with China only the previous year, and it was still rare for American businesspeople to get visas to travel there. Halston was under a lot of pressure, and he kept me and a few other key Halstonettes close to him throughout this trip because he knew he could count on us to smooth the way socially with all the people we were meeting and speaking to through translators (who, incidentally, were often the only nonwestern women anywhere in sight). Between the constant toasts with mao-tai, a distilled liquor that the Chinese men, clad in identical uniforms of gray, blue, or green, drank with abandon (often with what they claimed were thousand-year-old eggs that we unofficial goodwill ambassadors dutifully choked down), and our jam-packed schedule, we were worn out and had almost no downtime. Martin and I did not fight—there wasn't a spare minute for that—but he stopped talking to me about midway through the trip. It was upsetting, but I chalked it up to stress and figured he'd get over it as soon as we were back in the United States.

He didn't. I had to turn around and leave for Milan to do the collections almost as soon as we landed in New York City, and when I returned from Europe a few weeks later, he wasn't at the apartment. He had moved in with Alban. After a week or two of sitting around feeling sorry for myself, I started venturing out to parties and other events on my own and spending weekends with Halston at his beach house in Montauk, at the tip of Long Island, where we'd sing, watch old movies, make homemade fettuccine with his state-of-the-art pasta maker, and leaf through his collection of exquisite art books. It was pure heaven to relax with Halston on Sunday afternoons, as he reclined on a chaise longue beside his living room bookshelves, blowing perfectly formed smoke rings into the air. We'd talk about our dreams and also our disappointments. During walks on the beach, he and I would cheer each other up. He was worried about his company and feeling a lot of stress, and I was licking the wounds of my failed marriage. He'd remind me how important my friendship was to him and how lucky we both were.

As I think about Halston now, more than a quarter century after he died of AIDS (like so many of the men I dearly loved in the seventies and eighties), those quiet walks are what I recall most vividly—more vividly, even, than our wild nights at Studio 54, where in its heyday he and I would party into the wee hours with Liza Minnelli, Bianca Jagger, Jerry Hall, Steve Rubell, and a host of other fashion-forward friends. Those were insanely fun times, but the weekends with H in Montauk restored my spirit again. Come Sunday evening, I'd always return to the city feeling renewed. Slowly and surely, I adjusted to being a single woman again.

My divorce was finalized on December 30, 1981. Clueless about legal matters, Martin and I used the same law firm, Jacoby and Meyers, which we found through their ubiquitous ads on New York City subways and television stations. I remember with crystalline clarity the feeling I had when I walked out of their offices that day. I was wearing a Thierry Mugler "power suit" (very eighties!) with big Joan Crawford–style padded shoulders. I felt light, unencumbered—I'd just signed over to Martin some property in the Pocono Mountains that I'd bought for us—and ready for whatever came next. As I stepped into the sunlight of upper Broadway, I lifted my chin and shouted to anyone within earshot, "Happy New Year!"

chapter 47

MAD ABOUT THE BOY

Paul van Ravenstein on the day I met him
in 1977. A few weeks shy of his nineteenth
birthday, he was the photographer's assistant
on a shoot at Club Hurrah in New York City.
Courtesy of Ara Gallant.

You need a very bad man." Those were among the first words spoken to me by Lukas Fischer, an extremely tall German rock musician, part-time model, and full-time deadbeat whom I met at a Hot Sox fashion show that we were both modeling in. Unfortunately, when I became involved with Lukas (I blame loneliness and his skills at seduction), "a very bad man" is exactly what I got. He was so very, very bad that I'm not sure I would have come out on the other side of the relationship in one piece had it not been for a very good man whom I was fortunate to meet a short time later.

Ah, that good man. I first saw him in 1977 when I was shooting for *Playboy* with the Dutch model Apollonia van Ravenstein—everyone called her "Apples" for short—who was a close friend and one of the kindest people I've ever known. The photographer, Ara Gallant, promised I could keep my clothes on. (I'd never be able to explain naked pictures in *Playboy* to my mother.)

The shoot was at Hurrah, the hot disco where I'd met my dance partner and former beau Sterling, from whom I'd recently separated. I arrived early in the day with Ara, and then Apples and I went into the ladies' room to do our makeup. We emerged to total darkness. "Turn the light to the set," Ara said to his assistant. Ara liked to use an intense tungsten light because it helped create the glamorous "old Hollywood" look for which he was known. I was chatting with Apples when I looked into the light and saw the silhouette of a tall, slim man who then shifted slightly so that his profusion of layered blond hair was backlit in such a way that it formed a halo. Whoever this person was looked actually divine. "Whoa!" I said to Apples. "Do you see *that*? I want some." I was just joking around in the bawdy style we used when talking about guys. I expected her to join in, especially since she and I usually had similar taste in men. But she looked at me with a half smile, decidedly less enthusiastic than I was.

It was puzzling. How could this perfect specimen of manhood not be up to her standards? Before she could say anything, I was off to meet him. "Hello," I said, looking up in the darkness. I couldn't really see him, but I could feel the warmth of his body. And then a moment of paralysis overtook me and we were engulfed in silence. "Uh, hi," I finally stammered. "I'm Pat. I'm a Cancerian." Sharing your astrological sign was usually a safe bet.

A deep, accented voice replied, "I'm Paul. I'm a Cancerian, too."

Excellent! Now I knew we could get along. The lights came back on and Apollonia gave me another odd smile. I walked over to her and she said something that solved the mystery: "That's my little brother, Patty Cakes."

Okay, I thought. *That explains her apathetic response. But there's no reason . . .*

"He's only nineteen," she said. "He's too young for you."

Nineteen. I would turn twenty-seven in a couple of months and had to admit that Apples was right. So I marched over to Paul and said, "You're too young for me now, but I'll get back to you later."

Later turned out to be the spring of 1981, in Paris. I'd just seen Apollonia in Milan, where we both walked the shows, and she'd told me she was headed to Paris to meet her new boyfriend, Todd, and to work the collections there. She called me at my hotel on Rue La Boétie shortly after I arrived. "Pat, I need a favor. Todd and I need some time alone, but my brother, Paul, is staying with us in our hotel room," she said. "Can you take him off our hands for a while?"

"Don't worry," I said. "I'll take care of him." After a long week of fashion shows, with all the changes of clothes and performing on the runway, I was grateful for a companion in Paris, especially the tall, handsome Dutch guy I recalled from the *Playboy* shoot.

He was waiting with Apples and Todd just outside the show garden. Tall Paul, with his straw-blond hair and wide shoulders, dressed in a T-shirt and loose jeans. Simple, easy, honest, so different from the overdressed fashionistas who were exiting the garden. The four of us strolled along the Rue de l'Université, and it was as if I'd known him for years.

"Okay," said Apples, whose adorable Dutch accent was identical to her brother's, "we'll see you guys later." She and Todd walked swiftly away, leaving Paul and me alone.

Paul seemed ready for whatever I had in mind, so I said, "You're coming with me." I was fearless: I was single (Martin and I were legally separated, and I'd filed for divorce); it was spring; it was Paris. What more is there to say? To seal the deal, I pushed him up against a garden wall and kissed him on the lips. I pulled back and then kissed him again. This time he kissed me back. And even though he was seven years my junior and I was supposedly the worldly woman of experience, Paul was more mature than any man I'd ever kissed. He knew what to do and when to do it. We spent the rest of the afternoon and evening in my hotel room, breaking only to meet up with Apples and Todd for a little picnic dinner by the Seine.

Todd brought his guitar, and Apples and I brought the wine and cheese. It was like a scene by Pierre-Auguste Renoir. As we ate, drank, and sang American folk songs along the banks of the most romantic river on earth, I felt happier than I had in years. Paul moved out of Apples and Todd's hotel room and stayed with me in my little room at the Hotel Boétie, and we made love between the shows day and night until it was time for me to return to the United States. We made plans to meet again for the next fashion season, in autumn.

In the meantime, I carried on with my life and career in New York. Lukas was one of those mistakes a woman makes when she lets her hormones make bad decisions for her. A woman I knew who'd once been his girlfriend tried to warn me about him. "Steer clear," she said. "He's bad news."

Smart girl. Me, not so smart. Sometimes I wonder how I could have been so naive. In retrospect, Lukas's violent mood swings—which would be rectified after he disappeared for a few hours—were clearly a function of his addiction to heroin, though it took me an inexplicably long time to put two and two together. In desperate need of a fix, he'd raid my pocketbook, leave without telling me where he was going, and come back calm and smiling. Until he'd get twitchy again. It was a nightmare that for some reason I felt I couldn't reveal to anyone, not even Mom. She and I would talk for hours on the phone, but I never let on how despondent I was or how much Lukas mistreated me. I simply couldn't tell her; it would have caused her too much pain, and the last thing I wanted was to add to her many woes. If I'd confided in her, she surely would have recognized the symptoms of heroin addiction and advised me to get help. Instead, I bottled up my misery and pretended that things were fine.

I finally wised up and broke it off—or at least I tried to. Every so often Lukas would show up at my apartment and I'd have a hellacious time getting rid of him. I'd refuse to buzz him in, but he'd wait until another tenant opened the door, then sneak up to my apartment and beg me to let him in. I wouldn't, and eventually, he'd go away.

There were a couple of other men in my life around that time (including a very nice podiatrist who gave the best foot massages ever!) but no one who made my heart leap. I started to make peace with the idea that perhaps the kind of true love and companionship I'd long craved just wasn't in the cards for me. For some reason, I still regarded the beautiful Dutch boy as a lovely diversion, not a potential life partner.

My third encounter with Paul came in autumn 1981, when I went back to Paris for the collections. He was there as a freelance photographer, taking photos of the runway shows. We decided that after the shows ended, we'd go to Normandy for the weekend. We rented a car in Paris, and Paul drove. We spent the journey talking, laughing, and kissing. He was so young, sexy, and alive. There was something absolutely energizing about him. It sounds corny and melodramatic, but I'll say it anyway: I'd look at him and my life would feel brand-new. Plus, he was *so* much fun. I don't think I stopped grinning the entire weekend.

We spent the night in Normandy in a hotel room decorated entirely in orange. The next day we made a pilgrimage to the fortified rock island of Mont Saint-Michel, which appeared out of the ominous gray sky like a Gothic mirage. I was dressed in a black Thierry Mugler jacket, Issey Miyake leather pants, and knee-high boots, and the autumn chill encouraged us to be cozy. We were nearly the only tourists there because it was off-season. It got dark early and rather abruptly, and because the tide was coming in fast, we had no choice but to find a place to spend the night. There was no way off the island. So we cuddled up in a little room overlooking the bay, drinking beer and eating crepes.

We left in a hurry the next morning, because I had a flight to catch at Charles de Gaulle. We returned our rental car and I grabbed a taxi. As it pulled away, I saw Paul standing on the curb, looking abandoned and sad. Tears streamed down his cheeks. I was shaken to the core. No one—*no one*—had ever cried because I was leaving.

He stayed in my mind. In January 1982, just after my divorce from Martin became final, I went to Brazil to film *Rio Babilônia*. I brought along a gay friend as security, but he kept going off with a guy he met on the film set, leaving me alone. I would take solitary walks on the Copacabana and see Paul's face in every guy I passed. It was eerie and like nothing I'd ever experienced. This young man had gotten under my skin, and I realized I didn't want to go through life without him.

A friend of mine has a theory that you must be with someone seven separate times before you can know for sure that the two of you are destined to be together. I think Paul had me at four, when we took the train from Paris to Amsterdam to visit his big, happy, wonderfully welcoming family (he's the youngest of seven children). For our fifth and sixth times together, he was able to accompany me as a photographer on fashion shoots to the Caribbean and to Greece. He was such a joy to work with. So often in my career, I'd had to hang off rooftops or worse, always to please the photographer, to help him "get the picture." All I had to do to please Paul was relax and let him do the rest. At the end of the day, he would take the hundreds of hairpins out of my hair, which would be pulled into a tight chignon, and set it free into its loose and natural state. It was though he released me from the character I was playing on the outside and let me know he accepted without qualification the person I was inside.

It was in Greece that I asked Paul how he felt about kids. I was deliberately casual in my phrasing and braced myself for the answer, expecting to be disappointed, as I had been so many times before, with Martin. "I love kids," Paul said instantly. "I can't wait to be a dad." *Oh my God,* I thought. *Be still, my heart.*

Our seventh time together, when he accompanied me to New York for the spring collections, solidified our union, though not in the way I would have scripted. Nevertheless, Paul came through an ugly episode with flying colors.

When we got to New York, we discovered that Lukas had taken over my apartment. Evidently, he had convinced my friend Robert—a painter friend who was staying there while I was away in Europe—that he was my still my boyfriend and needed a place to stay. Now Robert had left and Lukas was in residence. I didn't know what to do and was afraid of confronting Lukas; by then I knew about his heroin addiction and had realized that all the bizarre occurrences and erratic behavior were signs that he was scoring drugs.

Paul and I decided to check in to the Gramercy Park Hotel for a couple of nights until we figured out the next step. In the morning, I went to my bank and made the horrifying discovery that Lukas had emptied out my accounts, stolen my checkbook, and bounced dozens of checks in my name. From there, I set off for the garage where I kept my car and found it missing. He had stolen it. (I never saw it again, and months later, I was billed for thousands of dollars' worth of parking tickets he'd received.)

By this time, I was really starting to panic. Lukas had now made his biggest score: my home. Paul and I took a cab over to 100 Central Park South. My hand was shaking so much that I couldn't get the key to work in the lock. Paul got the door open and we switched on the light. The place was empty except for the piano in the living room. Every window was open and the curtains torn off. My white wooden floors and white walls were covered with threats and profanities inked in red Magic Marker: "YOU'LL GET YOURS!" "YOU BITCH!" "YOU ASKED FOR THIS!" "I HOPE YOU DIE IN HELL!" Every surface was defiled.

Paul and I could tell that no one else was there, so we walked into the bedroom. My television had been ripped from the wall, and all the stereo equipment was missing. The bed was turned over along with every drawer. All my designer clothing was gone. All twenty of the beaded dresses that Halston had given me (he'd said, "One day these will be worth something")—*gone*. All my jewelry, including diamonds from Halston—*gone*. The Versaces, the Kenzos, the Fendis—*all gone*. (Fortunately, I still had most of my Stephen Burrows clothes because I'd taken them with me to Europe.)

Paul held me close. I told him about Lukas and how he had come into my life and wreaked havoc. I was close to bursting with despair. Paul listened and stroked my hair, exuding his usual tranquility and quiet competence and bringing everything into perspective. A feeling of peace settled on me and I turned to him. "You know what?" I said. "This has set us free. Now I have nothing to take care of."

"You're right," Paul said. "Still, you should still report it to the police, so you can make a claim on your insurance."

We went to the police station, where we spoke to a Lieutenant Larkin. As I did, I kept seeing the threats Lukas had scribbled all over my wall: "IF YOU REPORT ME TO THE POLICE, I'LL HAVE YOU KILLED!" and "I KNOW WHERE YOU ARE!" Maybe he was bluffing, but I was scared. I happened to look up just then, and there on the wall of the police station was a picture of Jesus Christ. Jesus had said to His followers, "Turn the other cheek," and now it was as if He were speaking those words directly to me. *Walk away. Move on. Forgive and forget.* The message was powerful and I heeded it. "I can't," I whispered to Paul. And he understood. We left the police station without filing a crime report.

That week I worked the New York collections, staying with Paul at the Gramercy Park Hotel. I arranged to give up my apartment. The lease was coming due soon anyway, and the management company was encouraging tenants not to renew because the owners wanted to renovate the building and turn it into a luxury residence. Paul and I booked a flight to the Netherlands. We'd stay with his parents for a couple of weeks before going on to London, where I had several editorial bookings and Paul would be photographing runway shows. Together, we'd figure out our next steps.

The day before we left for the Netherlands, we returned to 100 Central Park South. We packed up the few books and pictures that remained—all the bastard had left behind were items with no conceivable street value—and took them to the post office to mail to my mother's house in New Jersey. Movers had already picked up the piano, which we shipped to Mom as well. (I told her merely that I was moving and giving up the apartment; I'd spared her the gory details about Lukas before, so I certainly wasn't going to burden her with the even gorier ones now.)

After the post office, Paul and I went back a final time to make sure we'd left nothing behind. The apartment was utterly barren and almost unrecognizable. Already, the pain that Lucas had caused was receding into a past that I was all too happy to put behind me.

In front of me—or should I say beside me?—stood my much rosier future. Paul took my hand, squeezed it, and flashed me a smile that said, *We're in this together, kid, from here on out*. I squeezed his hand in return. Then we let ourselves out of the apartment, closed the door behind us, and didn't look back.

AT LONG LAST LOVE

Finally, a dream come true:
in Bali with Paul, 1983.

June 23, 1983. Paul leaned over my sleeping form and kissed me as our plane landed at the Kuta airport. "Happy birthday, darling," he said. I was turning thirty-three, and after months of nonstop work, Paul and I were about to embark on a much-deserved vacation.

I smiled at him, drowsy but exultant. "My prayer to the Lakshmi Murti has been answered," I said, reaching up to cup his face in my hands. "I'm in Bali with my true love."

The next eleven days in paradise passed like a dream as Paul and I walked, holding hands, along the beach or on dirt roads scented with the divine fragrance of frangipani and cooked simple meals by candlelight on an ancient wok. One lazy afternoon, at a little bar we stumbled upon, we sat beside trumpet-shaped hibiscus, drank coconut water, and played with the bar owners' pet monkey, which sat on my shoulder and got lost in combing its fingers through my curly hair, which I'd let go completely natural. For the first time in years—maybe for the first time ever—I felt myself truly, and totally, relax. In that moment I thought, "Finally, I have it all." And I did.

Vacations, of course, can't last forever, and the real world soon intervened, as it inevitably does. My agent in Paris sent a telegram informing me it was "urgent" that I fly to Milan to walk the collections. So Paul and I packed our things and off we rushed, still hand-in-hand, to catch a plane to Europe. It was a scene that we would find ourselves repeating many times over the next three decades as we entered into a shared, full-to-bursting life that has proved to be equal parts love and work and, eventually, family—a combination that continues to enrich and surprise me on a daily basis.

acknowledgments

I want to thank my editor, Dawn Davis, for having faith in me; you are magic. Also, thanks to all the teachers who have kept my spirits high: Amma Sri Karunamayi for your hugs, Swami Satchidananda for the Hatha, Abraham Hicks for the Vortex, Burt Goldman for the Quantum Jumping, and Gurumayi Chidvilasananda for being my guru.

Gratitude from A to Z to the many friends, photographers, and designers who have inspired me; you are all *my* muses.

Matt Zipin, I'm indebted to you for saving all my files. Maja and my Siddha Yoga friends, thanks for listening to my stories. Thomas Eubanks, you kept me moving forward. Paul Caranicas, I cherish you and your loyalty to our "Antonio Gang." Mauricio and Roger Padilha, I'm so lucky to have you—and MAO PR—on my side. Roxanne Lowit, you magically turned the beat around for me. Zac Posen and Christopher Niquet, you spoke up for me when I needed an agent; I'm thrilled you've kept my family and me on your list of friends. Karl Lagerfeld, we'll always have Paris. Antonio, I feel your spirit still; it lives on in everyone who knew you. Kevin Arpino, you are like a brother, and Massimo Cuviello, I owe you so much for getting me started on this book.

Thanks to David Kuhn, my wonderful literary agent, for taking me under your wing, and to Becky Sweren, for being the bridge between myself and the publishing world. Your patience should be trademarked. Thank you, Lorraine Glennon, writer and vegetarian cook extraordinaire (those lunches were terrific). Your talent, enthusiasm, and dedication to making my life story a great read mean everything to me.

Simon Doonan, you are so witty, so quick to help. I feel your joy. Joel Schumacher, we did follow the yellow brick road and discovered something like Oz. My dear friend Stephen Burrows, you wrapped me in your colorful creations and put me on the map of fashion. There are no words to express my gratitude. And a huge shout-out to the always-elegant André Leon Talley. You are a constant inspiration. Finally, a profound thank-you to my husband, Paul van Ravenstein, for helping me every day in every way, and to our two beautiful children, Noel and Anna. You are my world.

about the author

Pat Cleveland was born and raised in New York City. She has worked in the fashion industry for fifty years, splitting her time between the U.S.A. and Europe. She has collaborated with Antonio Lopez in his work for Karl Lagerfeld at Chloé. She has modeled for designers as diverse as Halston, Valentino, Oscar de la Renta, Stephen Burrows, Yves Saint Laurent, Kenzo, Thierry Mugler, Zac Posen, Tom Ford, Lanvin, and Christian Dior, and has been photographed by artists ranging from Richard Avedon, Bert Stern, and Irving Penn, to Steven Meisel and Bruce Weber. Cleveland lives in New Jersey with her husband, Paul van Ravenstein. They have two children, Noel and Anna.

OR DAY